Geo. F. Heath

# The Numismatist

vol. 7

Geo. F. Heath

**The Numismatist**
*vol. 7*

ISBN/EAN: 9783741143311

Manufactured in Europe, USA, Canada, Australia, Japa

Cover: Foto ©Thomas Meinert / pixelio.de

Manufactured and distributed by brebook publishing software
(www.brebook.com)

Geo. F. Heath

# The Numismatist

# THE NUMISMATIST

## Table of Contents.

## 1894.

An Illustrated Monthly devoted to the Science of Numismatics.

GEO. F HEATH, M. D. Monroe, Mich..

VOL. VII.

# Contributors to Vol. vii.

Isaac M. Bates,
Geo. F. Bauer,
H. Russell Drowne,
Ed Frossard,
Geo. F. Heath, M. D.
A. G. Heaton,
Joseph Hooper,
Daniel F. Howorth, F. S. A.
Chas. H. Howes,
Rev. Henry Kingman.
Joseph Lathrop.
O. W. Page,
Geo. W. Rice,
Major Adam Smith,
Luther B. Tuthill,
J. B. Walker,
Ph. Whiteway, F. I. Inst.
D. C. Wismer,
Rev. Jeremiah Zimmerman

# Index.

## INDEX.



*Illustrated.

# THE NUMISMATIST

**January, 1894.**

An Illustrated Monthly devoted to the Science of Numismatics.

Geo. F Heath, M. D. Monroe, Mich.

Vol. 7. No. 1.

## CONTENTS:




# The Numismatist:

A MONTHLY JOURNAL FOR COIN COLLECTORS,
AND OFFICIAL BULLETIN OF

## THE AMERICAN NUMISMATIC ASSOCIATION.

ONE DOLLAR A YEAR.

Editorial and publication office. Monroe, Mich.


THE NUMISMATIST is the only Illustrated Monthly Journal devoted to coins and their collecting published on the American continent.

ADVERTISING RATES very reasonable. Made known on application.

SUBSCRIPTION $1.00 per annum in the United States, Canada and Mexico. Other countries $1.50. Post free. Remittances may be made by money order, postal note, registered letter, or, when these are not obtainable, in unused postage stamps of low denominations.

# The Numismatist.

VOL. VII. MONROE, MICH., JANUARY, 1894. NO. 1.

## WHAT THINK YE OF THIS SCIENCE, MY LORDS?

*President's address, delivered at the Third Annual Convention of the American Numismatist Association at Chicago, Ills., Aug. 21, 1893.*

[GEO. F. HEATH, M. D.]

To the student of history, mythology and art does the science of numismatics especially appeal.

Most of us collect and study along these lines, and the association of the coins linking them with the history and art of the time in which they were struck, or the event they commemorate, renders them important and interesting witnesses of their times.

The coins of a Darius, an Alexander, a Charlemagne, a William the Conqueror, Charles the XII, or a Napoleon though mute, and possibly enveloped in its green shroud of twice ten hundred years, may speak to us of Arbela and Issus, or perhaps of Hastings, Narva, or when "Marengos' field was won" or of "Jena's bloody battle."

The coin corroborates history if it does not make it. Ancient manuscripts have brought down to us the chronicles of their times, but it has remained for the coin or medal to put upon the page of history the seal of authenticity.

Says Rawlinson, "The importance of coins is no doubt the greatest in those portions of ancient history where the information derivable from authors—especially from co-temporary authors—is the scantiest: their use, however, is not limited to such portions; but extend over as much of the historical field as admits of numismatic illustration." And over two hundred and twenty-five years ago Count Lewis Henry Lomenius wrote: "Coins are the breviaries of antiquity, the torch light of history; the supplements of the old vacillating and darkening faith, the fabulum of reading;" and as if this were not enough he further emphasizes "The papyraceous sea has its ebb and flow; all do not break through by force, nor do all written pages go forth to immortality. The coin alone scorns the power of death, glorying in a metallic eternity. Whatsoever the various pages report of the past,—the sorrowful, the doubtful, this the wise hand of the coin sculptor exhibits, and he commands us to behold the very face of Pompey and Brutus! What instructive light we derive concerning the actions of these men by the inspection of their coins! The likenesses so guide the eye that the pictures of those they represent even fasten eternity upon the mind;" and Cicero, the eloquent, realized the value to history of the light reflected from the coin when he said nearly two thousand years ago, coin legends are historical events abbreviated by technical ways, and 'tis the task of the student to arrange the extracts in due sequence: the disposition to penetrate the unknown is one of the strongest of human passions; ancient coins are histories in suggestive epitome; he holds possessions in coins."

Who can read the genial and classic Addison in his "Dialogue on Medals" without feeling that our collecting never had a more devout and loving defender? He says: "For this too is an advantage medals have over books, that they tell their story much quicker and sum up a whole volume in 20 or 30 verses. They are indeed the best epitomes in the world, and let you see with one cast of the eye the substance of above a hundred pages."

In speaking of the great value of coins as historical aids Dean Swift has said that they were "of undoubted authority, of necessary use and observation, not perishable by time, nor confined to any certain places, properties not to be found in books, statues, pictures, buildings or any other monuments of illustrious actions."

"It has been truly remarked," says Sir John Benering, "that the coins of ancient nations are among the most interesting and the most reliable of historical records," and Alexander Pope exclaims

"The medal faithful to its charge of fame,
Thro' climes and ages bears each form and name
In one short view subjected to our eye,
Gods, emperors, heroes, sages, beauties lie."

And this from one of Numismas' most galliant knights, one who has lately passed over the other side, but whose devotion to our science is yet to us a pleasant memory: I refer to that distinguished numismatist, traveller and orientalist, Robert Morris, L. L. D.

"A piece of antique money is even more redolent of the past than the tower, pillar, statue, or foundation wall; because the latter are always seen in ruins; defaced, mutilated, scarred by foes, and that worst foe time, suggesting chiefly the imbecility of man, who labors to build for eternity. But the coin, after the kind rusty crust with which mother earth envelops it is softly removed; looks upright in the face, entire, *incolumis*, a perfect piece of human workmanship, portrait, epigraph, attributions, legend, allegory, mintmark executed (frequently) in a style that modern art vainly strives to reach."

"Old Time yields up his precious hoards,
Calm Science gives her just awards.
By tarnished coin the 'long hidden part restored,'
Proves history's truth completes the grand record."

Were all the written records of Greece and Rome blotted out of existence, the history of their rise, their glory and their fall might yet be read on their coinage left behind. And what is true of Greece and Rome, would be equally true of Egypt, Parthia, Syria, Macedonia and other Nations once possessed of national or medallic coinage. We might not know all of Alexander or of a Ptolemy or a Cæsar should all written records be lost, and yet a tolerably complete history of them might be constructed from their coins.

We might not know all of Hadrian from his coins, yet Gibbon says, "If there were no other record of Hadrian his career would be found written upon the coins of his reign."

In our own time, perhaps within the times of some of us present, our science has brought to light a nation long dead and forgotten in antiquity, and whose history has been made out from finds of coin in Central Asia. I refer to the kingdom of Baltria. Leonard Schmitz, the historian, in speaking of this says, "A kind of Greek civilization, the result of Alexander's conquests, had thus maintained itself for several centuries in the distant East, until in the end it was exterminated by barbarians: and were it not for the numerous coins with Greek inscription found in these parts we should hardly know anything of the existence of a Greek empire in the northeast of Ivan." And again he says "the kings of Baltria succeeded Alexander's immediate successors; their names are known only from coins found in modern times at Balkh and Bokhara and bearing Greek Legends."

What numismatics has done for mythology, look at the magnificent features of Preserfine on the medallion of Syracuse, of Bacchus on the coins of Makos, of Pallas on the coins of Athens and Corinth, Arethusa on the coins of Clazomenæ, Apollo on the coins of Caria and Rhodes, and Zeus on the coins of Cyrene, and know the truth of what has been said, that, "in grandeur of treatment some of these idealized impersonations surpass any modern efforts of a similar class."

Since 750 B. C. coins have always represented the best art of the people. Show us the coins of any period and we will tell you of the status of the art and civilization of that period. To illustrate, contrast the magnificent specimens of coinage (unequalled in our own day) of 400 B. C. when Phidias touched the marble into life and Scopas could almost make it speak, with the rude coin of Postumas 800 years later, when art had almost reached the lowest ebb, when the barbarians of the north: Goth, Vandal and Hun, were prevailing against the gates of Rome, and the world seemed entering upon a troubled sleep.

The lovers of the poetic, artistic, the rare and curious, have also ever had a warm place in their hearts for our collecting.

Says Dr. Johnson to his biographer, Boswell: "When you receive silver in exchange for a guinea look carefully at it, you may chance to find a curious piece."

Ewlyn writing his friend Pepys, "to begin the collecting of coins," and after dilating on the beauties and benefits of the science concludes with, "if they can be purchased together as occasionally they may, it will save you a great deale of paines and enrich you at once. But otherwise they are likeliest met withal amongst the goldsmiths, and casually as one walkes the streetes on foot, and passes the stalls."

Robert Burton, in his Anatomy of Melancholy, says that the science instead of tending to melancholy, that, "to peruse old coynes of several sorts in a fair gallery is an antidote to the blues."

The late Jas. Ross Snowden, the veteran director of the mint, says, "the pleasure derived from the study of the history of the art of coinage is greater than is generally thought. The comparison of the present state of the art with what it was, furnishes a gratification to the student of the present day which amply compensates for the time and trouble attending the research.

Over sixty years ago Appel, the celebrated numismatist, wrote, "Among the remarkable manifestation in which our time is so rich is that interest in collecting coins, which is so widely extended in the educated classes, especially those which related directly to our present social condition. It would be difficult to find a considerable city in the civilized countries of Europe, where no collectors, or at least friends of the science, are not found."

As to the value of coins to the artist and designer, the Rev. Chas. Boutell says: "Not only are many of the coins of past countries executed with a genuine feeling for art, but in their types and legends they also exhibit truly felicitous conceptions expressed after the most effective forms." W. C. Prime as you all know had two "hobbies." "Coins, medals, and seals," came as the result of one and "I go a fishing" the other. One he could follow *adignem*—by the fireside, the other *adumbram*—beside the shady tree.

Mr. Prime held that every hard working man should have a "hobby" on which to rest the overworked brain and body: that at the end of the day's work one should find surcease from business and mental work and worry in an entire change of thought and occupation. Were this done our asylums would be less populated, and our undertakers find fewer premature subjects for the cemetery. Mr. Prime writes, "the science of numismatics has a claim on all intelligent persons that no other subject of study can surpass. In coins and medals, more than in any other monuments, the past is preserved, and its heroes and great events are kept memorable. Possibly it was to the almost imperishable nature of the splendid medals of the Augustan age that Horace alluded when he spoke of a fame more enduring than brass—*monumentum aere perennius*. Then, as now, the records of coins and medals were regarded as most lasting; and it may be safely affirmed that we owe as much of our historical knowledge of the remote past to the coins of nations long since passed away, as we owe to their written chronicles on paper or parchment."

John Ruskin says: "In coins we find wandering fancies and odd guesses, hints of familiar accents and imaginative suggestions: if a copy of any work of art creates the desire to see the original, it is a *good copy*."

"Numismatics, it is vain to deny, is a veritable passion, but one that is noble, agreeable and useful in its effects, because it predisposes the spirit to labor and to study, while it purifies the sentiments and the taste, it removes *ennui*, that most dangerous enemy of our race," says Sabbatier.

And so we might go on indefinitely calling forth from the shadowy depths of the unknown, these mighty ones who once were with us, and as they came in obedience to our call we would see besides those named, Plutarch, Chaucer, Spencer, who tells us of "great ingots and to wedges square,"

"Some in round plates with outer monument,
But most were stampt, and in their metal bare,
The antique shapes of kings and Kesars strange and rare,"

Sir Isaac Newton, Dryden Lord Clarondon and others who would enrich but not complete our list.

Our collecting is not a new one. It began in antiquity, was cherished in the mediæval and loved in modern times. We have no doubt that there were collections of coin made in Old Rome and Greece. We have the best of evidence that some of our most beautiful and perfect specimens of ancient art have been preserved to us from cabinet to cabinet for many centuries, and they will still be handed down—down the centuries—and centuries after our dust has returned to earth and our frail lives and deeds been forgotten, they will continue to tell the stories of Darius, of Philip, of Antony, and Cleopatra, of Vespasian, of Cromwell. Such has been and will be history.

The catalogue of over nine hundred and fifty cabinets of coins, not one formed later than three hundred and thirty years ago, and all formed in Holland, France, Italy, and Germany, have been handed down to us in all their completeness and minuteness to testify the attention paid to numismatics in the years past.

The comparisons of the present state of our science with the past can but be gratifying to the student of our day. In no other branch of science has advancement been more marked than in this which calls us together today. In no time in the past has so much attention been given to numismatics, or so many learned men been attracted to it, or such exact information been furnished on the science as at the present time.

All honor to these pioneers: Vailluent, Spanheim, Mionnet, Sestini, Rashe, Newmann, Wesseling, Eckhel and others of their day for the work they have done, as pioneers they did it well, and considering their times and opportunities exceedingly well. Upon their foundations have we built our superstructure, from such beginnings have Babelon, Madden, Akerman, Gardner, Head, the Pooles and others whose names are well known to you completed the edifice: from such beginnings has our collecting become a science.

And yet with a finished structure, the furnishings are far from complete. The work is not yet done, and herein lies the charm of our collecting—the charm of incompleteness. Within a few weeks we had the pleasure of conversing with a friend and classmate just from Asia Minor where he has spent the past eight or ten years. He returns with many a coin exhumed from that historic locality. Coins with strange devices, coins that as yet the British museum does not possess, coins whose strange characters have not been read, coins that are as silent as the sphinx that marks the sands of Egypt; but their history will be told, their hierglyphics deciphered, their tongues interpreted.

This gentleman informs us that he has stood and from a single spot gazed upon the tumuli of over forty cities, many of whose ruins have not yet been stirred. What possibilities remain in store for the archæologist? What victories for the numismatist and historian? We seem to stand but upon the threshold of our science, and when we stop and consider that there are over 500,000 varieties of coins already known we feel the insignificance of our feeble efforts in comparison with the work. 'Tis not given for but one to possess that prince of brilliants, the Khorinoor. 'Tis not given for but one to possess that numismatic brilliant, the twenty stater of Eucratides, but "there is many a gem of pures tray serene" that we can possess, and these possibilities in store are the great incentives of our enthusiasm for the work.

On our own side of the water such workers as Dickinson, Maris and Crosby, have seemed to exhaust their subjects, and yet Messrs. Frossard and Hayes have supplemented Dr. Maris' work, and Tatman has given us the completed chapter on the coinage of Virginia. Dr. Stores has delved deep in the field of medical, as has Marvin in that of masonic numimatics. Lerona and Breton have almost exhausted the Canadian field. Shiells has eloquently spoken of the Church Token, and Heaton has given us the long waited for work on the mint-marks of the United States. These names and efforts are well known to all of you and reflect credit upon our science.

It has not been our intention in this paper to tell you what you think or I think of this science. It has not been our design to tell you of the benefits you or I derive from this collecting, or the pleasures and profits you or I obtain in this most entrancing study of these "face to face vestiges of vanished aeons." Let our presence or representation here testify to that; but rather have I sought the words of those mighty men unto the manor borne and from the manor gone. These men of the past, who by their influence of tongue and pen, have left their footprints besides the still waters and pleasant path of our science, and the sheen of whose armour yet illuminates and leads us on the numismatic way. From them do we bring you words of encouragement. From them do we bring you answer to the question, "What think ye of this science my Lord."

## THE CONVENTION OF THE THIRTEEN SILVER BARONS.

*A paper read at the Third Annual Convention of the American Numismatist Association, at Chicago, Ills., Aug. 21, 1893.*

[BY A. G. HEATON.]

ELECTORS.

DOLLAR 1804, CHAIRMAN.

| | | | |
|---|---|---|---|
| Dollar......1794 | Dollar......1851 | Half Dol.......1796 | Quarter......1827 |
| " ......1838 | " ......1852 | " ......1797 | Dime........1804 |
| " ......1839 | " ......1858 | Quarter........1823 | Half Dime....1802 |

One quiet night without official hint
The showcase of the Philadelphia mint
Witnessed a new convention for among

Its ranks of silver strange reports had sprung
Of loss of caste and slavery to gold.
The silver Barons, therefore, willed to hold
Upon their "mettle" requisite debate.
And, thirteen all, they came in lofty state
To hear of general issues and the woes
Their hosts of poor relations might disclose.

---

Boldly the dollar 1804, more rare
Than the united Barons, took the chair
And to his presence general homage drew,
Though noble '94 beside him knew
This princely heritage, but chanced to be
Through loss of nearly all the family,
And that, to his own claim as first in line
And rank undoubted, all should there resign,
Feeling his stately visage could not fear
In all the coinage of the land a peer.
Then dollars '38 and '9 were placed,
Their handsome shields with living eagles graced
Instead of varied poultry badly stuffed
That others carried. So they were not huffed
When gossips called them patterns in despite,
But far more polished gave their proof of right.
Then yet more radiant '51 and '2
And '58 the chair's attention drew—
These "nonveaux riches' of modern days and men
Whom chance had thrust amid the 'upper ten.'
But passing far from such to sit beside
Old '94 came with a kindred pride
Half dollars '96 and '97
Of such high-toned, aristocratic leven
As to provoke the chair and he implored
These gentry not to seem so often bored
When they attended, adding, with a shrug,
The "nineties" often seem to need a "plug."
At this the entering quarters '23
And '27, mighty in degree,
And of a fixed expression lest disgrace
Of dignity should come with "altered" face,
Suggested caution, as the vandal's hand
Had harmed too many of their little band.
This 'roused the dime of 1804 intent
To hope that nothing personal was meant
And ask his elder brother not to show
Judgment by halves and here no quarters know.
So when assured, he gave his "better half"

The little 1802 a chance to chaff
  The company, a dwarfed, unruly elf,
  Who thought none other equal to himself.
He joked his large associates of weight
By saying that in spite of all their state
  They ueeds must come to him to intercede
  When of the people's favor having need;
He said it was a fifty dollar crowd
Except the noble chair as they avowed
  In varying condition sucu a price
  Would always fetch them. Some were over nice.
But the demand for him, he said with pride
Was such he often wished he could provide
  Some three cent piece with value he could spare
  And make it fit their noble set to share
For since from vulgar coinage he was free
He felt a sort of sacred rarity
  And pitied his companions who must still
  See millions of their sort the country fill
Each weary year, of such degraded kind.
Thus onward did the elf relieve his mind
  And only with the Barons cease to strive
  When dubbed "a small, abolished bunch of five."

---

Then all were called to order and the chair
Said that the business they came to share
  Concerned depreciation of their race
  By unrestricted coinage. They must face
The issue frankly, bold "impression" give
And if the fateful "die" were cast, must live
  In spite of their "reverses." As for those
  Assembled near him, age gave proud repose
And dignity and honor, but the host
Of silver pieces spread from coast to coast
  What would their life be worth? He wished to know
  If '51 and '2 and '8 could show
As they had from the modern rabble sprung
How it impressed them. These bright dollars stung
  By Chairman 1804's attempt at mirth
  In such insinuations on their birth,
Began by saying they were bright enough
To cast reflections on the dingy, tough
  And "very good for date" old fellows there
  Who took more time for gain than they could spare
And were not worth their interest figured out,
But they were there for business, about,
  Not the dissensions of the upper ten.

But the financial schemes of mining men
Which they had heard from relatives would kill
All standards and all values, make a mill
Of every mint, cause outpour uncontrolled
And give the sway of silver up to gold.
"What think you?" said the Chair. "I ask the floor,"
Exclaimed the ancient dollar '94.
And then he said, "My friends the thing is plain
Men must be stopped abusing us for gain,
We serve their needs too long and work too cheap,
Even when young and, if we are to keep
Our dignity, the commonest of dates
And issues must be guarded from the fates
Of evil financiering to upraise
The sounder values of the olden days."
Here all the noble Barons loudly sang
Approval and the ancient halves upsprang
To boast how pieces of their time surpassed
In grace and size and purity the last
Degraded coinage of our greedy land
Where every section struggles for command
Where few prize any rarity above
The metal where, not only adult love
For the "almighty dollar" all avow,
But even little children love the doll.
The half dime, 1802, alert and sly,
With lifted hand here caught the Chairman's eye,
And, given hearing, spoke his feelings thus:
"Oh, silver haired companions, why this fuss?
We cannot hinder men from being fools
And politics and finance make no rules
Which give to us a majesty and rank
Before the world. We surely do not thank
The '50s if the remnant of a date
Can give us title to a high estate
Through past associations. Why concern
Ourselves about the coins men pay and earn
The common dates in millions spread about
That pass through dirty fingers in and out,
Scratched, dented, bent with all the wear and tear
Of circulation? We who are the rare
And precious of the land should surely take
A different test of worth and henceforth make
Those noble sages called "numismatists"
The rulers of the nation. See the lists
Of coinage dealers where in proper place
Our value counts by hundreds over face

When in our Sunday clothes. Why, look at me,
If I am on the worst kind of a spree,
All bent and worn and tattered, they delight
To give their fifties and I'm out of sight
When I'm very good and feeling prime.
Yes, Barons, for audacity sublime
The dealers "take the cake," but even more
We owe to those with whom they wipe the floor,
The feverish collectors who will pay
Whatever price they ask in eager fray
And waste their hundreds or economize
And borrow to attain each single prize
For which the knowing ones will coolly wait
To get in lots or catch with cheaper bait
At auctions or from others who collect
And wish exchanges. Of these circumspect
We must beware for, if they truly say
Coins are but worth no more than dealers pay
To put aside for stock, their spirit tame
Assuredly would spoil our little game
Of lordly dignity and priceless worth.
We can remain the chosen of the earth
By taking stringent measures and as well
Relieve the common coinage. To compel
Mankind to come to reason I oppose
Free silver utterly and here propose
We bind the issue of each yearly date
To half the sum that men would circulate,
Have some years extra limited and see
That no two dies exactly shall agree,
And no two mints, and then, if any dunce
Make ugly dies, that he shall die at once.
I further move, our ballot henceforth gives
In young collectors representatives,
That those advanced be to the Senate sent,
And he among them shall be President
Who most to buy our noble band has paid
As for the dealers, let the best be made
The members of the cabinet." "And who,"
The Chair asked, dazed by little 1802
"Shall be the Court Supreme?" As down he sat,
The half dime answered, "We can see to that."
The Barons looked about them when he ceased
Until the Chairman said he would be pleased
The sense of all the meeting to attend,
"No cents are here," the dime said, to offend
The blacks are not admitted. "Any wit

Of this kind," spoke the Chair, "is counterfeit.
From 1804, my little brothers here,
The lower tens must upper tens revere,
Has anyone suggestions to propose?"
The lordly quarter '23 arose
And stated he was very much rejoiced
To second what his little friend had voiced,
Except the unkind criticism made
Upon the dealers. They would be repaid
He well believed in some awaiting sphere
For generous deeds and shining virtues here,
For unity of spirit, love of truth,
Protecting care of ignorance and youth
And forasmuch as, by report, they gave
Sweet flowers for each young collector's grave
Who at the sale of his collection forced
Received about a third of what it cost.
Without the dealer,s guidance death were gain
For sad collectors would but group in vain.
At this the Barons wept a little space
And then the noble chairman to efface
Emotion and provide against delay
Asked for a vote and all responded, "aye."
"It is so ordered," said he, "let us stand
United to enforce throughout the land.
A coinage, not for loosened anarchists,
But stringently disposed numismatists
Since, though 'tis very true that neither know
A jot of finance nor can either show
A sane idea of values, it is plain
That we should favor what would be our gain
And therefore honor (this the Chair enjoined)
Not those who count us "cash" but call us "coins."
If there are no remarks we now adjourn.
Mint julips here await the thirsty turn
Of noble members and that proofs prolong
Their brightness brief, we have ammonia strong.

## AMERICAN NUMISMATIC AND ARCHÆOLOGICAL SOCIETY.

(17 WEST FORTY-THIRD ST., NEW YORK CITY.)

A regular meeting of the Society was held on Nov. 20, 1893, President Parish presiding.

The Executive Committee reported that the propositions for corresponding membership of Rev. Charles M. Parleman and William L. Stone has been received and approved. Attention was called to the death of resident members. Gaston L. Fenardent and José Maria Munoz. The resignation of Isaac N. Seligman has been received and accepted. Acceptances of election have been received from life members, Louis C. Tiffany and Charles Morris; from resident members Julius T. Auger and George L. Rives, and from corresponding member William M. R. French. The Secretary read a letter from F. A. Castle Secretary of the Grolier club, announcing the presentation to the Society of a large, bronze medallion of Nathaniel Hawthorne, made for the club by Mr. A. Illzach. On motion the Secretary was directed to send vote of thanks to the Grolier club for their very acceptable gift. The Librarian announced that the new acquisitions since the May meeting had been greater in extent than during any previous year of the Society's history, 246 bound volumes, 107 pamphlets, 5 reports, 149 periodicals and 3,369 catalogues, total 3,876 had been received. The principal donors were Daniel Parish, Jr., Isaac F. Wood, William Poillon, S. O. Avery, Jr., Ralph F. Cutter and Thomas Cunningham. Special mention was made of the donation of 50 handsome pamphlet cases from Andrew C. Zabriskie and 28 from Charles H. Wright. The curator of numismatics reported the receipt of 13 coins, 144 medals, of which 38 were of Columbus, and 8 badges, total 215 pieces. The principal donors were George G. Williams and John S. Kennedy, executors of the estate of Robert L. Stuart, Daniel Parish, Jr., J. W. Ellsworth, G. Cavalli, James Kirkwood, Grolier club, Graham Mfg. Co., J. Sanford Salters and William Poillon.

The curator of archæology reported donations of a collection of miscellaneous curiosties from A. C. Zabriskie and an amphora from Isaac F. Wood.

The president presented a letter from Messrs. Tiffany & Co. accompanied by three Columbus medals in silver, gold bronze and bronze.

"Mr. Daniel Parish, Jr., Chairman Columbus Medal Committee. Dear Sir: The members of your Society having invited us to strike a medal in commemoration of the four hundredth anniversary of the discovery of America by Columbus, we shall be pleased to have them accept the three copies sent herewith and trust that the entire approval of the Society will be met.

Nov. 20, 1893. Very Respectfully, TIFFANY & Co.

On motion of Mr. Tonnell the medals were accepted and a vote of thanks tendered.

Mr. John M. Dodd, Jr., presented the following resolution:

WHEREAS, Messrs. Tiffany & Co. have done honor to numismatic art in America by the medal they have designed and struck in commemorationof the four hundredth anniversary of the discovery of America by Columbus. Therefore be it

RESOLVED, That the members of the American Numismatic and Archæological Society in recognition of this event do hereby tender to Messrs. Tiffany & Co. the assurance of their hearty appreciation of the artistic and successful result of their efforts. Carried unanimously. H. RUSSELL DROWNE, Secretary.

## SACRED CASH OF EMPEROR KANG HSI.

[BY HENRY KINGMAN.]

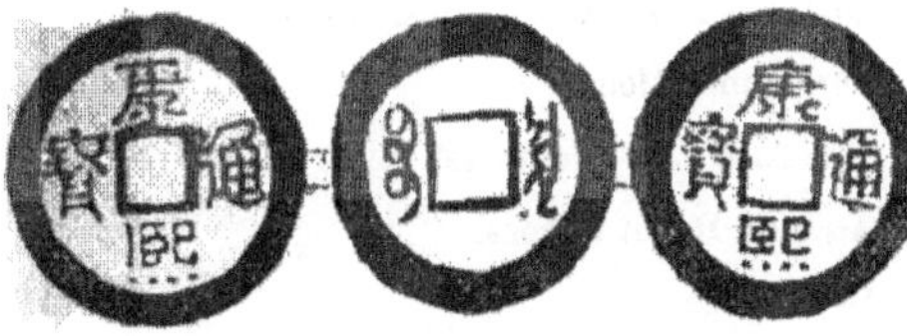

Common Cash of Kang Hsi. Lohan Cash of Kang Hsi.

A peculiar feature of Chinese cash, not generally known to the collector, but much valued in China as talismans or trinkets, is the Lohan cash of the Emperor Kanghsi (1662-1723.) It is so called because made of the brass of confiscated images of the Lohan, or eighteen attendants of Buddha, usually ranged on either side of the principal idol in Buddhist temples. It is said that the Emperor seized these images and melted them down into cash to show his contempt for Buddhism, and to gratify the Jesuits, then in power at court. The brass thus melted up is said to have contained a considerable proportion of gold, and in any case it is true that a genuine Lohan cash can be immediately distinguished from ordinary Chinese coins by the yellow, brassy lustre. Their only other distinguishing mark is the peculiar writing of the character "Hsi" at the bottom of the cash. The common coins of this reign have an additional line at the left side of the character; the sacred cash have not, as shown in the cut.

The term sacred cash, or Lohan cash, is also given to a certain issue of the Chou Yuan (A. D. 954), the copper of which was taken from more than 3,300 Buddhist temples that were suppressed. Both these varieties are much sought for by the Chinese and are seldom to be picked up except at good prices. The characters for "sacred cash" are inscribed on the reverse of all coins issued by the Tai Ping rebels, thirty years ago, but, though not often seen, this particular variety is not much prized, probably because the species of "sacredness" it represents is not up to the mark.

CONTENTS:




# The Numismatist:

A MONTHLY JOURNAL FOR COIN COLLECTORS, AND OFFICIAL BULLETIN OF

## THE AMERICAN NUMISMATIC ASSOCIATION.

ONE DOLLAR A YEAR.

Editorial and publication office, Monroe, Mich.

THE NUMISMATIST is the only Illustrated Monthly Journal devoted to coins and their collecting published on the American continent.

ADVERTISING RATES very reasonable. Made known on application.

SUBSCRIPTION $1.00 per annum, post free to any portion of the civilized world. Remittances may be made by money order, postal note, registered letter, or, when these are not obtainable, in unused postage stamps of low denominations.

Entered at Monroe, Mich., Postoffice, as second class matter.

# The Numismatist.

VOL. VII. MONROE, MICH., FEBRUARY, 1894. NO. 2.

## THE HISTORIC VALUE OF THE ANCIENT COINS OF GREECE AND ROME.

*A paper read at the Third Annual Convention of the American Numismatic Association at Chicago, Ill., Aug. 21, 1893.*

[REV. JEREMIAH ZIMMERMAN.]

When traveling in Egypt, and looking at the tombs of the ancient empire, with the walls covered with frescoes representing the events of over 4,000 years ago, I was impressed with the historic value of archaic art, and that the art of the ancients is an interpreter of history. This same view interested me in the study of the historic Coins of Greece and Rome, for they not only form the links in the long chain of history as it extends dcwn through the Centuries but invests with peculiar interest certain great personages, and prominent events in the life of these nations.

Whether it be true or not, that by tracing the series of Roman coins to the time of Gallienus we have "from an artistic point of view, an epitome of the rise and fall of the Roman Empire," *it is* true that by such a study we shall find many interesting and important facts of cotemporaneous history recorded on these ancient coins, and they not only inseparably connect us with that distant period of the past, but they tend to bring it much nearer and invest it with a realism that every student of Numismatics feels, giving us a keen personal interest in those times and well known characters, cridging over the intervening centuries and making those once stirring scenes vivid to our minds and feelings,—as though the great curtain that has fallen on the past Centuries should rise once more and the chief actors appear on the stage again to reenact their parts.

If it be true that when you touch a man's pocketbook you touch his heart, what shall we say of that intimate and vital relationship created when we take the money of the old Roman emperors and consuls into our hands, and gaze upon their original portraits as we study their individual characters in the light of history, and read the identical inscriptions which they themselves ordered to be recorded thereon. There you behold him in his own remote age expressing himself as a noble Roman, or as some cruel monster.

I do not know of any method within the range of human possibilities that seems so intimately to connect the past and present, and which makes those times and characters so real as the handling and study of these perfect numismatic monuments of cotemporary historical art which have come down to our times. Here we have, within the limits of an ordinary cabinet, an interesting portrait gallery of the famous men and women of those times, many of them with a strong individualism that shows their marked personality.

A comparison of the many portraits of emperors as given on their coins with existing marble busts of the same persons leads us to the conclusion that the portraits were realistic and not merely conventional, and hence at least to the days of Gallienus we have for the most part the actual likeness of those rulers, as struck on gold, silver or bronze.

These portraits are interesting too because in some instances they give us the likeness of the ruler at different periods of life as in the case of Augustus, Marcus Aurelius and Commodus.

How touching to look upon that sweet and beautiful face of the original portrait of that little boy who was murdered at the age of twelve with his father Philip. In all probability that attractive face was brightened by the spirit of Christ within, for the verdict of history seems to be that not only was he and his mother, Otacilla, christians, but even his father Philip also, although fearing openly to espouse the cause of the new and despised religion. We learn to know those ancient personages from their true original likenesses as we could not otherwise know them, and we carry this picture in our minds, and connect with it the various important events in their lives, and by this power of association we also remember those events, and enjoy them with a personal interest not otherwise possible. As truly as that youthful, attractive, pure and noble face of Philip the younger as given on his coin can not fail to touch the heart and awaken the interest of any true man or woman if viewed in connection with this history. Not only will the study of such portraits increase everyone's interest in history but their practical value to the student of history can not be easily over estimated

How great interest centers in the large tetradrachm of Antiochus IV (Epiphanes) as we study the well defined portrait of this mad Syrian King on his own coin, and read the wicked audacity in his inscriptions, for he dares to call himself "God," and as we examine this ancient and realistic portrait, and read the inscription, and study them in the light of history we appreciate the shocking irreverence of this monster of cruelty as we follow him in the year

Antiochus IV., Epiphanes. 176-164 B. C.

168 B. C. when he invaded Palestine, captures the city of Jerusalem and desecrates the holy Temple with all the outrageous insult of a mad demon, their sacred writings being burned, whilst to reach the very climax of sacrilege, a swine was slaughtered within the sacred precincts of the Temple itself, and "the broth of its filthy flesh sprinkled, amid shouts of laughter, on the sacred parchments."

How vividly, and with what intense realism that monster character of history, and this awful scene of sacrilege is brought to our minds as we study the face in connection with his cotemporaneous record; stamped on his own coin, and by his own order,—and hence out of his own mouth we condemn him.

But we are more especially interested in that class of Roman coins that were struck to commemorate some particular event—the memory thereof perpetuated on the imperishable metal. Hence they become an unfailing source of interest and information.

Gibbon expresses the historic value of such ancient documents when he declares that "If all our historians were lost to us, medals and inscriptions would alone record the travels of Hadrian."

Barclay V. Head tells us that, "The coins of Trajan record his conquest of Dacia, Armenia, Mesopotamia and his descent down the Euphrates and the Tigris to the Indian Ocean, the only Roman General who accomplished this feat" and he further states that his coins illustrate his extensive journeys into the Roman province from Britain to the far East.

The coins issued by the Romans and circulated in every province throughout the empire were like so many military despatches of the great General, whether making conquests or bringing help to the conquered, and looking at his coins and seeing the records on the reverse was something like reading a modern daily bulletin board.

In the early days of the Roman Empire the issue of an "*Egypta Capta,*" told all the people of the conquest of Egypt, and the overthrow of Mark Antony and Cleopatra by the proud Augustus.

Augustus (denarius) B. C. 28

When the "*Judea Capta*" was struck, it was something like the telegram; in 1865, which caused the ringing of the bells throughout the North, East and West, as it flashed the joyful news over the Country that Richmond had fallen, and the Country was saved.

1st Br. Vespasian A. D., 69–79.

In the numismatic monuments, the student of ancient history, handles authentic, original, unrevised records that have come down from those early times with the stamp of imperial and senatorial authority upon them that have silenced speculations, and put an end to the most learned controversies, by the presence of this cotemporaneous monument of the historical fact itself, and which furnish accurate and unmistakable testimony to the subject in question, for they are like so many original and autograph letters.

It is because of this manifest historical value of the ancient coins of Greece and Rome that many of our great historians and archæologists, like Mommsen of Germany, Lenormant of Paris, Lanciani of Rome and Gardiner of Cambridge are also numbered among the leading numismatists.

I will mention only one or two coins in this connection, but an exceedingly interesting one, especially to the student of the New Testament, is the Greek coin of the proconsul Proclus, struck at Cyprus during the reign of Claudius Cæsar. In this coin we have a remarkable and important confirmation of the accuracy of the writer of the Acts of the Apostles. For more than a century St. Luke's statement was questioned in Chapter 13: 7 wherein he calls Sergius Paulus, the ruler at Paphos, a deputy or proconsul.

Cyprus under Claudius Cæsar. Proconsul Proclus. 41 54 A. D.

The ground of the objection was that a proconsul was appointed by the Senate and only to provinces where no military force was required, but that a military force was needed on this island at this time, and hence the ruler could not have been a proconsul, but a proprætor or procurator and appointed by the Emperor.

The controversy was a long and interesting one as it impeached the historical accuracy of the sacred narrative. All doubt was removed and controversy ended by the discovery of three coins struck at Cyprus during the reign of Claudius bearing his portrait on the obverse and on the reverse the name of Cominus Proclus, bearing the title of proconsul ἀνθύπατος, the identical Greek word employed by St. Luke, and as St. Paul visited this island during the reign of Claudius, therefore Sergius Paulus was also a proconsul, for Cyprus at this time was a senatorial and not an imperial province. I will give another example wherein the discovery of ancient coins have enabled us to correct erroneous views previously held. Prof. Ramsey in his work, "The church in the Roman Empire" page 40 shows how the unmistakable evidence of *coins* must overthrow the account of Iconium as given in the works or Mr. Lewin and Canon Farrar who hold that it was "The capital of an independent tetrarchy, and not in the province of Galatia, and hence concluded that "The diversity

Coin of Iconium (Nero Cæsar Augustus 54 68 A. D.

of political governments which at this time prevailed in Asia Minor was so far an advantage to the Apostle that it rendered him more able to escape from one jurisdiction to another." This position must be abandoned in the face of numismatic evidence for we have coins which were struck by Iconium as a Roman city from the days of Claudius, and it was doubtles Roman long before.

The fact that Lystra was a Roman Colony was unknown until 1885. A marble pedestal on its ancient site revealed the fact, and the same was confirmed by the discovery of three coins of the Colony of Lystra, thus establishing the fact beyond all question.

It is an interesting fact in connection with the value of numismatic evidence that we are almost wholly dependent upon the coinage of Bactria for our knowledge of that country during a period of nearly 400 years.

From certain gold and silver coins alone do we know that Vitellius had children, and which representations correct Josephus, when in the history of the Jewish War, (Book 4, chapter 10, sec. 3.) he states that this emperor was childless.

In the famous early romance of "The Acta of Paula and Thekla," Prof. Ramsey shows, by the existence of certain coins that the hitherto unknown Queen Tryphaena who granted the protection to Thekle and became a second mother to this Christian Virgin was really a historical character, and no less a distinguished personage than Tryphaena, Queen of the independent Kingdom of Pontus, for on certain rare coins of the Kingdom of Pontus we have on the obverse the bust of the youthful king her son with his title Basileos Polemonos, and on the reverse the bust of the elderly Queen with the title Basilisses Tryphaines. The discovery of this important historical fact from the coins adds vastly to this remarkable and interesting romance. Acta Pauli et Thekla, for as Ramsey states, "It is the only extant literary work which throws light on the character of popular Christianity in Asia Minor during this early period."

Inasmuch as the Romans began as early as 150 B. C. to present certain facts on their coinage and this desire to record achievements on the money increased during the empire, we have therefore thousands of different types, and among this large number there are many of special historical interest and it is not so easy to select nor refrain from mentioning many favorite ones, and yet I am reminded that I must confine myself to the limit assigned me.

Of course among the early denerii we have the familiar legendary or mythological subjects as the rape of the Sabines, Tarpeia crushed beneath the shields, and Aeneas carrying the aged Anchises on his back.

[To be Continued.]

## NUMISMATICS AT THE EXPOSITION.

It is much to be regretted that no exhibit worthy of our science was attempted at the World's Fair. Whose fault it was is beyond our ken, but we are not disposed to believe it due to the indisposition of our association, other societies, or collectors of coin, who were not only abundantly able, but willing and anxious to have loaned from their valuable collections for this purpose. It is vain now to indulge in regrets; the time is past, and when such an opportunity may occur in this country again, few if any of us will be here to care.

The main exhibit was naturally that of the mint in the Government building, but this was arranged in so jumbled and amateurish a manner that but little benefit could be derived from it. If, however, the exhibit was designed to interest the novice, as we must believe it was, it was a decided success. All day long the space around the cases was crowded by an anxious and expectant mass of humanity, and the comments on the coins, one could hear from the tyro was decidedly refreshing and interesting, and the explanation often gives the gaping looker on by some one more or less "up" in the matter, proved that a little learning may be an amusing as well as a dangerous thing.

The main attraction to the laity was the "widow's mite" and the coin as old as "Adam himself," while the amateur and professional lingered longest over the little group presided over by the 1804 dollar and 1849 double eagle.

Here were specimens illustrating the money systems of the ancient Greek and Roman Republics from 700 B. C. to about the Christian era. The Roman Empire from Julius Cæsar B. C. 49 to the end of the Western Empire. The Byzantine Empire from 395 to 1453 A. D. France was represented by a series of coins extending from 814 A. D. to the present time, and Germany from the end of the Roman Empire. England's coinage was well illustrated, beginning from the coin struck in Britain by the Romans in the beginning of our era down to and including these struck for Victoria known as the "Jubilee Coinage." China and Japan of the oriental nations were best represented, the former excelling.

As would be expected the coins and medals struck by our own mint since 1793 were well represented, the exhibition being all that could be desired.

The coining press, as used in our mints, in operation also attracted considerable attention, and souvenir medals struck in brass found ready sale at twenty-five cents each. In this connection it is worthy to note that while medals of the cheaper class struck in brass, copper, bronze, aluminum or white metal, were offered for sale and hawked about all over the grounds and the city, the better class representative of a higher art so much sought after and obtained at our centennial Exposition in 1876, were conspicuous for their absence.

In another part of the building was the government exhibit of U. S. Colonial and Washington medals, which is easily excelled by many private collections.

One collection stowed away in a little side room of this building deserves more than a passing notice, and that is the valuable and rare collection of decorations, military and naval medals belonging to W. H. Harris, ex-sheriff of London (Eng.) Here are decorations and medals for gallant service at Waterloo, Egypt, Salamauca Tollouse, Pyrenees, Trafalgar, Seringapatam, Balaklava, Alma, Sebastopol, etc; Medals to commemorate peace and great events, Victoria crosses, crosses of the Legion of Honor, Stars of the most illustrious Order of St. Patrick, of the most Honorable order of the Bath, etc. Some of these decorations and medals are in gold; some ornamented with precious gems: all associated with brave men and great events; all replete with stories of war and victory. A collection unequalled, a collection representing a life time with unusual advantage for collecting, a collection that means a fortune expended in its accumulation.

In the gallery of the Mining building was really the finest exhibit in its line. This was the collection of coin belonging to Mr. Geo. Kunz, the gem expert of Tiffany & Co., of New York City. The collection illustrated the metals used in coinage. The exhibit was not large but every piece was of numismatic value either as a work of art or from a historical point of view.

The Scott Stamp and Coin Co. of New York City had quite a comprehensive exhibit in the gallery of the Anthropological building, in which we noticed some fine early Greek Tetradrachm, large German quadruple, triple and double crowns, besides a good variety of the plate money of Sweden, an extensive collection of modern copper coins of all nations. This firm with W. A. Fletcher & Co., have also a branch in the Plaisance, presided over by Mr. Wm. Rudley.

Small collections of coins were also offered for sale in the Algerian building in Midway, the Costa Rica building on the grounds, also at the Siamese building or booth could be obtained coin of that nation arranged in sets, comprising full series of the gold, silver, copper, and pewter, including the eight pieces of "bullet" money; all for $72. In the East India building Messrs. Tellery & Co, had a fine lot of Indian and old Graeco-Bactrian coins. Kashmere, Afghanistan. Delli and the late English coins for India were also represented. Here was the finest lot of oriental coins to be seen on the grounds, and an hour here was profitably spent.

Again in the Midway a visit to Mr. Dikran G. Kelekian of the Turkish village was in order. Several stands of dilapidated copper and silver, there were before you got to the "holy of holies," but when you could make them understand that you wanted to see coin, not trash. a fine line of old Greek silver would be shown you. Here were tetradrachms of Athens, Macedon of Philip II and III. and Alexander the Great, Syria of the Selencides and Antiochus I, IV, and VIII. Tigranes: early Parthian and Persian: early Roman Colonial for Asia Minor, etc: also late Persian, Turkestan and Turkish in silver and copper.

In the centre of the rotunda of the Administration building, enclosed by a railing, was a model of the treasury building made up as far as the eye could note of Columbian souvenir half dollars. Just how many pieces entered into its composition it would have been interesting to know, but this secret was carefully guarded. The clipped pieces noticed in the make up of the angles, etc., were of white metal of similar size and design to the half-dollars.

In the center of the Liberal Arts building was a plain shaft some twenty feet in height, apparantly made of these half-dollars. Both these models were evidently intended to advertise the sale of the Columbian half-dollars, but in spite of all the efforts put forth in this and other ways by the World's Fair authorities, a large proportion of these pieces are returned to the mint for recoinage into standard silver coin.

In the Woman's building only, could be obtained the Isabella quarter-dollar. They are a beautiful little piece, that sold on their merits; no outside efforts as far as we could learn being made for their disposals. Owing to the limited number coined, they will always command a higher premium than her half-dollar brother. This piece is the first authorized United States coin to bear a crowned head. G. F. H.

## SOUVENIR BELLS.

A curious prevailing custom in vogue in the casting of souvenir bells is the placing in the retort of molten metal by private parties of metal souvenirs, more or less valuable, to enter into the composition of the bell. Whether this adds to the tone is a matter of grave doubt, but no one will deny but that the bell might have a greater interest to those who thus contribute.

During the past year a Columbian liberty bell was cast in Rutland, Vt., and the following contributors became incorporated in the product:

From Washington, 10,000 pennies.

Benton Hussey, of North Berwick, Me., gives two "widow's mites" found in the pool of Bethesda.

W. L. Hill, of the Brooklyn Navy yard, a piece of cannon captured from the Coreans in 1871.

Cornelius R. Stark, of Hamilton, Ont., one gold watch case.

Mrs. I. C. Morton, of Boston, a Turkish coin dated 800.

William Gray Brooks, of Boston, a Roman coin dated 161 A. D.

Mary M. Babcock, of Warren, Penn., a silver ring made from a half dollar found on the battlefield of Petersburg.

Elizabeth P. Stark, Manchester, N. H., two silver spoons, several coins and a copper cover from the home of Gen. John Stark, of revolutionary fame.

Charles Tryon, of Newark, N. J., a Brazilian coin 136 years old.

I. Bruckell, of Durham, Conn., a penny found in Swathel's tavern, which was once occupied by Washington and Lafayette.

Besides the above, donations of a minor character were received by every mail and express up to the time of the casting.

Speaking of souvenir bells, there is a locomotive on the Boston and Maine R. R. that carries with it a bell of unusual interest. It is related that when they were about to cast this bell, the superintendent of the road came along and counted out twenty silver dollars and threw them into the melting pot. It is further related that the bell has a beautiful tone, but the silver lining of the superintendent's pocket is not as bright as before.

## AMERICAN NUMISMATIC AND ARCHÆOLOGICAL SOCIETY.

Abstract from minutes American Numismatic and Archæological Society:

A regular meeting of the Society was held on Jan. 15, 1894, President Parish presiding. The executive committee reported that the nomination for corresponding membership of George McArthur, of Malden, Victoria, had been received and approved. Acceptance of election had been received from corresponding members Charles M. Parkman and William L. Stone. The resignation of Dr. John S. White has been accepted. Attention was called to the decease of corresponding member Walter Trumbull, of Chicago, Ill. The committee on revision of constitution and by-laws reported at length on the proposed changes, and on motion the committee were authorized to prepare copies for use at the annual meeting. The chairman of the commitee on papers presented the following resolution:

RESOLVED, That this Society sends to Dr. Theodore Monimsen, of Berlin, Germany—one of its honorary members—a cordial greeting upon his celebration of the fiftieth anniversary of his obtaining his diploma as a doctor of philosophy. Carried.

The librarian reported that since the last meeting, 7 bound volumes, 43 unbound volumes and pamphlets, 42 catalogues, total 92 had been received. The curator of numismatics announced 131 separate donations. Particular attention was called to a collection of over 50 medals of the Columbian Exposition, secured for the society from exhibitors, officials, etc., by Mr. George F. Kunz. On motion the special thanks of the Society were tendered to Mr. Kunz for his successful exertions to secure all the medals struck at the Columbian Exposition for the Society's collection. A donation of 20 Australian tokens of historic interest was announced from Mr. George McArthur, of Malden, Victoria. The curator of archæology reported donations of an old duelling pistol, a blue Revolutionary Washington plate and a Roman tear bottle—all gifts of Mr. Isaac F. Wood. On motion adjourned. H. RUSSEL DROWNE, Sec'y.

## CONSTITUTION AND BY-LAWS OF THE AMERICAN NUMISMATIC ASSOCIATION.

### Preamble.

The objects of this Society are: To assist its members in acquiring knowledge in regard to numismatics; to cultivate a feeling of friendship among collectors and to enable them to affiliate with collectors of similar societies in America and Foreign Countries; and the formation of a cabinet and library of numismatic literature for the use of its members.

### Constitution.

ARTICLE I.—NAME and OBJECT.

SEC. 1. This organization shall be known as the American Numismatic association.

SEC. 2. Its objects shall be the encouragement and promotion of numismatic science and the formation of a cabinet and library relating to the same.

ARTICLE II.—MEMBERSHIP.

SEC. 1. The membership of this association shall be divided into two classes: Active and Honorary.

SEC. 2. The first class shall constitute the governing body of the association, from which all officers shall be chosen.

SEC. 3. Only Active members residing in the United States or Canada, shall be eligible to hold office in the association.

SEC. 4. The second class shall comprise those persons who are considered deserving of the distinctive title of Honorary. Honorary members shall be elected only at the annual convention, upon the written nomination of five Active members.

SEC. 5. All applications for Active membership shall be addressed to the secretaryon the form prescribed by Sec. 6 and accompanied with the initiation fee of fifty cents. In case the application is rejected, the initiation fee shall be refunded.

SEC. 6. Form of application. I hereby make application for active membership in the American Numismatic association, subject to the constitution and by-laws of said association.

Name.................................Address.................................

Age............Occupation.................................Date.................

Recomended by...........................................A. N. A. No.......

And.........................................A. N. A. No.......

SEC. 7. Upon receipt of such application in due form, the secretary shall cause the name and address of the applicant and his references to be published in the next number of the official organ, and if no objections are received by him within one month from the date of publication, the applicant shall be entitled to membership in the association.

SEC. 8. In case objection is made to the admission of an applicant, the secretary shall refer the matter to the board of trustees the secretary of which shall at once notify such applicant, stating the name of the objector and the nature of the objection and request a statement of his side of the case. As soon as this has been received, the board of trustees shall consider the matter and either accept or reject the application and notify the secretary of its decision.

SEC. 9. Whenever written charges have been brought against a member the secretary of the board of trustees shall notify such member, giving a written copy of the charges; the member so accused shall be permitted to enter a written defense, after which the board of trustees shall determine the case under such rules as it may adopt and may censure, suspend or expel such member.

SEC. 10. Appeal may be made from the decision of the board of trustees to the next annual convention of the association, the decision of which shall be final, but the president must be notified of such appeal within thirty days after the decision of the board of trustees has been published.

SEC. 11. No member shall be permitted to resign from the association while he is in arrears for dues or indebted to it in any manner whatever, or while there are charges pending against him.

ARTICLE III. OFFICERS.

SEC. 1. The elective officers of this association shall be:

President, Vice-President, Secretary, Treasurer, Librarian and Curator, Superintendent of exchange, Detector of Counterfeits and Board of Five Trustees.

They shall be elected at the annual convention and hold office until their successors have duly qualified.

SEC. 2. The official board shall be composed of the President, Vice-President, Secretary, Treasurer and Chairman of board of trustees.

SEC. 3. In case of a vacancy in any office the official board shall appoint a member in good standing, to serve for the remainder of the term.

SEC. 4. Whenever ten members of the association prefer charges against any officer for dereliction of official duty or violation of the constitution, such officer shall be tried by a court composed of one of the trustees acting ex-officio as presiding officer and two members chosen by the board of trustees. The finding of such court shall be final and binding both upon the association and the official tried.

SEC. 5. All officers are to be elected yearly and such election shall be by ballot under the direction of the board of trustees. Each member shall enclose his ballot in a sealed envelope marked "ballot" and such envelopes shall not be opened until after the polls are closed on the day of election. The polls shall close at noon on the first day of the annual convention. A plurality of the ballots cast shall elect.

SEC. 6. At least sixty days prior to an election the board of trustees shall call for nominations and the names of all candidates shall be published in the official organ at least thirty days prior to the election.

ARTICLE IV.—DUTIES OF OFFICERS.

SEC. 1. The President shall preside at all meetings of the association. He shall sign all warrants on the Treasurer. In case of a vacancy in any office he shall appoint a member to act until the official board fills the vacancy. In case any officer is prevented by sickness or other causes, from performing the duties of his office the president may appoint a substitute to act during such disability.

SEC 2. The Vice-President shall act as President, in the event of the death, absence or inability of the President.

SEC. 3. The Secretary shall keep a true record of the transactions of the association and preserve all documents. He shall collect the dues and balances due the association and pay the same to the Treasurer at least once a month. He shall draw and countersign all warrants on the Treasurer. He shall publish in the official organ all applications for membership (as provided by Article II, Sec. 7) list of new members and any other information he may receive in his official capacity. He shall give the board of trustees an approved bond for one hundred dollars for faithful performance of his duties.

SEC. 4. The Treasurer shall receipt for all monies received from the Secretary. He shall not pay out any money except upon warrants duly drawn and signed by the President and Secretary. He shall have charge of any securities belonging to the association. He shall present to each convention a complete statement of the financial condition of the association and report of his transactions during the term, accompanied by the proper vouchers. He shall furnish an approved bond for two hundred dollars or as much more as the board of trustees may require.

SEC. 5. The Librarian and Curator shall have charge of all coins, medals, books, papers, etc., which the association may acquire and shall permit access thereto by the members under such regulations as are prescribed by the by-laws. He shall compile accurate catalogues of the same, with the names of donors, or price, if purchased by the association, together with any other information concerning them and keep them in order and safety.

SEC. 6. The Superintendent of exchange shall conduct the exchange business of the association under the rules and regulations provided by the by-laws. He shall furnish an approved bond for five hundred dollars or as much more as may be required by the board of trustees.

SEC. 7. The Detector of Counterfeits shall pass upon the genuineness of all coins, medals, etc., which may be submitted to him by the members of the association for that purpose.

SEC. 8. The Board of Trustees shall elect its own Chairman and Secretary. It shall have general oversight of the interests of the association and perform such duties as may be required of it by the constitution and by-laws. Its Secretary shall be the custodian of the official bonds.

SEC. 9. All officers shall report quarterly through the official organ and also present a complete report to each convention which reports shall be published in full in the official organ.

SEC. 10. All officers at the expiration or their terms of office, shall deliver to their successors, all books, papers, monies or other property of the association which may be in their possession and shall not be relieved of their bond or obligation until this requirement has been complied with.

## ARTICLE V.—CONVENTION.

SEC. 1. This association shall meet in convention once each year. A quorum for the transaction of business, shall consist of one-third of the active membership, either present in person or represented by proxy.

SEC. 2. Each convention shall provide for the place of the succeeding one, the date to be announced by the official board at least three months prior to the date of the meeting.

SEC. 3. Upon written request of at least twenty-five members, the President shall call for a general vote of the association upon any desired question.

SEC. 4. Such vote shall be taken under the direction of the board of trustees and a majority of the votes cast shall determine the question.

SEC. 5. Whenever a general vote is taken at least thirty days shall elapse between the call for such vote and the closing of the polls.

## ARTICLE VI. BRANCHES.

The organization of branch associations shall be encouraged in every locality containing five or more members of the association and such branches shall be subject to the provisions thereof in the by-laws.

### ARTICLE VII.—Amendments.

Sec. 1. This constitution may be altered or amended only by the consent of two-thirds of the members voting upon such alteration or amendment.

Sec. 2. The President shall order a general vote upon the reconsideration of any amendment or alteration passed in convention whenever requested to do so by one-third of the voting membership of the association, but no reconsideration shall be taken if notice of such amendment has been published in the official organ not more than sixty nor less than thirty days prior to the meeting of such convention.

Sec. 3. All amendments or alterations shall go into effect at the close of the convention in which they were made, or if made by a general vote, upon official announcement of the result of such vote.

Sec. 4. Any by-laws, not in conflict with this constitution, may be made or amended by the official board, but such by-laws may be subjected to a general vote as provided by Article V, Sec. 3.

Sec. 5. It shall require only the assent of a majority of the members voting to make or amend a by-law in convention.

## By Laws.

1. The dues shall be one dollar per annum, payable to the Secretary in advance, on the first day of October of each year; members admitted during the last half of the fiscal year, will be required to pay only fifty cents for dues until the following October. In case a member neglects to pay his dues before the first day of November, the Secretary shall notify such delinquent member and unless the dues are paid within thirty days, his name shall be stricken from the roll. Any member dropped for non-payment of dues may be reinstated by the board of trustees, upon payment of all back dues.

2. At the annual convention the President shall appoint the following standing committees of three members each:

Credentials, Finance, Standing Rules, Library and Cabinet, Exchange Department, Official Organ, Constitution and By-Laws.

The president shal' be ex-officio Chairman of the committee on constitution and by-laws.

3. The order of business of the convention shall be as follows:

Call to order.
Appointment of standing committees.
Reports of officers.
Report of committee on credentials.
Roll call.
Reading of minutes.
Report of committee on rules.
Communications.
Reports of committees.
Deferred business.
New business.
Election of officers.

All questions of order and parliamentary law not covered by the standing rules of this association shall be determined by reference to Cushing's Rules of Order.

4. In order to facilitate the transaction of business and provide for a rapid decision of questions requiring the vote of the official board, the following shall be the order of proceeding:

Whenever any member of the board desires to submit any matter for its action, he shall reduce the same to writing, in the form of a motion, and mail a copy thereof to each member of the board. Any comments or observations he may desire to make thereon, shall be written upon a separate sheet. Upon the reception of such motion, each member of the board shall write upon the back or bottom thereof his vote for or against the same or any correction or amendment he may wish to make and then forward to the President. In case any amendment has been offerred the President shall mail to each member of the board a copy of the motion as amended, who shall return same at once, endorsing on it his vote for or against the amendment, or his preference for the original motion. Upon receiving the votes of the other members, the President shall certify to the Secretary the motion and vote, accompanying the same with the original papers. The Secretary shall file and record the vote and notify the members of the board of their decision.

5. The Librarian and Curator shall collect, in advance, the necessary postage from any member desiring any book, etc., from the library. Any book, etc., taken from the library shall be returned, without expense to the association, within two weeks after the receipt of same by such member. Any member receiving books, etc., shall be responsible for the safe return of the same in as good condition as when given out, and if damaged, lost or destroyed, he shall be required to replace the same, or pay the cost value, at the option of the Librarian, The Librarian must impose a fine of ten cents a week, for each book, pamphlet or other publication retained longer than the prescribed time, and shall not permit such delinquent member to obtain any more books, etc., until such fine is paid, Fines imposed by this by-law can be remitted only by the board of trustees. The surplus of receipts from fines shall be paid to the Secretary at the end of each fiscal year or term of office.

6. (See Appendix A.)

7. The board of trustees shall prepare a "black list" of individuals who have dealt in counterfeit coins or who have been engaged in questionable transactions with collectors, and also a list of bad debtors and furnish a copy of either list to any member upon payment of a fee of twenty-five cents.

8. The committee on official organ shall make provision for the publication of the proceedings of the association. It shall furnish a copy of each number of the official organ to each member and an additional copy to the President, Secretary, Superintendent of Exchange and Secretary of the Board of trustees. The expense of the official organ shall be paid out of the general treasury.

9 No officer shall incur any expense on account of the association except

for postage and expressage, unless the same has been authorized by the official board.

10. Five or more members residing in the same neighborhood may associate themselves as a branch society. Upon notifying the Secretary of the formation of such branch, he shall assign to it a number, which number shall be assigned in numerical order. Each branch shall be entitled to send a delegate to each convention, but such delegate must be a member of the branch he represents. Collectors, not members of this association, may belong to such branches, but shall not be entitled to the privileges of the association members. Each branch may make by-laws for their own government, provided the same are not in conflict with this constitution and by-laws.

APPENDIX A. (By-Law, 6.)

6. The Superintendent of Exchange shall conduct the exchange business under the following rules and regulations:

a Envelopes in which to enclose coins, etc., shall be furnished by the Superintendent at cost. After properly filling up the description etc., on same, the members will return them to the Superintendent, charges paid.

b The Superintendent will arrange same in packages at his discretion and start on a circuit, expressage paid.

c Each member will forward to next on the list, value declared and expressage paid. Members may retain each lot not longer than four days. A fine of ten cents shall be imposed for each day a package is retained beyond the prescribed time.

d Each member retaining anything from a lot will report and remit to the Superintendent the same day the package is forwarded.

e In case a lot is missing, or any discrepancy exists, the member discovering the same must report at once to the party ahead of him on the circuit and also to the Superintendent. Failure to do so will make the last party responsible.

f Members will be held responsible for all lots lost or injured while in their care.

g The Superintendent will send lots only to such members as request the same, and they must satisfy him regarding their responsibility, before being placed on the circuit.

h The Superintendent will settle with each member when his sales amount to ten dollars or when his lot is returned or sold.

i The Superintendent shall deduct ten per cent of all sales, to cover the expenses of his office. Any deficiency shall be paid out of the general funds: any surplus shall be paid to the Secretary.

j The Superintendent shall have first choice of all exchanges and be entitled to circulate his own lots free of commission.

k The Superintendent may make additional rules and regulations, not already provided for, as will facilitate the exchanging of coins, medals, etc., between members of the association, but such rules, etc., must be approved by the official board before being put in force.

l The board of trustees shall decide all cases of misunderstanding which may arise in this department.

## WITH THE EDITOR.

It is with no small degree of satisfaction that the editor is enabled to fulfill, in some measure, past promises and to come a little nearer that mark he has set out to reach. Though yet at a distance from the goal of his ambition, the breakers ahead are less formidable and the mists seem less dense and he hopes from now on to gradually arrive at the haven of his desires.

He expects a gradual developement of this journal in its interest to collectors of coins. He will endeavor to make it a necessity in every numismatist's home, a fit associate with the treasures of his cabinet and a welcome visitor to any one interested in our science. To this end, the upbuilding of the journal in the interest and growth of our collecting, would he ask your friendly criticism and co-operation.

After due deliberation the subscription price has been placed at ONE DOLLAR per annum, there to stay, and for this price it will be sent post paid anywhere in the civilized world. All who have been fortunate enough to have sent in their subscriptions at the old rate, for their confidence and promptness will be credited the year's subscription.

Unfortunately many typographical errors crept in our January issue. The publisher says the editor's writing is a cross between the ancient Hebrew and Phœnecian and the editor supposing he (the publisher) was conversant with these tongues is the cause of all the trouble, but now that a better understanding exists, of course the errors will be as few as possible—we hope obsolete.

No one can appreciate better than the editor, that what The Numismatist is today, is what you have made it and no one knows better than he what it will be in the future, depends also upon you. Your influence has made it called for beyond the confines of this continent. It goes now to every portion of our globe and wherever it goes, at home or abroad, an oasis for the extension of its influence is formed.

The life of the American Numismatic association and of this journal is so intimately blended that anything that would tend to militate against the one would injure the other and what will build up the one will develope the other. It will, therefore, be the part of wisdom for the two to continue on together in the work of popularizing our science.

The Association, now well along in its third year, is recognized as a power throughout the numismatic world. It always stands ready to strike hands with any kindred organization in work for the advancement of our science. Its dues are merely nominal and any collector of coins or any student of numismatics, whether amateur or professional, is invited to join with us. Further particulars cheerfully given at any time on application to the secretary, Mr. O. W. Page, Waltham, Mass.

# Wants, to exchange, etc.

Wanted—An Isabella quarter. Mrs. Mary O. Mills, Bloomington, Wis.

To Exchange—Colonial paper money. J. A. Bolen, 25 Bay St., Springfield, Mass.

Wanted— Coin Collector's Journal for January, February and March, 1886. Dr. Geo. F. Heath, Monroe, Mich.

To Exchange—Coins, medals and tokens. Correspondence solicited. F. X. Paquet, box 387, Ottowa, Ontario.

Wanted—A specimen of the decoration of the Order of Cincinnati. H. Mansfield-Bullner, Copenhagen, Denmark.

Wanted—May, 1893, issue of The Numismatist. Foreign coins to exchange for Greek, Roman or U. S. coins. Send list with wants. W. H Taylor, North Wales, Penn.

Wanted—The Numismatist for July and August, 1891; February, 1892, and May, 1893, to complete files. Geo. W. Rode, Hazelwood Ave., Pittsburg, Pa.

Wanted—Complete proof sets of silver and copper prior to 1855 except 1850. Also Coin Collector's Journal for October, 1888. W. M. Friesner, 2217 Figueroa St., Los Angeles, Cal.

I have broken bank bills, copper cents, fine minerals, some Indian relics and a lot of curios to exchange for U. S. dimes 1821, '22, '23, '28, '32, '33, '34, '36 and 37. Cent 1811. Store cards, medals, or tokens. J. B. Goldsmith, Beverly, Mass.

---

THE undersigned offers for sale a number of duplicate coins of all denominations and mints (gathered largely while studying "mint marks") his half dime accumulation being especially large and varied. Also a duplicate set or two of copper cents complete with many varieties and a number, good to uncirculated, singly.

A. G. HEATON, 1618 17th St., N. W., Washington, D. C.

---

# Continental Currency

And old copper coins for sale. Address

**D. C. Wismer, Richland Center, Pa.**

---

**CONFEDERATE MONEY**

**Of all kinds, Broken bank bills, State notes, etc. Also confederate stamps.**

**F. C. SAWYER, BEAUCLERC, FLA.**

---

## David Harlowe,

3002 Mt. Vernon Ave. Milwaukee, Wis.

Duplicate Coins for sale or exchange.

---

## AUTOGRAPH LETTERS.

What have you in signed letters from noted literary people, American and Foreign? Send description and price to C. H. Conover, 32 Lake St., Chicago.

---

**H. D. SMITH,**

**NUMISMATIST AND ARCHAEOLOGIST,**

53 Gratiot Ave., Detroit, Mich.

When in Detroit come and see me.

---

**CLARENCE MATHIS, GREENWOOD, NEB.**

*COLLECTOR OF COPPER COINS.*

Duplicates for sale or exchange. War tokens and store cards, 1834-64, to exchange for same, or other coins and medals not in my collection.

---

JOSEPH HOOPER,

Box 105. Port Hope, Ont.

Collections of coins bought or appraised. The best bank and other reference and security given.

---

Roman Denarii, in fine condition, of Antoninus Pius, Caracalla, Geta, Septimus Severus, and Commodus, 2s. ea., or five for 6 free. Several reverses of each.

**T. FORSTER,**

101 High Street. Colchester, England.

---

GEO. F. HEATH, M. D.,

NUMISMATIST,

MONROE, - - MICH.

Specialty: Ancient and Oriental Coins. Will buy, sell or exchange.

TYPES OF EXTINCT CIVILIZATION
MORE HISTORIC THAN WRITTEN HISTORY

# THE NUMISMATIST

**April, 1894.**

An Illustrated Monthly devoted to the Science of Numismatics.

GEO. F HEATH, M.D. Monroe, Mich..

Vol. 7. No. 4.

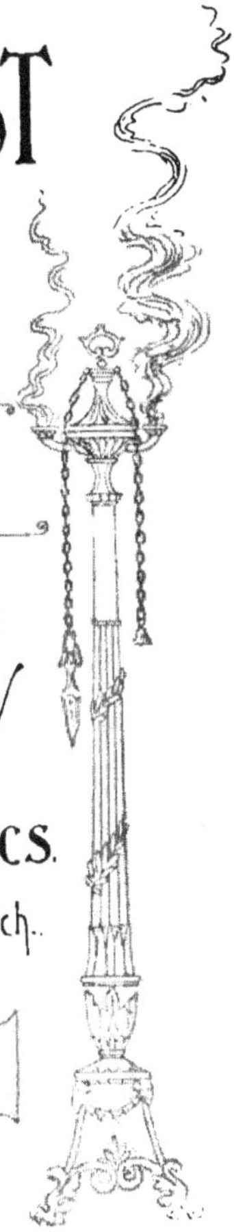

"Press" Steam Ptg. Co., Waterloo, Ind.

## CONTENTS:




# The Numismatist:

A MONTHLY JOURNAL FOR COIN COLLECTORS, AND OFFICIAL BULLETIN OF

## THE AMERICAN NUMISMATIC ASSOCIATION.

ONE DOLLAR A YEAR.

Editorial and publication office, Monroe, Mich.

THE NUMISMATIST is the only Illustrated Monthly Journal devoted to coins and their collecting published on the American continent.

ADVERTISING RATES very reasonable. Made known on application.

SUBSCRIPTION $1.00 per annum, post free to any portion of the civilized world. Remittances may be made by money order, postal note, registered letter, or, when these are not obtainable, in unused postage stamps of low denominations.

Entered at Monroe, Mich., Postoffice, as second class matter.

# The Numismatist.

VOL. VII. MONROE, MICH., APRIL, 1894. NO. 4.

## THE COPPER COINAGE OF FRANCE.

*A paper read at the Third Annual Convention of the American Numismatic Association at Chicago, Ill., Aug. 21, 1893.*

[D. F. HOWORTH, F. S. A. SCOT.]

The political changes which France has undergone during the last century or more makes its series of coins a peculiarly interesting study, and offer ample excuse for the exclusion from the following paper some branches of the subject which might perhaps be expected from the title. I wish, therefore, at once to state what I do *not* propose to attempt, so that readers (or hearers) may not be disappointed.

1 The copper coins of the French Feudal princes, many of which are not uncommon, will not receive attention.

2 The coins of the French colonies will not be noticed. Those who wish to study these are referred to the valuable work on the subject recently published by W. Zay.

3 Siege pieces and money of necessity will be omitted despite the great historical interest which they possess.

4 The Tokens issued by bankers and others during the Revolutionary period will also be omitted. These, with all other issues of that very interesting period, are exhaustively described in "L histoire numismatique de la Revolution Francaise."

5 Mere "Essais" will also be omitted, together with the issues in the names of Napoleon II, Henry V, etc.

The omission of these leaves the way clear to examine the issues of the various Royal mints of France itself, whether under regal imperial or republican forms of government. One other caution, however, may be added—viz: that no attempt will be made in this paper to describe every separate issue, the aim will be rather to so indicate each similar group of coins—if one may so apply the word—that no difficulty will be found in arranging the series.

The first part of the paper will have to deal with Deniers and Doubles. The denier was the twelfth part of a Sou, or Sol, which itself was about one cent in value. The issues in old time from the mint at Tours, which were known as Deniers Tournois and Doubles Tournois, found most acceptance with the people; hence the name was given afterwards to those also which were issued elsewhere.

Later the coins were Sous, Half Sous, and Quarter Sous. The last named were also called Liards, which word is explained by M. Blanchest as corrupted from "le hardi," which itself means the fourth part.

Following these the decimal system will claim attention, the copper coins being the centime and its multiples; the franc being the bases of value.

In former times it was necessary to have many more mints engaged in supplying the demand for currency than is now requisite. The ruder machinery, worked by manual labour only, together with the absence of ready means of transport and communication, quite accounts for the necessity of having a mint in every important centre of population. The following list shows the principal mints in operation during the period under review with the dates of of their closure:

| | | | |
|---|---|---|---|
| C | Cacu, closed 1772 | M | Toulouse, closed 1794. |
| * | Besancon, " " | R | Orleans, " " |
| E | Tours, " " | a cow | Pau, " " |
| G | Poitiers, " " | H | LaRochelle, " 1837. |
| O | Riom, " " | I | Limoges, " " |
| P | Dijon, " " | L | Bayonne, " " |
| S | Rheims, " " | M | Toulouse, reop. 1810, closed 1837. |
| V | Troyes, " " | Q | Perpignan, closed 1837. |
| X | Amiens, " " | T | Nantes, " " |
| Y | Bourges, " " | B | Rouen, " 1858. |
| Z | Grenoble, " " | D | Lyons, " " |
| * | Rennes, " " | * | Marseilles, " " |
| * | Aix, " 1786. | W | (L crowned, 1886) Lille, closed 1858. |
| AA | Metz, " 1794. | BB | Strasbourg, closed 1870. |
| N | Montpelier, closed 1794. | K | Bordeaux, " 1878. |

A Paris. †

The adoption of all recent improvements in machinery, etc., now enables the Paris mint to meet all the demands of the French nation and its colonies.

The sixteenth century was drawing to its close when France first commenced the use of a copper currency, during the reign of Henry III. This king, the last of the Valois line, reigned from 1574 to 1589. Being the third son of Henry II it seemed unlikely that he would be called to occupy the French throne and he was elected to that of Poland in 1572. But the death of his two elder brothers in early life, both of whom were kings of France, brought him into the direct line of the succession, and he left Poland and relinquished its

*Have no characters to represent these mint marks.

†The closing of the mints in 1858 followed on the cessation of the great issues of bronze money intended to replace the old currency. Strasburg was lost to France as one result of the Franco-German war; and Bordeaux, although closed, is held in reserve for use if required.

crown in order to wear that of his native country. He continued however to call himself king of Poland, as the coins will show.

The copper coins of his reign are the Doubles Tournois and the Deniers Tournois. The king's bust is found on the obv. of both, looking to the right usually clad in armour; the head laureated or plain; and the whole generally surrounded with a circle which cuts it off from the legend. In some coins the bust projects beyond the circle, which on some other coins is wanting. The type of rev. is, for the Deniers, two fleurs-de-lis with the m.m. below; for the Doubles, three fleur-de-lis; in both cases a surrounding legend within outer and inner circles. The legends found are,

*Obv: HENRI - III - R - DE - FRAN - ET - POL - and the m.m.
" " " ROI " " " " "
" " " R " FRA " PO - "

Rev: DENIER - TOVRNOIS - date and devise.
" DOVBLE " " "

The period immediately following the death of Henry III was one of civil war between the Protestants, who wanted to place Henry of Navarre upon the throne, and the Catholics, who advocated the claims of the Cardinal Charles de Bourbon. Although the latter cannot be said ever to have been king de facto, and although he died in the midst of the struggle his adherents issued doubles in his name as late as 1595 when their opposition to Henry IV ceased after his adopting the Roman Catholic faith. These coins, struck at Dijon and Troyes only, bear the crowned bust of the Cardinal looking to the left with the legend: CHARLES X - R - DE FRANCE and m.m.; while the rev. is similar to the doubles already described.

So early as 1590 coins were being issued in the name of Henry IV, the son of Jeanne d'Albret, last queen of an independent though curtailed Navarre, and the heir to the French throne through his father, Antoine de Bourbon. The deniers and doubles of this reign bear the king's bust in armour facing to the right, a high collar surrounds the neck, the head is laureate and the face bearded. The legend varies thus:

Henry IV—Double Tournois.

French { HENRI - IIII - R - DE - FRAN - ET - NAV - and m.m.
" " " " " NAVAR "
" 4 " " NAVA "

Latin { HENRI - IIII - D - G - FRAN - ET - NAVAR - REX - and m.m.
HENRIC " " FRANC - ET - NAVA " "
HENRICVS " " " " NAVAR " "

The reverse differs in no way from that of the coins in the previous reign.

---

*The legend usually commences at the lower left hand side and reads round the top; but on one issue, at least, it commences at the upper right hand side and reads round the bottom.

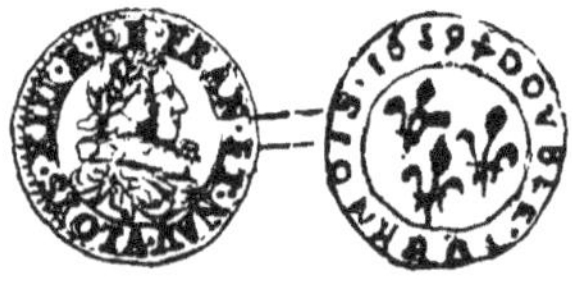


Louis XIII. Double Tournois.

Louis XIII succeeded his father in 1610 and reigned until 1643. During his reign no change occurred in the denominations of the copper coins issued: but some of the varied types must be noticed. The earliest coins bear a boyish looking bust facing to the right, the neck covered with a high collar or a ruff and the head laureate. About 1620 a rather older aspect is given to the face: and in 1629 appears a newly designed bust with draped shoulders and the face for the first time moustachioed and bearded. In this one year there is no surrounding circle and the bust extends at the bottom almost to the outer edge of the coin, thus quite separating the end from the beginning of the legend. A similar, but not usually so large a bust, adorns the various issues until 1642, when an entire change occurs. No longer a bust but the head and neck of an older looking and beardless man facing to the opposite direction is now found. The legend *again* varies:

LOYS XIII [or LOVIS XIII] - R - D - [or DE] FRAN - ET - NAVA - and m.m.
" " " " " " " " NAVAR "
" " " " " " " " " NAV - "

Latin: LVD - XIII - D - G - FR - ET - NAV - REX -

The legend on the deniers is

LOYS - XIII - R - D - FRAN - ET - NA - [or NAV - ]

LOVIS - " " " " "

The reverse remains unaltered.

The long reign of Louis XIV presents a greater variety of coins though it commenced with a repetition of the deniers as the previous reign. These, issued in 1649, bear the youthful king's head laureate and looking to the right with the simple inscription:

LOVIS - - XIIII -

and reverse as before.

Louis XIV Liard de France.

The principal copper coins of this reign, however, were the liards, which naturally fall into two groups—(1) those issued in 1655-7, and (2) those bearing date after 1690.

(1) In the first the young king's bust draped and with the head crowned faces to the right and it extends to the outer edge in the lower part of the coin. Legend:

L - XIIII - ROY - DE - FRA - ET - DE - NA -

and the date. The reverse bears in the three lines the words,

LIARD | - DE - | FRANCE

below which is the m.m. with a fleur-de-lis on each side of it and one below.

(2) In the second group the king's bust with plain head and flowing locks no longer wears so youthful an appearance. The same legend is found, but a rayant sun above the king's head divides the words after the first DE, and and sometimes NAV is found in place of NA. The reverse presents no change.

There were also issues of 2, 4, and 6, deniers, which, although they bear no provincial name, were intended rather for local than general use. The two former were struck only in Strasburg, after the annexation of Alsace. The four-deniers piece bears a similar head and inscription to the liards last described: while the same head on the two-deniers and the later issues of the four bear the legend in Latin, viz:

LVD - XIIII - D - G - FR - ET - NA - REX

The reverse bears three fleurs de lis under a crown surrounded by the words.

PIECE - DE - IIII - [or II -] DENIERS the date and m.m.

The six deniers piece, called a Dardenne, was coined for Provence. It bears on the obverse six L's in three addorsed couples, their bases forming a triangle within which the m.m. finds accommodation: each pair of uprights of the letters is crowned, and each couple of the contiguous "toes" is capped with a fleur de lis.

Legend, LOVIS - XIIII - ROY - DE - FRANCE - ET - DE - NAV

The reverse bears an ornamental cross each arm of which terminates with a fleur de lis. Legends SIX - DENIERS - DE - FRANCE and the date.

With Louis XV an apparently more settled system prevailed during his long reign, when coins of three values of a uniform type were issued. These were the Sou, (of 12 deniers) half-Sou and quarter-Sou or liard. The earliest issue bears the king's bust facing to the right as that of a boy with pleasant open countenance and long wavy hair. The legend is LUDOVICUS XV DEI GRATIA. The reverse bears the crowned Shield of regal France with the inscription continued from the obverse, FRANCIÆ ET - [m.m.] - NAVARRÆ REX and the date. These were struck when the king was about 10 to 12 years old, and then an interval of nearly fifty years elapsed before another issue of copper money. The same three values then bear the king's laureated head looking to the right; and the legend

LUDOV - XV - D - GRATIA

while the reverse exactly copies the last named. The issue from the mint at Aix (m.m.) differs from the others in having quite a distinct head, and a cartouche-like shield.

A sou bearing a design on the obv. similar to the Dardenne of the last reign was issued at the Pau mint in 1727, with the legend

LUD - XV - D - G - FR - ET - NAV - RE and m.m.

The reverse bears within an ornamental cartouche the words

PRODUIT | DES MINES | DE | FRANCE -

with the date in the exergue.

[TO BE CONTINUED.]

The subject of this sketch, well known to the readers of the Numismatist, was born near Snydersburg, Carroll Co., Md., April 26, 1848. He graduated at Pennsylvania College, Gettysburg, in 1873, and in the Theological Seminary at the same place in 1876. Immediately after graduating he entered upon the work of the ministry at Valatie, N. Y. Eighteen months later he resigned for an extended tour through Egypt, Palestine, and Europe. In June, 1879, he became pastor of the First English Lutheran church at Syracuse, N. Y., where he still labors. In 1889 he made another extended trip in Europe and will start again in June next to visit the most interesting places of the same continent.

Mr. Zimmerman is an honorary secretary of the Palestine Exploration Society and is deeply interested in its work as well as that of the Egypt Exploration Society. He has studied numismatics for its historical and archæological value to the student and assisted Funk & Wagnalls, the publishers of the Standard Dictionary, by furnishing the material for their subject on ancient coins. He is a student in the full sense of the word and has a very large and valuable library of standard works. The following we clip from a very late number of the Hudson, N. Y., Daily Republican: "Rev. Jeremiah Zimmerman, pastor of the English Lutheran church, of Syracuse, looks like, and is, a scholar. He is an Egyptologist, and is well posted in the science of numismatics, especially in the department of Biblical coins and medals; he has been honored with an invitation to lecture before one of the scientific assemblies of the World's Fair at Chicago. He is, too, a theologian, and we have been wondering why he has not, ere this date, been doctored. He is abreast of our first men in the pulpit, an active pastor, and a busy man generally."

G. F. H.

## HOOPER'S RESTRIKES.

---

### THE FIRST SILVER COINS.

According to an old tradition, silver was first used as a coin in Great Britain nineteen hundred years ago. A mint is said to have been established at Colchester. in the county of Essex, England. by one of the native kings during the reign of the Emperor Augustus, and gold, brass, and silver coins, to a small extent, were issued therefrom.

---

### RARE AMERICAN COINS.

Coin collectors have long felt great difficulty in making a complete collection of American specimens. The United States coinage of 1793 is very rare, and a dollar of the year 1794 has often sold for as much as $100. A 1796 half-cent is so rare as to sell readily for $15. and a half-dollar of the same year is worth sixty times its original value. While the half-cent of 1804 is common enough. all the other coins of that year are rare, the dollar of that particular date being the rarest of all American coins. Only eight are known to exist out of the 19.570 that were coined. The lowest price that one of these now changes hands for is $800.

---

### A CONFEDERATE COIN DIE.

S. H. Chapman. of Philadelphia. bought the original half-die. from which the Confederacy struck its half-dollar, for $31. on June 27, at the Herman sale, at No. 739 Broadway. The other side of the coin was made from a die in the New Orleans mint in 1861 Only four impressions were made. A cancellation of the die has been effected by a straight file-cut across the face, to prevent its further use. Otherwise it is in perfect condition.

---

### A DOLLAR OF 1804.

The belief that only seven of the 1804 silver dollars were in existence has been an error, for the eighth one has turned up. Rosenthol Bros., dealers in old iron, had a debtor in Virginia, from whom they tried vainly for some time to collect a bill of $500. Recently the Virginian sent the firm one of the much-sought-for 1804 dollars. He stated that he sent the coin in payment of his bill and if the Rosenthol Bros. could sell it for more than the total of the account they could keep the balance.

In explanation of how he came into possession of the dollar, the Virginian wrote that he had bohght it for $30 from an old negro, who was ignorant of its rarity and value, and in whose family it had been for a long time. The Rosenthols took the dollar to the mint here and it was pronounced genuine. A coin collector has offered $350 for the dollar, but they refused the offer, as at an auction sale of coins here one of the 1804 dollars sold for $1,000.

A perfect silver dollar of 1804, recently found with a skeleton in a tree in Illinois, sold for $1,350.—Cincinnati Enquirer.

---

The total coinage of gold and silver, of the reign of Henry III, was £3,898;

the total coinage of the reign of Victoria up to 1892 was £544,100,000, of which £312 300,000 were of gold and £231,800,000 of silver.

THE FIRST HALF-PENCE.

Half-pence were first coined when Mary, Queen of Scots, was a baby in her nurse's arms, and she appears so in the coinage of the year of her birth. In the broad vernacular of those days baby was pronounced "baw-bee" and to this day in many parts of Scotland a half-penny is invariably pronounced a baw-bee, though it has the matronly figure-head of Queen Victoria on one of its sides.

JOS. HOOPER.

## A FEW FINE COINS OF ANCIENT GREECE.

*Translated from the French in Numismatic Circular.*

[G. F. BAUER.]

An amateur from Vendée who collects antiquities, particularly of coins and medals, has gotten together a few fine types of the coin of ancient Greece, and speaking of their artistic character, he says they are, in fact, little triumphs of fine art that remind us of their ancient sculptors now unfortunately lost. The Greeks were superior in the science of numismatics as well as in art and letters. There is nothing more beautiful than the large silver medallions in relief produced in Syracuse at that time a Greek possession. They were designed and engraved by *Evainetos* and Kimon, the two best known artists in this special line at that time. The accompanying cut imperfectly represents this grand medallion.

Fr. Lenormant says in regard to this piece engraved by Evainetos: "In looking but for a moment at this medal we hold in our hand we forget its dimensions and see in our mind a few detached fragments from the prizes of the Parthenon, both representing the highest type of art in its perfection, illustrating as much granduer in the smallest as well as the largest objects, and as much beauty and harmony on a medallion six or seven centimetres in diameter as in a statue of colossal dimension."

ΣΥΡΑΚΟΣΙΩΝ: Head of Porserpine, surrounded by four dolphins; signature ΕΥΑΙΝΕ.

Rev: Victory flying toward a quadriga exergue, a helmet, coat of mail, shield and some leggins, called greaves.

It would appear that the French mint authorities could not find any better design to represent the Republic of 1848 than this head, so beautifully portrayed by *Evainetos* over twenty-two hundred years before. One of our best engravers, Oudiné by name, is thought to have imitated this magnificent and living profile which he transformed into a head of Ceres ornamented with flowers and fruits.

This medallion can be considered the triumph of the *art monétaire*, and authentic copies are rare enough to command a very high price: they are often found counterfeited.

All the other coins of Syracuse are of similar style, pure and gracious: they date from the highest development of Sicily under Denys after the Athenian war, 412-406 B. C.

From an artistic point of view the numismatics of Greece are exceedingly interesting and may be divided into eight periods, beginning about 700 B. C., and extending to the year 268 of the present era. The most interesting are:

1st. The one from 430 to 400 B. C. This period represents the naissance of art, so called, and ended with the Athenian supremacy.

2d. The period 400 to 336 B. C. The most beautiful, the period of the supremacy of Sparta and Thebes and the time of Philip of Macedon.

3d. 336-280 B. C.: the time of Alexander the great and his immediate successors. The art declines with the descendents of the successors of Alexander.

Dekadrachm Syracuse, about 400 B. C.

Up to the time of the successors of Alexander the Great the Greek coinage almost without exception exhibited religious symbols. The head of a mythological god or some animal or sacred object emblematic of a god on a coin, seems to have been the best guarantee of the weight and parity of its metal. Later on the divinity herself was placed on the obverse, while the reverse was occupied by the emblems, etc. Other types represent some of the games as illustrated by the quadriga on the coins of Sicily.

Lysimachus of Thrace had the head of Alexander the Great deified under the form of Jupiter Ammon with a goat's horn back of his ear. Ptolemy Sater of Egypt had his head also put on his coins; also Philip V, king of Macedon.

All of mythology is represented in the numismatics of Greece. Each country or city exhibits to us in their metal the gods to which they were consecrated. Athens shows us Minerva, after the statue of Phidias. The island of Crete, the cradle of Jupiter (his portrait is given). Apollo holds his lyre on the coins of Delphos, which reminds us of the temple he filled with his oracles, and this piece brings us back Diana, escaped from the ruins of the temple of Ephesus. We see on the coins of Teos the portrait of Anacreon, and that of Hippocrates on the money of Cos: also that of Homer on those of Amastris, etc.

The principal type of Greek coins are often followed by smaller types or symbols in allusion to the name of the peoples or the cities; for example, the goat for *Ægos Potomos;* the rose, for Rhode; the seal, for the Phoeceens of Ionia and of Narbonnaise; a grain of wheat, for Crete; an apple, for those of Millos, etc.

It is a small but choice collection of these artistic coins which our amateur has gotten together and I will give you an illustration of a few specimens with notes of explanation.

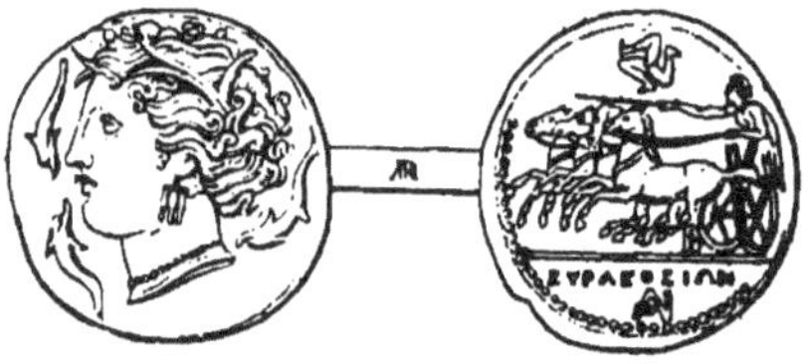

Syracuse, Tetradrachm. B. C. 317-310.

Here is another coin from Syracuse in silver. Obverse, head of the nymph Arethure, coronet of roses, surrounded by three fish (dolphins). The reverse is represented by a quadriga, a *triquetra* above formed of three legs joined together, alluding to the triangular form of the island of Sicily. In exergue ΣΤΡΑΚΟΣΙΩΝ (money of Syracuse) and a monogram composed of the letters AT.

Athens, Tetradrachm. B. C. 525-430.

*Athens.*—FIRST EPOCH.—Since the time of Pisistratus (563-527 B. C.), says Fr. Lenormant, Athens adopted the type of money representing the head of Minerva on the obverse and the owl on the reverse. This design with slight modifications remained up to the time of Alexander the Great.

Obverse: Head of Minerva in archaic style, head ornamented with laurel leaves.

Reverse: ΑΘΕ., beginning of the word ΑΘΕΝΑΙΩΝ (money of the Athenians), the owl, bird of Minerva, and a branch of olive leaves, the whole set in a hollow square.

[TO BE CONTINUED.]

## REVIEWS.

---

ILLUSTRATED HISTORY OF COINS AND TOKENS RELATING TO CANADA.—By P. N. Breton, Montreal. P. N. Breton & Co., 1894. Pp. 240; price $2.

The last is always the best, and this publication is no exception to the general rule, for it is beyond doubt the best work on the coins and medals of Canada yet offered the public. The volume is one of 240 large octavo pages and is gotten up by the British American Bank Note Co., of Montreal, which is sufficient assurance that it is up to the times in the art typographic. The text is in both French and English and is illustrated with over 500 double cuts and describes in brief but comprehensive manner a like number of pieces giving as far as possible the history of the piece, engraver and issuer's names, the number struck, disposition of the dies and comparative rarity. In these respects the publication excels all previous attempts and the reader will be continually surprised at the accuracy and amount of information furnished.

One feature of the work we especially commend and that is the biographical portion containing portraits and brief sketches of some of the more noted Canadian numismatists. We need to know more of the men who have added so much to our science. It would have been better if the portraits instead of being scattered through the book had been relegated to the rear with the biographical sketches, but this can be remedied in the rebinding.

The compiler begins with No. 500, this we suppose in order to avoid all possible confusion with his former editions. The history of the multitudinous church tokens and religious medalets of Canada, to the credit of the work, has not been attempted. We notice that Mr. Breton has taken the cue from the Numismatist and at the last moment dropped his Nova Scotia mills taken from his Canadian list and given to England her due.

To any one interested at all in the collection or history of Canadian coins or tokens, including the card and paper money, legitimate colonial and dominion issues, together with the private issues of coin collectors; trade, bread, milk, shave, drink and pool tokens, this work will be found complete and invaluable.

---

VARIETIES OF UNITED STATES CENTS OF 1794.—By Ed Frossard and W. W. Hays. New York; privately printed 1893; pp. 18; plates 2; small folio cloth, $1.

Since the publication of Dr. Mavis' work on the cents of 1794 which so long has been the authority on the cents of this year, several new varieties and combinations of dies have been discovered rendering a new edition almost a matter of necessity. This has been accomplished by Messrs. Frossard and Hays, two men as well qualified by study and research on the subject as we have. Two photogravure plates of forty obverses and forty reverses taken from excellent specimens faithfully illustrate the text. In all fifty-six varieties are illustrated and described. A table is presented giving the corresponding number in Dr. Mavis work. The Scott Stamp and Coin Co. L't'd., of N. Y., have bought up the remaining edition and will send copies of the work postpaid for $1.25.

# THE CONFESSIONS OF A COIN CRANK.

[BY THE CRANK HIMSELF.]

The first full series of our cents I ever saw was one I used to see when a boy in the main hall way of a then prominent business college in the East. The coins were arranged *ad seriatem* in a large frame with many others and held in place by round-headed tacks, the tacks being driven close to the edge of the coin, holding it in place by the over-lapping head. I remember this frame well for it was the first effort of the kind I had ever seen or heard of, and stimulated me in my efforts to complete my set. The pieces were in an ordinary condition, the most of them, though the dates were distinct. There had been a space left for the 1815 and the probabilities are that the getter-up of the collection was not aware that no cents were struck in that year.

It was about this time that I got my first '99. It had originally served very likely for a '97 or '98, the last figure of the date having been cut out and a "9" substituted in its place. The work had been well done but the joining together was plainly discernable. It suited my purposes, however, for some eight years or until I began to look to the bettering of the condition of my series, when I got a good specimen and the other was parted with. But the strangest thing happened. Fully twenty years later, among a lot of coins received from a Philadelphia auction sale what should turn up but my old '99 (?) friend again, looking as natural as life and no worse for its long absence, showing that it had been well cared for. I parted with it again and years later it went down with a collection through a burning building and landed in a cellar cistern. Some of the collection was recovered in a damaged state, but the '99 "never came back." Strange to relate that while some of the larger silver and gold pieces were never found, a little twenty-five cent gold piece was returned unharmed.

And now I come to another confession, and I do it with all regret and humiliation—regret that I knew no better and humiliation that when I did know better I did not follow my best judgement, and this confession is that for twenty years and more when I should have known better. I tried to collect coins without studying them or knowing their literature—nothing further of them than that they were coins, and had been used as a medium of exchange by such and such peoples. Beyond that I had no care. To be sure I had never heard of Dickeson or Humphreys, neither had I heard of the efforts at coin periodicals so to some extent I was excusable and yet when I go back to the comparatively later years and realize that though collecting all this time I did not know of Crosby or Mavis, that my name never appeared on the subscription books of the American Journal of Numismatics or Coin Collectors' Journal but for one year, I now realize with much shame and mortification the great loss to myself, for I look back upon those long years with regret that I did not collect intelligently and therefore did not receive a tithe of the benefits I should have derived.

Given, the all important material, brains, with suitable proportions of white and gray matter, the test of a farmer's success will depend much upon the implements he has to do with. The test of the mechanic's skill or ability will depend much upon the tools with which he labors. The test of the lawyer's or physician's capability for successful and scientific work will depend very much on the books or instruments he has for use.

Given the same mental qualification, just as true will the test of the numismatist's ability for scientific work and his capacity for appreciating and enjoying his collecting will depend upon his library and the knowledge to be gained therefrom. There can be no questioning this truth. To get the most out of your collecting you must know about it; to know about it you must have good literature.

A "crank" is one who collects and knows nothing about what he collects, in other words, is not *sane* in his collecting. We often hear of him in the general press; he possesses the "only genuine shekel of King Solomon," the "coin dated B. C.," the one "so very old you cannot see the date," "the only Connecticut cent in the country,' the only "widow's mite known" he has the full pedigree of. You will always recognize this individual, for we often meet him. He has never heard of a coin journal and the only work on the subject he has ever seen is a pamphlet on prices paid for old coins issued by some peripatetic dealer, and this he guards with zealous care. There is no harm in the "coin crank," the disgrace is to *remain* one.

The coin "faddist" or "hobby-rider" belongs to the middle class, the mean between the "crank" and the numismatist. He is in a state of evolution. He collects and classifies, why or how he cannot explain satisfactorily to himself or others. He is endowed with the collecting sense. The germ is within and only needs the warmth and light of the numismatic sun and the refreshing rains of our literature to quicken him into a useful individual. There is great hope for this class.

The numismatist belongs to the highest type of the order *Collectores*. He belongs to some organization in the interest of his science. He is a liberal subscriber to the literature of his collecting. He is well and intelligently acquainted with his cabinet. He dwellest in the Seventh Heaven. He consorts with kings and queens, emperors and sages. The world from ihe dawn of history and all it contains is his. He is supremely happy. Of course the readers of the NUMISMATIST, whatever they may have been, are all numismatists.

---

That gentleman was surprised and he said so. He was surprised that Mr. Gruber did not know that he could not do such a thing. Mr. Gruber was surprised that Mr. Chase, then secretary of the treasurry, did not know that it could be done very successfully. He even produced a letter from the director of the mint at Philadelphia, in which that gentleman declares the Colorado coin superior in every way to the government coin and actually worth 1 per cent. more than Uncle Sam's money. .

## AUCTION ROOM ECHOES.

The following prices were realized at the auction sale of the Messrs. Chapman on March 6 and 7. Dickinson and Lindsay collections.

23 Judaea, Simon Maccabees shekel of Israel, triple lily, v. fine...... $16 00
24 Same, half-shekel........ 21 50
33 Rome B. C. 385, head of Janus; U. S. weight, 8¼ oz.; v. fine......... 8 50
191 1652, Massachusetts Pine Tree shilling, crosby 14—K, v. good...... 4 00
208 1791, Washington cent, bust left, sun-eagle, v. good........ 3 00
224 1855, U. S. Dollar, proof........ 13 00
264 1794, U. S. half-dollar, v. good........ 6 00
266 1797, same, good........ 43 00
268 1802, same, v. good........ 5 50
283 1815, same, fine........ 6 50
425 and 426 1877–78, twenty cent pieces, proof @........ 2 75
496 1805 half dime, good. 1846 same, v. good........ 5 00 and 2 25
578 1804 Cent broken die, fair........ 4 00
638 1856 Nickel cent, proof........ 5 00
643 1793 Half cent, very good........ 3 25
646 1796 " poor........ 15 00
760 Alfred, Saxon king, 872-901, AELF RED, fine........ 5 30
762 Eadgar, 959-75, EADGAR REX, penny, very fine........ 6 00
766 Harold I, 1035–40, HAROLD REX, penny, good........ 8 50
768 Harold II, 1066, HAROLD REX ANG, penny, v. fine........ 12 00
769 William I (the Conqueror), 1066–87, PILLEMUS REX, v. fine........ 8 00
790 Edward VI, crown 1552, royal arms on long cross, very good........ 8 50
794 Philip and Mary, busts vis a vis, shilling, fine........ 7 50
796 Elizabeth, crown 1601, bust in rich, dress fine........ 13 00
797 " type of last, same date, fine........ 12 50
801 James I, 1603-25, king in armor mounted, Rev: Square top shield, QUAE DEUS, crown, fine........ 30 00
806 Charles I, 1625, crown, Tower mint, CHRISTO, etc., fine........ 19 00
812 Commonwealth, crown 1652, "God with us," fine........ 13 00
813 " half-crown, type of last, fine........ 5 50
819, 820, 821 Oliver Cromwell, crown, half-crown, shilling, all 1658 and very fine 50 00
850 Anne, ANNE DEI GRATIA, 1714, copper farthing........ 5 00
878 William IV, crown 1831, proof, plain edge........ 67 00
1013 India, Delhi, Ghias-ad-din, 720-725 A. H., (goldmohur,) fine........ 10 00
1015, 1017, 1018 India, Mohurs of Akbar, Farrukhsiyar and Mohammed Ali, fine @ 8 50
1084 to 1103 Siam, porcelain money, ranged from........ 50 to 1 50

## AMERICAN NUMISMATIC AND ARCHÆOLOGICAL SOCIETY

(17 WEST FORTY-THIRD ST., NEW YORK CITY.)

Abstract from minutes American Numismatic and Archæological Society—A special meeting was held on Feb. 5, 1894, President Parish presiding. The object of the meeting being to consider a resolution relative to designs for the coinage of the United States.

Mr. George F. Kunz presented the following: Whereas, there is no more honorable way of perpetuating the history or the art of design of a nation in the hearts and minds of its people than by the issue of its mints either as coins or medals on account of their permanence and popular use, and, Whereas, the appropriations of Congress for the use of the United States mints have been, within the limit of the amount allowed, used in a way to reflect honor to all who have been concerned therewith, and, Whereas, the growth of the metric system throughout the world renders it adapted to our decimal system and would thereby give our mint issues a world wide circulation on account of their utility and beauty. Be it

Therefore enacted by the Senate and House of Representatives of the United States in Congress assembled that the honorable Secretary of the Treasury be directed to appoint a committee of five members to consist of two well known sculptors, artists or medalists to be named by the National Sculptors Society of New York, two well known numismatists or medal collectors to be named by the American Numismatic and Archæological Society, and a fifth to be a recognized authority on weights and measures to take into consideration all matters relating to the United States mints as appertain to the weight, design and execution of coins and medals for the future. Be it

Therefore enacted that in order that the investigations of this committee shall be of immediate benefit to the public that the honorable Secretary of the Treasury be directed to expend ten thousand dollars, five thousand dollars to be divided between artists or designers and five thousand dollars between die-sinkers who are willing to compete for said rewards upon the conditions that the said committee may indicate, one of which there shall be that the result of such competition shall be capable of being used by the United State's mints. Seconded and carried unanimously.

A letter was read from F. Wellington Ruckstuhl, Secretary of the National Sculpture Society, and Mr. Sturgis in behalf of that society stated that they wished to obtain the endorsement and co-operation of our Society. On motion a committee of three consisting of Daniel Parish, Jr., and Messrs. Geo. F. Kunz and Andrew C. Zabriskie were appointed to confer with the National Sculpture Society. On motion adjourned. H. RUSSELL DROWNE,
Secretary.

A square copper coin, struck by the Swedish government in the sixteenth century, is nearly one-half inch thick and weighs a pound and a quarter.

## THE AMERICAN NUMISMATIC ASSOCIATION.

BOARD OF OFFICERS:



## PERSONAL AND LOCAL.

### A Correction.

The address of C. W. Stutesman; 1730 Market St., Logansport, Ind., is incorrectly given in our March issue, Roll of Members of the A. N. A., as Indianapolis.

Secretary Page reports the following new members:

188 George Rowe. M. D. No. 2 Cayaduct St., Gloversville, N. Y.
189 Mrs. P. R. King, 552 Dearborn Ave., Chicago, Ill.
190 Jacob Weigel, 266 Burnett St., New Brunswick, N. J.
191 C. B. Norton, Box 127, Conneaut, O.

The application of B. H. Collins, Washington, D. C., has been received in regular form and if no objection he will be entitled to membership certificate on May 1.

Farrar Ineson (No. 9) has removed to Carleton West, Ontario.

D. C. Wismer write us that strictly speaking the U. S. dollar is size 24. The half-dollar 19 and the quarter 15.

One of our western members, C. S. Wilcox, of Chicago, has just secured the finest known specimens of half dollar 1805 over 04.

Mr. P. N. Breton has placed in the library of the A. N. A. a copy of his excellent work, The Illustrated History of Coins and Tokens relating to Canada.

An interesting letter has lately been donated to our library. It is dated from the U. S. mint December 1, 1857, and signed by James Ross Snowdon, the then director.

Wm. Rowley succeeds to the firm of Fletcher Rowley & Co. and has removed to 107 S. Clark St., Chicago, Ill. He is agent for the Scott Stamp and Coin Co., for Chicago.

Brother F. F. Budd, of Fort Wayne, Ind., is engaged in stirring things up there in the interest of our science. That ancient and historic town will soon be heard from numismatically.

Mr. H. E. Morey, 31 Exchange St., Boston, Mass., has issued his Numismatic Quarterly and Catalogue for January, 1894. It gives colonial coin history, finds and queries as well as bargains in coins.

Brothers Oatman, Mathis, Wismer and Budd write us to second the remarks of Mr. Walker in March Numismatist. They are all in favor of a membership medal. We want to hear from more in the matter or address Mr. J. B. Walker, Box 28, Agency, Ia.

It is stated by the highest authority that Mr. B. H. Collins, of Washington, has, as an entirety, the finest set of U. S. cents in this country. The basis of this grand set was once the personal collection of the oldest coin dealer in England if not in the world, Mr. W. S. Lincoln, 69 New Oxford St., London.

Brother Ph. Whiteway, after spending the winter in New Zealand is about to return to England. Mr. Whiteway is engaged in literary and journalistic work and his contributions to fiction and letters of travel have been published the world around. The readers of the Numismatist shall know more of this gentleman soon.

Two of our prosperous dealers in coins have lately taken in partners and enlarged their business. F. R. Kimball, of Waltham, Mass., has associated with him Mr. P. C. Turner under the firm name of F. R. Kimball & Co. and Mr. Steigerwalt, of Lancaster, Pa., has added a philatelic department to his business with Wm. R. Wilshaus in charge.

## A Tale of Woe.

Mrs. Numisma:—"So strange Jack that Arthur should have attempted suicide and only married two weeks."

Mr. N.—"But there were extenuating circumstances you know."

Mrs. N.—(meditatively) "Why Jack, to be sure Miss Ann Tique had been in the market some time, and was his senior ten or fifteen years."

Mr. N.—"Yes dear, but that 1804 dollar she has so long possessed and Arthur so much desired, to complete his set, he sent down to the Chapmans last week, who pronounced it a raised 1801, and Arthur accused her of obtaining a husband under false pretenses. She turns around and charges him with obtaining money under false pretenses, and—well, the poor fellow had nothing else to do."

In Tepe-Kermene, an ancient town in Crimea, a platina coin has been found bearing the image of Antiochus of Syria, who died B. C. 164. The coin is the only one of its kind known to exist and for this reason its value is inestimable.

# QUERIES.

This Department is open to all the readers of The Numismatist. A *non de plume* may be used if desired in either the asking or answering queries.

A saying we here commend to you
Ye learned, ye wise ye great ye small;
Far better to have aimed and missed,
Than never to have fired at all.

12—Of the 1836 half-cents which is the rarer, the original or the restrike?
*1811*

13—On the 1860 fine dollar Mormon piece (gold) there are some curious characters that look like a cross and recross of all the ancient alphabets. What are they, and what does it say? 1811

Ans.—Reverse:—A lion conchant occupying the field. Legend, same as on the obverse. Assay office G. S. L. C. only in the "Deseret" characters, an alphabet on phonographic principles.—*Dye's Coin Encyclopedia.*

A correspondent to whom we referred the query, answers: "In reference to the query by 1811 as to the language on the Mormon fine dollar gold piece of 1860, I would say that it is supposed to mean 'Holiness to the Lord.' This is said to be the reformed Egyptian or sacred language of the Latter Day Saints. The first plates exhumed by Jos. Smith were in this language. Personally I believe it to be all bosh."

14—Can you publish the whereabouts of the 1804 dollars and 1802 half-dimes?
C. Mathis.

Ans.—Yes, if some one will undertake to furnish the information.

15—I should like to know the value of this coin as a curiosity should I wish to sell it to a numismatist. Geo. Nusser, Plevna, Kan.

Ans.—This correspondent sends us a cast copy of a dekagram of Syracuse, bears the name of Evaintos. It is struck in bold relief in base silver and as far as the die work is concerned is evidently a good copy. What it was struck for we are unable to discern. As the originals weigh from 650 to 667-5 grains and this copy only 290, it could not have been meant to deceive, for the veriest tyro in ancient coins would not have been imposed on by it. We have submitted it to two of our best experts on this side who express no further opinion than that it is a modern cast.

16—Can anyone give me a description of the iron money of King Cyrus. I have three *facsimiles* said to be from original coins, but doubt their authenticity. F. F. B.

One million dollars in gold coin will weigh exactly 3,685.8 pounds or a ton and three-quarters. A million dollars in silver weighs 58,929.9 pounds. A ton of pure gold, without alloy, is worth $602,799.21; a ton of pure silver, $37,704.84.

# THE WORLD OF FAD.

The oldest known poem is the Song of Miriam.

Over 8,000 varieties of postal have been issued since 1870.

The notes of the Bank of England cost exactly one-half penny each.

There are 2,700 complete bibles in all languages in the British museum.

The finest collection of antiquities in the world is in the British museum.

What is the difference between a horse and a hobby? You can get off of a horse.

Three centuries ago only seven metals were known to exist. Now there are fifty-one.

Cakes of tea in India and pieces of silk in China and salt in Abyssinia and codfish in Iceland have all been used as money.

Mrs. Charles J. Barnes, of Chicago, Ill., rejoices in the collection of 218 tea-pots each one of which has an enviable history.

The herbarium and library of the late Dr. C. C. Parry, of Davenport, Ia., one of the most valuable in this country, has been purchased for the agricultural college at Ames. The only collection to rival it west of the Alleghany mountains is the Engelmann, of Missouri.

Of the 68 true specimens of the Great Auk's eggs known to exist, Great Britain claims 48; France, 10; Germany, 3; Holland, 2; Denmark, Portugal and Switzerland, 1 each, and the United States, 2. The specimen just sold in London to Sir Vauncey H. Crewe for 300 guineas is said to have been bought some seventy years ago by William Yarrow for a few francs, and to have been sold in 1856 for twenty guineas.

Such of the readers of The Numismatist as visited the World's Fair will remember the Tiffany exhibits of gems and precious stones which were displayed in the Tiffany pavillion in the Manufacturers' building. This collection contained a specimen of every known gem and the best examples the firm could obtain. One specimen, the famous Hope opal, once having sold in London for $26,310. This collection entire has been bought by the trustees of the Field Museum, of Chicago, and the price paid about $100,000.

Poodle and other diminutive dogs are these days taking back seats as ladies' pets. The latest live stock freak they now indulge in is the chameleon. These animals are chained to the hats and are sought so extensively that in our larger cities the humane agents of the Society for the Prevention of Cruelty to Animals have taken action to forbid their sale. Mme. Melba, the great prima donna, instead of a lizard, is bringing up a large, gorgeous-hued Mexican beetle that capers around her throat and down her back with the utmost abandon.

# GENERAL NEWS.

The gold coins of Great Britain contain one-twelfth alloy.

The Spartans had an iron coinage no other at the time being allowed.

A gold coin depreciates five per cent. in value in 16 years of constant use.

The city of Montreal claims to come into the possession of the finest(?) collection of coins in the world consisting of 1,600 specimens. They belonged to an exiled Russian family.

While excavating for the foundation of a house on Boyle street. Allegheny: James Dixon, a contractor, unearthed a crock containing nearly $500 in gold. It is supposed to have been buried by James Graham, an eccentric old gentleman who died fifty years ago.

The Scott Stamp and Coin Co. L't'd. have this to say regarding Mr. A. G. Heaton's treatise on the coinage of the United States branch mints: "This particular branch of the United States coinage has long been a matter of special interest to collectors and many have noted something connected with the various mints and the mark that is peculiar to each of them. But Mr. Heaton is the pioneer in placing a treatise on the subject, before the public. How well he has succeeded the large sale the book has met with since it was placed on the market expresses more than tongue, pen or printers ink can do. It is almost unnecessary to remark here that by reason of the intel'igent research, careful classification and scientific enthusiasm of the compiler, his work is entitled and likely to remain a hand-book of the highest authority on the subject for years to come.

## Private Coinage.

The talk of Colorado coining money on her own account has revived the story of the early days of Denver, when Clark, Gruber & Co., the Leavenworth bankers, made money at the old mint on Market street in the early '60's.

In this connection it may be interesting to readers to know that Mr. Gruber of the old banking firm above referred to is now a notary public of Cripple Creek and one of the most interesting characters of that interesting camp. He told me the story of the Denver mint and his experience at Washington when he showed some Colorado coin to Secretary Salmon P. Chase.

The matter was referred to the attorney-general, who surprised the administration by declaring that up to that time there was no law prohibiting the "uttering" of money by private individuals. In order to get out of a bad hole and prevent the issuing of money by citizens in the future the government then bought the Denver plant for $25,000, if I mistake not and congress passed a law which gives to the United States government the sole right to coin silver and gold into money.

# WITH THE EDITOR.

## Convention Papers.

The time of our convention meeting is rapidly drawing nigh, and before we are hardly aware of it, will be at hand, and it is important that all who have promised to give us papers on this occasion, or will give papers, should report at once. There is one thing certain, we shall make no mistake in regards to this—either the papers or reasonable promises of the same must be forthcoming or the feature will be dropped and when we part with this feature of our program we are taking a step backwards. Is the association going to do this? We believe not! The officers of the association will do their part, but before they will see this part of the program a failure or unworthy of our association, they will see it dropped altogether. We must not have a failure. For many reasons it is important that this question be settled very soon and we hope to hear at once from any and all members interested in this part of the convention work, so that proper arrangements may be made: It might be stated here that the following gentlemen have already given assurance of aid: Messrs. Brudin, Bauer, Howorth, Whiteway, Wismer, Stone, Tatman, Hooper and Heaton. We have reasons to believe Messrs. Zimmerman, Drowne, Fisher and Bingham may be relied upon also and we hope others will yet see their way clear to help us make this a lively and important part of our convention. Whatever else may be accomplished by the convention it is upon this the public will give verdict of our usefulness. Let us show them that we are not an association of "cranks," but of scientific work.

For the many words of encouragement and congratulation the editor has received over the appearance of the revised NUMISMATIST, he returns his grateful acknowledgements. He can assure his readers that the standard at present adopted will continue during the year. Whether the forthcoming years will see this magazine on the same plane as now, must and will depend upon the support received this year. THE NUMISMATIST needs and hopes to deserve all the aid and support its friends can give, and promises full return for all thus given.

The editor of THE NUMISMATIST does not desire his name considered as a candidate for renomination as president of the A. N. A., under any circumstances. This statement is made this early so that the members may be canvassing among the many available ones for the place, and that no embarrassments may result. The office of president of this association is an honorable one, and as such has been appreciated by the present incumbent, and as such deserves to be passed around.

As THE NUMISMATIST is published in the interest of collectors and students of coinage, the editor hopes all will feel perfectly free to use any portion of its pages or departments.

Contributions, news items, correspondence, clippings, queries, exchange notices, all will be gladly utilized for the common good. Let us fill our magazine to over flowing, and if it is not large enough we will tear down and build larger. Let us hear from you.

## Applications for the A. N. A.

The following have been received in due form:

Leslie W. Hills, 9 E. Main St., Ft. Wayne, Ind.

H. H. Walter, 274 W. Creighton Ave., Ft. Wayne, Ind.

Recommended by Messrs. Budd and Heath.

## Coins as Letter Weights.

Many are the uses of money; but Jos. Newton, late of the Royal mint, points out there is at least one use which is not generally known. This is the availability of coins for letter weighing when the ordinary postal weights do not happen to be at hand. Commencing with the sovereign, this weighs a very safe quarter-ounce, for foreign postage, two equalling, of course, a half-ounce and four one ounce. The next denomination, the crown piece, is just on the right side of one ounce in weight and the half crown of half-an-ounce. Five separate shillings, or two shillings and a six-pence for the ounce, and half-ounce will do as well. Descending from the gold and silver to hard-working bronze, it is found that either three-penny pieces or five half-pence, or ten farthings, will respectively make up one ounce. Another peculiarity in regard to the half-penny is noted by Mr. Newton. That is its diameter, which is precisely one inch, so that by using it as a measure it will be seen that twelve half-pence laid flat and in touch are equal to one foot and thirty-six to one yard.

## Bandit Treasure.

A few weeks ago a Spaniard arrived at Arneca, state of Jalisco, Mexico, from Spain. He had with him documents and drawings showing the location of hidden treasure secreted a century or more ago by a band of brigands. Perez has already had success. An iron box filled with gold coin and jewelry, valued at $500,000 has been unearthed.

# The Numismatist.

VOL. VII. MONROE, MICH., JULY, 1894. NO. 7.

## COINS, THEIR ORIGIN AND AID IN HISTORIC RESEARCH.

*A paper read at the Third Annual Convention of the American Numismatic Association at Chicago, Ill., Aug. 21, 1893.*

CONTINUED FROM PAGE 105.

[JOSEPH HOOPER, ESQ., PORT HOPE, ONT.]

The idea has prevailed that coined money was coeval with the race of man, or at least at as early a period as national organizations existed. It is evident gold and silver became valuable as ornaments long before they were used for coins.

We find Eleazer of Damascus carrying to Rebecca rings and bracelets of fixed weight, and in the same verse, 42d chapter of Job, we find each of Jobs friends brought him an ear-ring as well as a Lamb or "piece of money." That these rings and bracelets became frequently and at length commonly a medium of exchange, we have abundant evidence. The Egyptian monuments show that the common form of the valuable metals when in course of transfer was the ring.

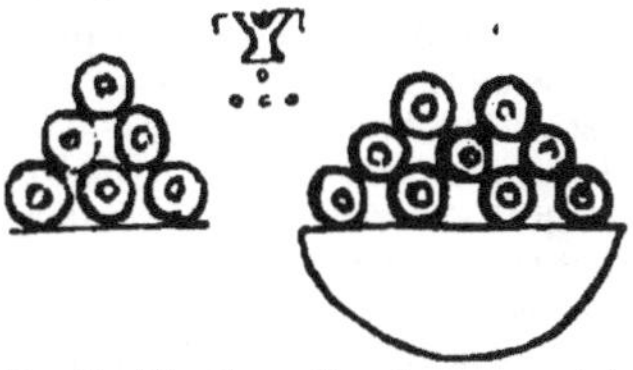

Egyptian Ring Money (from the monuments.)

Ancient writers refer to rings and bracelets as the usual form of gold ornaments, and modern customs in the east are doubtless accurately like the ancient.

The Oriental traveler is surprised to find the poorest woman sometimes wearing heavy gold bracelets and anklets; but his surprise ceases when he learns that there is no investment for money in the east which pays interest, and that as a consequence the poor and rich, when they accummulate more or less gold, are accustomed to call in the travelling tinker who with crucible, furnace and hammer, sits down in the court of the palace or on the ground floor of the hut, and out of the coins handed soon fashions a rude bracelet or anklet which adorns the dusky leg or arm of the favorite wife until necessity compels its transfer. When this necessity comes there is no delay or trouble about it in an Eastern Market. The owner goes into the street to make a purchase and tenders his bracelets as payment. The convenient money changer is at hand in every street with his scales, the weight is told—it is three, five, ten or twenty mejiddi, and the merchant takes it as readily as coin. This is regarded as one of the best evidences of the Ancient custom of using similar bands of precious metal for currency. We give also the illustrations well known to Numismatists "*the Ring money*" of the Ancient Britons dating before the Roman Invasion and at a period not many centuries later than the invention of coined money by the Greeks and continuing in use down to a late period in the Christian era. These rings have been found in various parts of England and Ireland. In 1832 a quantity valued at $5,445 (intrinsic gold value) was dug up at St. Quentin in varied forms. Some large ornaments were evidently worn over the shoulder, others on the arms and around the waist. Cæsar, in his account of England, distinctly relates that rings of fixed weights were used for money in Britain. He says the same of Gaul. We find the same sort of money spoken of in the north of Europe; the Bible contains so many allusions to similar ornaments that there is no reason to doubt that they had a fixed weight and passed current as coins. As yet no regular coin existed. The Greeks had been in the habit of using bars or spikes of metal. A bar was an abolus (translated a spike or small obelisk) six of these were as many as a man could grasp in his hand. Six obli made one drachma (a handful) thus originated the coins "obolus" and "drachm" the latter being to this day the coin of Greece, and having given its name to weights and measures in all the languages of the civilized world, it was about 800 B. C. that the first money was coined. There is doubt in the minds of antiquarians as to the precise spot where the custom originated. Heroditus ascribes it to the Lydians his authority is not conclusive. The oldest coins extant and probably the first ever made are from Ionia in Asia Minor. Miletus a city south of Ephesus, on the shore of the Icarian Sea, probably produced the first coined money the gold "stater," the coin was stamped on one side with a deep indentation. On the other it has a rude picture of a lion's head. This form is characteristic of coinage for a long period. A die was used and the lump of metal placed in it, and a punch struck with a hammer drove the metal into the die leaving the rude mark of the punch on the reverse of the coin. What induced the adoption of the lions head as a design is left for

Egyptian Ring Money, Gold and Silver (from the monuments.)

Early Ring Money of Britian.

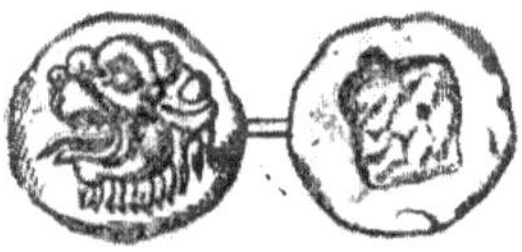

Stater of Miletus, 700 B. C.

conjecture. By some it is supposed to refer to the regal power represented by the lion while others think it had reference to the worship of Cybele, the goddess of the Ionians. A somewhat similar coin which some numismatists suppose to be of earlier date than the Ionian is of Lydian origin and is referred to by Herodotus, we give as a specimen of one of the earliest if not the earliest.

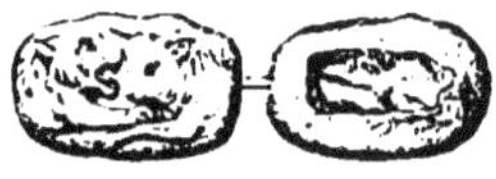

Gold Stater of Sardis, B. C. 568-554.

These have been found in considerable quantity at Sardis and there is reason to believe some are of the period of Croesus. The value of these two coins is the same. It was called a stater or standard, and it is worthy of remark that the value of this first gold coin known has been continued in European currency with slight variation down to the present time. These coins were the first specimens of stamped gold in the form of money.

Drachms of Aegina B. C. 700 [illegible].

Silver was coined in Ægina not long after the date of the Lydian and Ionian gold. When copper was introduced as a medium of exchange does not appear.

From this rude beginning the art of coinage advanced to a stage of beauty in early periods which has been hardly surpassed in our day. This advance was not instantaneous but measured, gradual, and slow.

## Addenda: Metals, etc., Used.

The only method of purifying gold, known to the Ancients seems to have been that of grinding and then roasting: by this process they succeeded in getting it very pure.

It was the boast of the Athenians that this coinage was finer than all other money in Greece, and Xenophon says they exchanged it with profit in any market. Iron was used by the Lacedaemonians and Bysantines, probably on account of the abundance of the metal in Laconia and on the shores of the Euxine.

Aristotle mentions iron and silver as examples of the materials of money, and tells us elsewhere that the people of Clazomenae had iron money; and there are some obscure testimonies respecting the use of iron money in the earliest age of Rome. Not a specimen of iron money is now extant, a fact easily accounted for by the liability of the metal to rust. Tin was coined by Dionysius at Syracuse, no specimens are extant. Leaden money is frequently mentioned by the poets and not a few coins or medals of it are preserved; but it is doubtful if they were true money.

Leather, wood and shells are also referred to as materials of money, but could only have been tokens. Leather money is said to have been used by the Carthaginians, Spartans, and Romans. The earliest denomination of money and the constant unit of value in the Roman and old Italian coinages was made of mixed metal called "ÆS" (Libra). Like all other denominations of money it originally signified a pound weight (of 12 ounces) of copper uncoined. The earliest copper were not struck, but cast in a mould. In the collection of coins at the British Museum there are four ases joined together as they were taken from the mould in which many were cast at once. In most "ases" the edge shows where they were several from each other. Under the Roman empire the right of coining gold and silver belonged only to the Emperors, but the copper coinage was left the "ærarium, which was under the jurisdiction of the Senate.

The words "Aes" or "As" signify both pure copper and a composition of metals, in which copper is the predominent ingredient. In the latter sense it should not be translated brass, but rather bronze. Brass is a combination of copper and zinc, while all the specimens of ancient objects formed of the compound material ÆS are found upon analysis contain no zinc, but with very limited exceptions, to be composed entirely of copper and tin, which mixture is properly called bronze electrum. A compound of gold and silver, and billon and patin alloys of silver and bronze were also used.

The material used and manner of construction in heavy reliefs with concave reverses, show intentional time resisting design, from which our coin-makers of the present day would do well to copy.

Thanking you gentlemen for your patient hearing.

FINEM.

PORT HOPE, ONTARIO.

A very much worn and sadly dilapidated carpet covered the floor of the cashier's office in the mint. A new one involved the expenditure of perhaps $75 and for weeks Superintendent Townsend has endeavored to secure permission from the department at Washington to buy one. The mass of red tape and the difficulty of obtaining money for any purpose balked him but he pegged away patiently and a day or two ago had the satisfaction of gaining permission to buy the needed carpet, which cost him a little more than $70. The wretched old covering was burned. The ashes were refined and they yielded $400 of gold.—Philadelphia Record.

# REBELLION COINAGE IN CHINA.

[J. A. BRUDIN.]

As a continuation of my paper, "The Coins of Wang Mang" (see the NUMISMATIST, Vol. III, April, May, June and July) the following list which contains some of those most often met with of the Rebel coins may be of interest to collectors of Chinese coins. The characters of Table II are mostly copied from original coins and the reading order is given by members of the four fields: 1, is the top; 2, the bottom; 3, is the right; ahd 4, is that to the left of the square hole.

Example: $\frac{1}{2}$ = Top, bottom, right and left.
$\frac{1}{3}$ = Top, right, bottom and left.
$\frac{3}{4}$ = Right and left.

The sizes are in millimetres (m). For some of the data the writer is indebted to Mr. Henry Kingman.

STATE OF CHENG. Rebel King Li Shou. Title, Han Hsing, began A. D., 291.

No. 1 Tsien, $\frac{3}{4}$, Han hsing, without borders. 20 m. (Table No. 1.)
No. 2 Tsien, $\frac{1}{2}$, Han hsing, 17 m. (Table No. 2 is the same characters in present style.)

STATE OF PEI LIANG. Rebel Tsu Chü Mêng Yu.

No. 3 100 Tsien, $\frac{3}{4}$ Yung An; $\frac{1}{2}$ Yi peh 29 m.
4 100 Tsien (iron), same legend as above 31 m. (Table No. 3).
5 1000 Tsien (iron). $\frac{3}{4}$ Yung an; $\frac{1}{2}$ Yi Chian, 57 m. (Table No. 4.)
6 Same as No. 5, 45 m. (Table No. 5).

TANG DYNASTY. Rebel King, Shih Szu Ming. Title, Te Yi.

7 Tsein $\frac{1}{3}$ Te Yi Yuan Pao. Reverse 1, —
8 10 Tsien, with 1, 2 and 3 — ( — on the reverse, 35 m. (Table No. 10.)
9 100 Tsien like No. 8, 36 m.
10 100 Tsien, Reverse 2 — 35 m.
11 100 Tsien, with plain reverse, 36 m.

Title Shun T'ien: began A. D. 760.

12 100 Tsien $\frac{1}{3}$ Shun t'ien yuan pao. Reverse 1 —
13 100 Tsien with 2 — on the reverse, 35 m.
14 100 Tsien with plain reverse (Table No. 11) 36 m.

STATE OF TSI. REBEL KING, LIU YU. TITLE, TOU CH'ANG A. D., 1120.

15 2 Tsien, $\frac{1}{3}$ Tou Ch'ang Yuan pao 26 m. (Table No. 12.)
16 2 Tsien, same legend in seal characters.
17 3 Tsien, like No. 15.
18 2 Tsien, $\frac{1}{2}$ Tou ch'iang tung pao, 26 m.
19 2 Tsien, same legend in seal characters, 26 m.
20 3 Tsien, like No. 19. 35 m.
21 5 Tsien, 35 m.
22 5 Tsien with seal characters, 35 m.

STATE OF SUNG. REBEL KING, HSIAO MING WANG. TITLE, LUNG FENG, 1360-1371.

23 Tsien, ½ Lung fêng tung pao, 24 m.
24 Tsien, same legend on obverse and reverse. 24 m.
25 2 Tsien, like No. 23. 29 m.
26 3 Tsien, like No. 25. 32 m. (Table No. 14.)
27 I have in my collection one like No. 23. On reverse, ½ yung — 23 m.

STATE OF HAN. REBEL, CHEN YU LIANG. TITLE, TA YI. 1355 A. D.

28 2 Tsien, ½ Ta yi tung pao. 23 m.
29 3 Tsien, like No. 28. 28 m.
30 3 Tsien, like No. 28. (Table No. 15.) 30 m.

REBEL, LI TZU CHENG. TITLE, YUNG CHANG, 1644 A. D.

31 Tsien, ½ Yung chang tung pao. 24 m.
32 5 Tsien, like No. 31. 38 m. Issued in Hsi An, capital of Shensi. (Table No. 16.)

REBEL, CHANG HSIEN CHUNG. TITLE, TA SHUN, 1644 A. D.

33 Tsien ½, Ta shun tung pao. 27 m.
33a Tsien, like No. 33. Reverse 2. Hu. 27 m.
34 Tsien, like No. 33. Reverse 2. Kung, 26½ m. Issued in Szuchuan. (Table No. 17.)

REBEL, SUN KO WANG. TITLE, HSING CHAO. 1655 A. D.

35 Tsien, ½ Hsing chao tung pao. 24 m.
36 Tsien, like No. 35. Reverse 2. Kung.
37 2 Tsien, like No. 36. 28 m.
38 5 Tsien, same. Reverse, ½ U Li. 33 m.
39 10 Tsien, same. Reverse, ½ Yi Fen. Issued in Kuei Chou. (Table No. 18.)

REBEL, KENG CHING CHUNG. TITLE, YU MIN. 1674 A. D.
All have the same legend in the obverse.

40 Tsien, ½ Yu min tung pao. 25 m.
41 2 Tsien. Reverse 3. Yi Fen. 29 m.
42 Tsien (silver value). Reverse, ½, Yi Tsien. 36 m.
43 10 Tsien. Reverse, 3, Yi Tsien.
44 10 Tsien. Reverse, ½, Che—Yi Tsien. m 38. Issued at Kwangtung. (Table No. 19.)

REBEL, WU SAN KUEI. TITLE, LI YUNG, 1673 A. D.
All have Li yung tung pao on the obverse.

45 Fen, Reverse ½ Yi Fen 44 m.
46 Fen, same, 42 m.
47 Fen, same, but Yi written in a more complicated form.
48 Fen, Reverse, ½ Yi Fen.
49 5 Li, Reverse, ½ Wu Li, 32 m.
50 2 Li, Reverse, ½ Erh. Li, 28 m.
51 2 Li, same as above, 27 m.
52 2 Li, same, 25 m.

53 Li, Reverse, 3, Li, 26 m.
54 Li, same, 25 m.
55 Li, Reverse, 4, Li, 25 m.
56 Li, " 2, Kung, for the Board of Works, 25 m.
57 Li, " 1, Kuei, Province Kuei chou, 24 m.
58 Li, " 3, Yün, Province, Yünnan, 27 m.
59 Li, " plain, 27 m.
60 Li, " " 26 m.
61 Li, " " 23 m.
62 Li, " " 21 m. (Table No. 23.)

TITLE, CHAO WU, 1673 A. D.

All have ¼, *Chao wu tung pao* on the obverse.

63 Tsien, Reverse plain, 23 m. (Table No. 20)
64 Tsien, " 2, Kung, 22 m.
65 Tsien, " ¼, Cheng chung. 21 m.
66 Tsien, same legend in seal characters, Reverse plain, 23 m. (Table Nos 21 and 22)
67 Tsien, same, Reverse, ½, Yi Fen in seal characters, 35 m.

REBEL WU SHIH FAN. Title, Hung Hoa, 1679 A. D.

Issued in Kuei chou. All have ¼ Hung hao tung pao on the obverse.

68 Tsien, Reverse, 3, Kung, 24 m.
69 Tsien, " 3 Hu, 22 m.
70 Tsien, " ½, Yi yi, 24 m.
71 Tsien, " ½, Yun-5Li, 25 m.
72 Tsien, " plain, 25 m.
73 Tsien, " " 24 m. (Table No. 24.)

REBEL, CHAO CHIN LUNG. TITLE CHIN LUNG. 1832.

Chief of the Yao, a mountain race in S. W. China.

74 Tsien ¼ Chin lung tung pao, current coin of the golden dragon, 23 m. (Table No. 25.)

REBEL, LIU LI CHUAN. Title, T'ai Ping. "Great Peace." 1853.

The chief of the Triad Rebels. (Shanghae)

75 Tsien, ¼ T'ai p'ing tung pao, Reverse, ¼ — ming. 24 m.
76 Tsien, like above, Reverse, ¼ • — 24 m.
77 Tsien, ¼ T'ai p'ing tung pao, Reverse, ½ Fu, in Chinese and Mantchu, ¼ ornaments. The body of the coin on both sides is net work design. White metal, (tin and lead.) 26 m. (Table No. 26).*

REBEL, HUNG HSIU CHUAN. TITLE T'AI P'ING T'IEN KUO. CELESTIAL STATE OF "GREAT PEACE," 1851-1864.

Chief of the T'ai P'ing Rebels, (Nanking.)

78 50 Tsien, ¼ T'ai p'ing t'ien kuo, Reverse, ¼-sheng pao (sacred coin) 43 m.
79 Tsien, same legend, Reverse, ¼ sheng pao. 25 m.
80 Tsien, " " " ½ " " 24 m.

---

*I have in my collection. J. A. B.

# Table II. Rebels of China

| | | | |
|---|---|---|---|
| 1 | 漢 興 | 16 | 永 昌 |
| 2 | 漢 興 | 17 | 大 順 |
| 3 | 永 文 一 百 | 18 | 興 朝 |
| 4 | 永 文 一 千 | 19 | 裕 民 |
| 5 | 永 安 一 十 | 20 | 昭 武 |
| 6 | 豐 貨 | 21 | 昭 武 |
| 7 | 豐 貨 | 22 | [illegible] 寶 |
| 8 | 豐 貨 | 23 | 利 用 |
| 9 | 豐 貨 | 24 | 洪 化 |
| 10 | 得 壹 | 25 | 金 龍 |
| 11 | 順 天 | 26 | 太 平 |
| 12 | 阜 昌 | 27 | 天 国 |
| 13 | 㕣 平 | 28 | 聖 寶 |
| 14 | 龍 鳳 | 29 | 皇 帝 |
| 15 | 大 義 | 30 | J. A. B-n |

81 Tsien, ½ T'ai p'ing, ½ T'ien kuo, Reverse, like No. 80, 27 m.

82 Tsien, ½ T'ai p'ing sheng pao, Reverse, ½ T'ai p'ing, 21 m.

83 Tsien, obverse like No. 82, Reverse, ½ T'ien kuo, 23 m. (Table Nos. 26, 27, 28.)

84 ½ Dollar, Imitation in pasteboard of a Spanish ½ peso, 34 m.

85 Tsien, ½, Huang ti tung pao, current coin of the Emperor, Reverse, ½ Pao Che, Province of che kiang. (Table No. 29.)

NOTE.—Maefarlane writes in his book "The Chinese Revolution;" as follows: "The attempt to murder the Emperor (1851) was soon reported through the provinces, and in the camp of the insurgents. Forthwith the rebels, assured that the emperor was dethroned or dead, issued a new coinage inscribed with the name of *Tien te*, (celestial virtue). The sudden appearance of this new coined money greatly puzzled the political traders of Canton. They turned it over and over and looked with sharp eyes at the seditious characters of the pretender. Perhaps they were of the same opinion as an old European politician who said 'I have a very simple method for recognizing the legitimacy of a sovereign: I merely ask to see a piece of money recently coined; the head upon it is to me that of Cæsar; for the true Cæsar is in my eyes, always he that coins money." I have not seen any other description of this money. Perhaps it is all mythical?

NEW YORK CITY.

---

## THE JETONS OF FRANCE.

### Their Importance in Numismatics: Historical and Otherwise.

*A paper read at the Third Annual Convention of the American Numismatic Association, at Chicago, Ill., Aug. 21, 1893.*

[GEO. J. BAUER.]

Although collectors in France have of late years taken an increased interest in the Jetons of their country, American collectors continue to remain indifferent to the study of this important branch of our study. The Jetons of France cover a wide period of usefulness and time. They originated sometime between the eleventh and twelfth centuries. The oldest Jeton now in existence was coined about the year 1237. This piece is described as having the Roman numeral IIII on the obverse with a small c immediately back of it, indicating hundred. This piece represented 400 marks value. It was a small coin about the size of an United States dime. This piece, or similar ones, were given as a certificate of deposit by Treasurers of cities or towns who issued them. The Jetons of France were minted in many sizes, mostly from 14 to 20 and a variety of metals were used in their manufacture, brass being the most popular metal. The oldest are of brass. Copper, silver, nickle and composition metals were also used.

Many are the uses to which the Jetons were put. The earliest, as indicated in the one described, were used for counting. From this field they spread out into many other uses as follows:

Jetons of exchangeable values.

Jetons made to recognize some person, some choice or some faith.

Jetons for merit, prizes, etc.

Political Jetons, as those issued during the reigns of Louis XIV, XV and XVI, and lastly, we find the Jeton not a Jeton, but called a "spiel-marke."

Of these later pieces the most of them are not commended to collectors and they should not be confounded with the real historical Jeton used prior to the nineteenth century. Of the inscriptions found on the Jetons of France, the greater part are in Latin which would indicate that the pieces with such inscriptions were not struck by ordinary individuals, but by men of learning—at least they were dictated by such.

The very early Jetons had no inscription, but later Jeton makers more than made up this deficiency. The most interesting are the political, especially those relating to war and peace, to treaties and to marriages, religions and reward Jetons. The greater portion of these pieces have the portrait of the king on the obverse. A Jeton of Louis XV has the inscription "Louis Protecteur de l Academie Francaise," showing that science was not forgotten by the Jeton makers, and in the history of France we find that the "Academecians" in the reign of Louis XIV were struggling with the making of the "Dictionary and were so slow about it (some thirty-five years) that the king sent his minister, M. Colbert, to enquire about it and to see if they earned their Jetons. These were the Jetons *de presence* or Jetons of attendance. It was this same gentleman, M. Colbert, who in 1662 established the Academy of Medals and Inscriptions. The chief intention of this academy was to render the acts of king immortal by deciding the legends and inscriptions on the medals and Jetons struck in his honor.

This Academy or Society had about forty members. They evidently studied the designs on many of the ancient coins, for we find on one Jeton the king seated on a throne; before him are four females offering him tokens of peace. On another is a figure of Peace standing with cornucopiæ. A Jeton of Louis XV has a four horse chariot on reverse very similar to the Roman quadriga. Another has a palm tree and many others have similar reverses.

Perhaps, in time, colllectors will take more interest in Jetons, especially French Jetons. Although there are many difficulties in getting together a collection of these interesting pieces. There is one thing certainly in their favor and that is their cheapness. At a sale not long since a lot of French Jetons, catalogued from good to uncirculated, sold at two cents each, and they can be bought at any sale at from ten to fifty cents each, only now and then one realizing more than this latter figure.

If you desire to buy Jetons always turn to the last page of the sale catalogue for it is there where these interesting pieces, despised by most collectors, are tobe found, and the cataloguer does not deem them worth while to individually describe so they are usually offered by the lot. Some day these Jetons will bring good prices, and collectors can do no better than make up their collections of the Jetons of France, a careful study of which will greatly add to their history of that country.

ROCHESTER, N. Y.

## THF 1838 HALF DOLLAR NEW ORLEANS MINT.

[ED FROSSARD.]

The comparative rarity of this half dollar has often formed a subject of discussion among collectors, some contending that only three specimens were struck while others conceded a coinage of from twelve to fifteen pieces. In the recent Friesner sale, 583, the famed 1838 Orleans mint half dollar, with 0 under the bust of Liberty on the obverse, was wrapped up in an old piece of paper on which was written the following statement which I have the pleasure to communicate to The Numismatist for the benefit of its readers:

"The enclosed specimen coin of the United States branch mint at New Orleans is presented to Pres. Bache by Rufus Tyler, the coiner. It may be proper to state that not more than twenty pieces were struck with the half dollar dies of 1838."

This certificate in the handwriting of Rufus Tyler, should forever settle the question concerning the number of half dollars of the year 1838 issued at the New Orleans mint. True "not more than twenty" is slightly vague—still it certainly means that the number was either twenty or a few less, say from fifteen to twenty and by these figures numismatists will hereafter have to abide.

The half dollar in question was purchased by Mr. A. G. Heaton, author of "Mint Marks" and of the "Twelve Silver Barons" and other very original and worthy compositions in verse which lately appeared in The Numismatist and the certificate has been presented to him by me through B. H. Collins, Esq.

Mrs. Potter Palmer and the board of lady managers wish to establish four scholarships with four 25-cent pieces. They will be called the Isabella scholarships, for they will be founded with the proceeds which will be derived from the public sale of the four great Isabella quarters—the first one minted, the 400th, the 1492d and the 1892.

They are now in Mrs. Palmer's custody, but will soon be exhibited in New York and then will be put up at public auction.

## HOOPER'S RESTRIKES.

[JOSEPH HOOPER]

WHO DEMONETIZED THEM.—The Carthagenians had leather coins. The first Roman brass coins weighed 4,000 grains. Tin coins were cast by Dionysius, of Syracuse, about 405 B. C.

COINAGE IN 1893.—The total value of the coinage of our mints during 1893 was $66,934,749, about $18,000,000 greater than in 1892. It was made up of $56,997,620 in gold, $8,702,797 in silver and $1,134,932 in minor coin. The Columbian half dollars coined were 4,052,105 in number and the Columbian quarters 40,023 in number. There were 13,370,195 five cent and 46,642,191 one cent pieces turned out by the mints.

THE OLD DIES DESTROYED.—The laborers at the mint in Philadelphia lately destroyed the dies of the coins issued during 1893. The 733 pieces of very hard steel were hammered with heavy sledges until their utility was entirely destroyed. They were as follows: Double eagles, 13; eagles, 81; half eagles, 28; quarter eagles, 6; silver dollars, 14; half dollars, 21; quarter dollars, 68; souvenir quarters, 4; dimes, 45; nickels 143, and cents, 310.

RARE AMERICAN COINS. Coin collectors have long appreciated the difficulty of making a complete collection of American specimens. The United States coinage of 1793 is very rare and a dollar of the year 1794 has often sold for as much as $100. A 1796 half-cent is so rare as to sell readily for $15, and the half dollar for the same year is worth sixty times its original value. While the half-cent of 1804 is common enough, all the other coins of that year are rare, the dollar of that particular date being the rarest of all American coins. Only eight are known to exist out of the 19,570 that were coined. The lowest price that one of these now changes hands for is $800. These prices are encouraging to collectors.—New York Commercial Advertiser.

A RARE FRENCH COIN.—A certain New York woman possesses one of the rarest coins in the world. It is a twenty-franc piece and at the first glance does not appear to differ greatly from the ordinary French coin of that denomination. Upon those inspection, however, it will be seen that while one side is plainly marked "Napoleon Empereur," the other side says quite as plainly and contradictorily "Republique Francaise." The answer to this seeming numismatic enigma is as follows: The coins were in mint at the time of Napoleon III's accession to the Empire. One side was already stamped "Republique Francaise," when word came that France was no longer a Republic and Napoleon had been crowned. The obverse side was therefore marked with respect to the latter historical developement. But few of these coins are now in existence and hence the possession of one of them is a matter of much moment to the collectors. The best known authority on such subjects declares the coin to be simply invaluable.—Exchange.

---

RARE AMERICAN COINS.—Although the American people enjoy the distinction of being the best informed people on the face of the globe, there are, perhaps, not to exceed five persons in every thousand who have anything like a correct idea of the early coinage of this country. All are familiar with gold, silver and copper coins now in circulation, and, perhaps, a few remember the large coppers and half-pennies in vogue and a few decades ago, but further than that their knowledge does not extend. Yet according to the Globe Democrat there were scores of varieties of coins in circulation in the early years, some of which have now become so scarce that fortunes are offered for a single specimen by numismatists, as, for instance, the gold 20 shilling "Bermuda" piece" as it is technically known, for which $20,000 is offered for a single specimen in good condition. Nearly every one who reads the daily papers has heard of the dollar of 1804 and the majority of readers harbor the idea that that this is the most valuable coin searched for by collectors. This is not the case, however, by far, as there are dozens of coins which command a much greater premium than the 1804 dollar, for which from $750 to $1,250 has been paid by various collectors, says the Baltimore American.

The condition of coins has nearly as much to do with the price as their age. Numismatists classify coins as proof, uncirculated, fine, good, poor and mutilated. Proof coins are struck from polished dies at the mint, especially for collectors and present a burnished mirror-like surface. Uncirculated coins are those which retain the original lustre just as they came from the mint. Fine coins are those which have lost this original lustre, but which do not present the least appearance of wear. Fine coins might be tarnished or blackened, but the least scratch would prevent them from being thus classified. Good coins must show every feature plainly, especially the date, and must not be scratched, hammered or in any manner mutilated. Fair coins may be scratched, but every feature must be visible plainly. Poor coins are those which are much worn and on which the features are almost illegible. It is not surprising that there are in existence many counterfeits of rare and valuable specimens. These counterfeits may be divided into five classes. There are restrikes, which are coins struck from the original dies but at later dates. Among the restrikes of American coins are some of the early colonials, the 1804 dollars, the half-cents of 1831, 1838 and 1840 to 1849.

These do not command the prices offered for genuine specimens. Formerly it was the practice of the government to preserve all the old dies and on several occasions employes of the mint surreptitously coined counterfeits of rare specimens. But all the o'd dies were destroyed some twenty years ago and the present practice is destroy them yearly, so there is no more danger of this sort of spurious specimens. There are also counterfeits which have been struck from false dies, but no expert is deceived by them as they lack the characteristic appearance of the originals, and, as a general rule, are much sharper and more distinct.

Casts from the originals are also made, but they are always much lighter than the true coins and the imposition may be detected by weighing. Electrotypes are found occasionally, but they are necessarily of false weight and the edge shows the marks of joining the two sections. The fifth class of false coins are those on which the date has been changed, either by skillful engraving or by boring out the obnoxious figures and inserting in the hole thus made a plug that has been cut from another coin bearing the desired figure. The microscope readily discloses this trick and no expert is likely to be deceived in this manner.—Philadelphia Inquirer.

## AUCTION ROOM ECHOES.

The following quotations of prices realized at Frossard's 125th sale (The Friesner Collection) is of unusual interest to collectors of the American series and will be quoted from liberally. It seems always a misfortune to see a collection like this broken up, and in this case the necessity that compelled it is especially a matter of regret to us all.

| | | |
|---|---|---|
| 120 | Dollar 1794, good impression, head bold | $77 50 |
| 121 | — 1795, Flowing hair, star sharp, fine | 3 00 |
| 122 | — 1795, Fillet head, seven berries to branch, ex. fine | 8 00 |
| 123 | — 1795, Fillet head, six berries to branch, fine | 2 60 |
| 124 | — 1796, Large wide date, 8 berries to branch, fine | 3 30 |
| 125 | — 1798, Large close date, 7 berries to branch, v. fine | 5 00 |
| 126 | — 1797, Six stars facing, fine | 2 50 |
| 127 | — 1797, Seven stars facing, very fine | 3 90 |
| 128 | — 1798, Fifteen stars, small eagle in wreath, fine | 7 80 |
| 129 | — 1798, Thirteen stars, small eagle in wreath, v fine | 7 00 |
| 130 | — 1798, Heraldic eagle, v fine | 3 00 |
| 131 | — 1799, Extremely fine | 2 20 |
| 132 | — 1799, Five stars facing, fine | 5 00 |
| 133 | — 1800, Stars sharp, extra fine | 2 50 |
| 134 | — 1801, " " fine | 4 10 |
| 135 | — 1802, Almost uncirculated | 7 00 |
| 136 | — 1803, Small 3 in date high, v fine | 3 90 |
| 137 | — 1803, Large 3 in date low, v good | 2 20 |
| 138 | — 1836, Liberty seated *C. Gobrecht* at base, proof | 9 25 |
| 139 | — 1836, " " " " in field, proof | 43 00 |
| 140 | — 1836, " " in semicircle of 13 stars, Rev. Flying eagle without stars in field; reeded edge; proof | 66 00 |
| 141 | — 1839, same type, proof | 39 50 |
| 152 | — 1850, proof $12, 153-154; 1851 and 2 proofs, each | 50 00 |
| 155 | — 1853, stars to right rounded, ex fine | 4 00 |

156 — 1854, sharp, extremely fine.......... 7 50
157 — 1855, proof.......... 15 00
158 — 1856, " .......... 13 75
159 — 1857, " .......... 11 50
160 — 1858, " .......... 29 00
204 Half Dollar, 1794, well centered, very good.......... 5 20
205 — 1795, strong impression, fine.......... 2 50
206 — 1796, fifteen stars, very good.......... 71 00
207 — 1797, small nick on reverse edge, very good.......... 42 50
208-9 — 1801-2, bold impressions, fine.......... 6 50, 7 50
210-11 — 1803, large and small 3 in dates, fine and extra fine.......... 1 25, 8 60
213 — 1805, Five berries, ex. fine.......... 4 00
214 — 1806, pointed six, without stem, uncirculated.......... 5 60
227 — 1815, bold impression, fine.......... 5 25
251 — 1836, reeded edge, ex. fine.......... 3 00
267 — 1850, proof, $4 50. 268 — 1851, uncirculated.......... 1 55
269 — 1852, uncirculated.......... 6 00
272-3-4-5 — 1855-6-7-8, brilliant proofs.......... 9 00, 7 75, 4 00, 3 50
312 Quarter Dollar, 1796, date close to bust, broad milling, very fine.......... 11 25
313 — 1804, very good.......... 4 00
314 — 1805, sharp, extremely fine impression.......... 3 50
315 — 1806, beautiful impression, uncirculated.......... 16 25
323 — 1822 over '22, bust worn, date, stars and reverse good.......... 39 00
324-5-6 — 1824-5-6, fine, very fine and semi-proof.......... 5 00, 2 00, 5 10
354-5-6-7 — 1855-6-7-8, brilliant proof.......... 5 90, 4 10, 2 40, 2 00
396-7 Twenty-cents, 1877-8, proof,.......... 2 10, 2 00
398 Dime, 1796, break in dye over lower left star, uncirculated,.......... 7 60
399 — 1797, thirteen stars, fine (hair lines a trifle worn).......... 22 50
400 — 1798, perfect date, very good.......... 3 15
401 — 1800, scratch or cut over head, otherwise fine.......... 9 00
402-3-4 — 1801-2-3, all very good.......... 3 00, 3 80, 3 60
405 — 1804, very good, (the rarest of the dimes).......... 19 75
406 — 1805, fine.......... 3 00
407 — 1807, small break in die under chin, very fine.......... 4 80
410-1 — 1814, large and small date, very good.......... 2 10, 1 00
415 — 1822, very good.......... 2 95
436, 37, 39, 40, 41 — 1842, 43, 45, 46, 47, uncirculated.. 2 10, 1 00, 70, 8 75, 3 00
450, 52, 53 — 1855-6-7, brilliant proofs.......... 3 50, 3 60, 1 55
472 Half Dime, 1794, extremely fine.......... 4 60
473 — 1795, perfect die, uncirculated.......... 4 10
474 — 1796, sharp, struck on polished planchette.......... 13 50
478 — 1802, circulated while in slightly bent condition rubbing off two stars to left, hair rubbed, but upper locks, face, legend, stars to right, very good; date bold, three small nicks on breast; rev. much more circulated than obverse, very good for this rarest half dime; cost Mr. Friesner $75.......... 60 50
479-80 — 1803-5, fine and nearly fine.......... 7 50, 13 50

| | | |
|---|---|---|
| 501 | — 1846, brilliant sharp, uncirculated.............................. | 10 00 |
| 503 | — 1848, large date, uncirculated.............................. | 3 60 |
| 506, 11, 12, 13, 14 | — 1850-5-6-7-8, brilliant proofs,.....1 20, 2 50, 3 05, 2 50, | 2 00 |
| 535-6-7-8-44 | Three cent, 1855-6-7-8-64 brilliant proof,3 50, 3 00, 4 25, 1 50, | 1.30 |
| 555-6 | Two cent nickel, 1866-7, without and with rays, proof.........3 70, | 4 20 |
| 557 | Three cents nickel, 1865 to 1889, complete series, proof, each......... | 19 |
| 558 | Two cents bronze, 1864 to 1873, brilliant proofs, each................ | 38 |
| 562 | Nickel cents, 1856, flying eagle, proof.............................. | 5 00 |
| 563 | — 1857, sharp, proof.............................. | 1·05 |
| 564 | — 1858, large and small legend; sharp proof, each.................... | 41 |
| 565 | — 1858 to 1864, Indian head, uncirculated, each...................... | 10 |
| 566 | Bronze cents, 1864 to 1893, complete, all proof, each.................. | 11 |

On June 27 and 28th, Charles Steigerwalt, of Lancaster, Pa., sold at auction at 59 Fifth Ave, New York City, the collection of Charles Luckenbach, of St. Louis, Mo. The collection was of United States silver and copper, foreign copper, ancient coins, medals, etc; 963 lots. Mr. Steigerwalt will also sell on July 13th the collection of Geo. T. Crawford, of Carlisle, Pa. This collection is said to be a very choice one and will foot up the neighborhood of $8,000 in cash value.

Frossard's 125th sale took place at the Central Auction Rooms on June 29th. It consisted of several properties, mainly of modern coins of various countries, medals numismatic literature, etc: 563 lots.

The largest collection of American medals offered lately at auction is that of Isaac F. Wood, catalogued by S. H. & H. Chapman and offered for sale on 11th and 12th of this month. The index includes American Colonial, U. S. pattern piece, American medals, Washington medals and coins, medals of merit, political and store cards, Masonic, theatrical and presidential medals, Jackson cents, foreign medals, numismatic literature, etc. 1127 lots.

## EAST INDIA NOTES.

[MAJOR ADAM SMITH, POONA, INDIA.]

The Numismatist for April to hand today (May 15.) Hearty congratulations on its improved appearance and interesting contents. I will try and help you, but the want of parcel post is much felt.

Five per centum customs duty has been imposed in India on medals and coins, based on the weight of the metals and not on the value a person may place on them. This imposition is much felt by collectors and others interested in numismatics.

The collection of coins made Major General Gossett, C. B. British army, consisting of some 153 gold, 700 silver and 500 bronze coins is for sale in India. The coins are being catalogued by the Honorary Numismatist to the Government of India. Major General Gossett has left India for England.

Amongst other steps taken by the Government of India in the last two or three years for the encouragement of that archæological research may be mentioned the purchase for six thousand rupees, of a valuable collection of Gupta coins for the Indian Museum from Mr. Rivett Carnac, opium agent of Ghazepur, Bengal.

The late Sir Alexander Cunningham, the renowned Asiatic coin collector and honored numismatist, used to clean his silver coins, covered with the rust of ages when taken from the earth with a mixture of one ounce citric acid, half ounce glycerine in ten ounces of water; in this he soaked the coins to be cleaned from a half to three hours. If not then cleaned he soaked them in a solution of ammonia for half an hour. Great care must be observed in not allowing any of the acid to remain on the coins. Then protect with a thin coat of transparent varnish.

I have got, for sale or exchange, one hundred copper and bronze coins of crude design, beaten out and stamped from guns taken in action. These coins were dug up in front of the ruins of a Hindu temple standing near the historic battlefield of Corygaum, where on the first of January, 1818, seventy-five native non-commissioned officers and men of the 2d Reg't. Bombay (grenadiers) Infantry, under the command of Lieutenant Swanston, aided by Assistant Surgeon Wyllie, withstood the attack of the whole Mahratta army. The coins were treasure trove and purchased from the government.

Mr. C. Rodgers has sent to the government of the Punjab the first part of the catalogue of coins purchased from him two years ago. It is a book of 273 pages of text and 18 of preface. In it are described 1,816 coins, of which 1,559 are Mogul and 257 Suri. The latter are inserted so that the coins may be shown without any interruption from Babar, the founder of the Mogul Empire, to Bahadur Shah, the mutineer, who died in Rangoon. Of the coins 53 are gold, 1046 silver and 717 copper. The British Museum collection of Mogul coins consists of 1,235 coins, of which 40 only are copper. Mr. Rodgers' collection has 485 copper Mogul coins. When we remember that the revenues were assessed in copper coins, and that silver and gold were very little used by the people at large, it will be seen that this collection shows better than any other what money common folks used in the times of the Mogul emperors. The 232 copper coins of the Suri emperors contain very many novelties not heretofore published. As the British Museum catalogue was the first published information as to what that institution contained of copper coins, it will be seen that the Lahore collection must have coins from many more mints than the London one. In all there are coins from 12 mints in the Lahore collection. At present the catalogue is not illustrated, but we hope the Punjab Government will see its way to publish an illustrated edition. We understand that this matter is under consideration. Never before in India has so complete a collection of Mogul coins been made; but complete though it be, we understand that Mr. Rodgers has already discovered several other coins not in his previous collection and not in the British Museum. The manuscript of the second part of the collection, which comprises over 6,000 coins, will shorty be presented to Government. The work of preparation has occupied over two years and the whole work will show what a vast field the Punjab offers to a coin collector who goes about his work with system and knowledge. We hope the Punjab government contemplates some reward for Mr. Rodgers over and above the stipulated remuneration for this vast work; for we are told that the remuneration, when spread over three years, (it will take a year to see the second part through the press) amounts to the pay of a second clerk in one of our public offices.

## OBITUARY.

### Henry Allen Chaney, M. A.

On June 6th Henry A. Chaney made application for membership in the American Numismatic Association; eight days later, on June 14th, he was suddenly stricken down to "take up his abode in the silent halls of death." Though the elements so graciously mixed in him and moved upon by his gentle spirit—though his kindly clay has been mutilated—with his soul it is well.

Henry A. Chaney was born Burlington, Vt., in 1849. He came to Detroit, Michigan, in 1858 and has resided there since. He graduated from the Detroit high school in 1864 and from the University of Michigan in the classical course in 1869. In 1871 he was admitted to the bar. The following two years he served on the staff of the Detroit Tribune and later served in the office of the State Commissioner of Railroads and as reporter to the Supreme Court. But it was in the literary world that his light shone the brightest. Several volumes of law reports and manuals are the result of his efforts and his newspaper and magazine articles are innumerable. Mr. Chaney was one of the founders of the Detroit High School Alumni Association, has served on the Detroit Board of Education and was Professor of Medical Jurisprudence in the Michigan School of Medicine.

In 1877 he married Miss Francis M. Hall, who with five children survive him. He was a member of the Congregational church and the Michigan Club.

To a cultured mind like Mr. Chaney's the science of nnmismatics has ever proved attractive, and with him this was especially true. Collecting in a modest wayfor years it had only been of late that the full beauties of the science had burst upon him and less than two weeks before his death a column and a half article in Daily Journal announced him as a full convert to numismatics. When organization of the Detroit Numismatic Club was agitated he was one of the first to put his shoulder to the wheel and only a few days later, as before said, made application for membership in the American Numismatic Association.

What the North lost in an Ellsworth, a Baker, or a Lyon we may never fully know. What our science has lost in Mr. Chaney we may also never fully know, but this we do know, that a most lovable, genial, cultured knight has fallen from among us. G. F. H.

## DETROIT NUMISMATIC CLUB.

The Detroit Numismatic Club met at the office of Dr. Joseph Lathrop, eight members being present, and was called to order by the president. The minutes of the last meeting were read by the secretary and approved.

The secretary read a communication from Dr. Heath, president of the American Numismatic Association relative to the appointment of committee on exhibition, programme and reception, and at his suggestion Messrs. Rice, Griffith and Bates were appointed a committee to receive, care for and place the exhibits at the convention, August 23 and 24 next, and Messrs. Seymour, Lathrop and Manton as the committee on programme, these being members of the American Association. Reception committee appointments were deferred to a later date.

The constitution and by-laws having been transcribed in the club record book, it was signed by the members present.

Mr. J. H. Valpey, exhibited an extensive collection of ancient coins which he had secured while at the Columbian Exhibition at Chicago last summer. They were arranged and mounted in an original manner and gave evidence that considerable time had been devoted to them.

Dr. D. R. Bogue exhibited an over-date five cent nickel of 1889, the date having been originally cut 1899. It is an uncatalogued variety, of which none of the members had heard before.

Mr. Rice reported that, anticipating the appointment of a receiving committee, he had ascertained that arrangements could be made with a Safety Deposit Vault Company to have the exhibits sent directly to them and held in fire and burglar proof vaults until the owner himself could receive and place them.

As the next date for a regular meeting would fall on July 4, it was decided to defer it for one week, to July 11, 1894. The meeting then adjourned.

June 13, 1894. GEO. W. RICE, Secretary.

## THE AMERICAN NUMISMATIC ASSOCIATION.

BOARD OF OFFICERS:

President: Dr. Geo. F. Heath, Monroe, Mich.
Vice President: Joseph Hooper, Port Hope, Ont.
Secretary: O. W. Page, Box 296, Waltham, Mass.
Treasurer: Dr. A. L. Fisher, Elkhart. Ind.
Librarian and Curator. W. C. Stone, 384 Union St., Springfield, Mass.
Superintendent of Exchange: W. J. Luck, Adrian, Mich.
Counterfeit Detector: S. H. Chapman, 1348 Pine St., Philadelphia, Pa.
Board of Trustees: J. A. Heckelman, Daggers, Va; David Harlowe, 3002 Mt. Vernon Ave., Milwaukee, Wis; C. W. Stutesman, 1730 Market St., Logansport, Ind; W. K. Hall, Peterboro, Ont; Hiram E. Deats, Flemington, N. J.

### Secretary's Report.

To the President and Members of the American Numismatic Ass'n.

Greeting:

The following report covers the period from May 20 to July 1:

Cash receipts during this time, $8.00, of which $3.00 was for initiations. The amount of $3.50 in my hands, May 20, has been turned over to the Treasurer, leaving still in my hands a balance of $8.00.

The new members are as follows:

195 J. Rochelle Thomas, Granville Chambers Portman Sq., Orchard St., London, England.
196 Jos. M. Potichke, 652 Michigan Ave., Detroit, Mich.
197 H. P. Bellinger, 1917 W. Genesee St., Syracuse; N. Y.
198 A. H. Griffith, Detroit Museum of Art. Detroit, Mich.
199 W. P. Manton M. D., 32 Adams Ave., W. Detroit, Mich.
200 Rev. B. Fresneborg, St. John's German church, New Brunswick, N. J.
201 J. B. Bowell, Plymouth, Ind.
202 Fred H. Seymour, 44 Fort St., W. Detroit, Mich.
203 J. R. Straub, 238 Lake St., Rochester, N. Y.
204 Wm. S. Disbrow, M. D., 151 Orchard St., Newark, N. J.
205 W. H. Clark, 109 E. 7th St., St. Paul, Minn.
206* Henry A. Chaney, 120 Edmund Place, Detroit, Mich.

### Applications for Membership.

Albert Howver, Cambridge, N. Y.
Vouchers: Messrs. Oatman and Page.

Theron Y. Sebring, Kalamazoo, Mich.
Vouchers: Messrs. Heath and Luck.

A. B. Ragan, Monroe, Mich.
Vouchers: Messrs. Heath and Page.

Also the applications of Dr. D. R. Bogue and C. C. Deuel, of Detroit, Mich., in due form. If no objections are received these candidates will be entitled to Certificates of Membership on Aug. 1.

Expense of Secretary's office, (postage) 39 cts. Respectfully submitted,

O. W. Page, Secy.

*Deceased.

## AMERICAN NUMISMATIC AND ARCHÆOLOGICAL SOCIETY

(17 WEST FORTY-THIRD ST., NEW YORK CITY.)

A regular meeting of this society was held on May 21, '94. President Parish presiding. The Executive Committee reported that the following nominations had been received, approved and recommended for election. For Resident Membership Francis G. Himpler, James TenEyck, Samuel P. Avery, Frank Sherman Benson, and J. Douglas Sparkman. For Corresponding Membership Charles T. Tatman and Luther B. Tuthill. The resignation of J. H. TenEyck Burr has been accepted and attention called to the decease of Robert Harris. Acceptances of election have been received from Resident Member John F. B. Lilliard and from Corresponding Members Dr. Anton Blomberg, of Stockholm, Sweden, W. C. Goddard, of Watford, England, George McArthur, of Maldron, Victoria, and Frank B. Lee, of Trenton, N. J. The resignation of Walter Tounele, as Cor. Secy, has been received and accepted, and Mr. Herbert Valentine has been unanimously appointed to that office. The Librarian, Mr. Belden, reported donations of 4 bound volumes and 41 pamphlets catalogues, etc. Special mention was made of three valuable works from S. P. Avery. Curator, Mr. Wright, announced additions since the last meeting of 102 coins and medals being donations from Dr. Brush, Jr., J. M. Dodd, Jr., Jno. A. Hadden, N. P. Peterson, B. L. Belden and Isaac H. Wood, also by purchase 51 pieces. Attention was called to the fine collection of medals of the "Renaessance" including a number of pieces from the noted Spitzer collection exhibited by Mr. Tonnell, also to the collection of oriental coins of Bauman L. Belden as fully described in the interesting paper printed in our annual proceedings.

H. Russell Drowne, Recording Secretary.

At the annual meeting the following officers were duly elected: Daniel Parish, Jr., President, Andrew C. Zabriskie and John M. Dodd, Vice-Presidents; H. Russell Drowne, Recording Secretary; Herbert Valentine, Corresponding Secretary; Charles Pryer, Treasurer, Charles H. Wright, Curator, and Bauman L Belden, Librarian.

## WASHINGTON NOTES.

(*From our regular correspondent.*)

J. M. Clapp also obtained a long line of prizes at the Freisner sale. He has lately taken up the collecting of gold as well as silver mint marks.

A. G. Heaton will pass July at Childwald, a resort in the Adirondacks. He obtained at the Friesner sale the 1838 O mint half-dollar and the 1842 O quarter-dollar, paying for the former $113.00. He only needs now, we believe, the 1873 s dollar and c. c. 1873 dime without arrows to complete his series of mint marks.

B. H. Collins, long known as a prominent collector, has lately established himself here as a dealer in coins, curios, fine old glass, antique silver, etc., and being a gentleman of great experience in these things and of unquestionable integrity deserves the patronage of all interested.

We Washington collectors flatter ourselves that between us all we could display an array of U. S. coins, etc., that the collectors of no other city could equal, for we could present a large representation of U. S. gold of all mints—the $3 and $1 being complete (except an 1870 s mint dollar: every silver date of all mints (except 1873 s mint dollar) and many varieties, mostly in the highest condition; the best set of cents in the country; the best set of 1894 cents in the country; a collection of Colonials, surpassed by but one: the best collection of Confederate and other paper money in the country; the best collection of minor coins: and a rich array of tokens, medals, patterns, etc.

## NUMISMATIC NOTES.

To avoid disappointment don't set your hearts upon possessing the U. S. series for 1802 and 1804.

The St. Gaudens design for World's Fair medals has finally been rejected, and the design of Chas. E. Barber, of the mint been taken in its stead.

One of the pleasures of the numismatist's life is the anticipation indulged in between the sale and the receipt of the prizes captured. The realization is often another matter.

The Field Museum of Chicago has purchased the Kunz collection of coins which was on exhibition in the gallery of the Mines Building at the World's Fair. We venture the prediction that this will be the nucleus of the largest and most valuable numismatic collection on this continent.

In the Cosmopolitan for the present month is an article that will interest all collectors of French medals, entitled, "Some Rare Napoleonic Medals," by J. Howe Adams.

In Harper's Magazine for March, 1860, may be found a very interesting article, entitled "Coin in America." with about seventy illustrations. It gives the history of one of the George Clinton coppers with its third narrow escape from being lost.

The mint marks of the Friesner collection formed the most profitable part of the sale Heaton's Treatise on the Coinage of the Branch Mints is the only guide to this line of coin study and indispensable to American collectors. It can be bought of all prominent dealers or of The Numismatist.

A Lafayette, Ind., dispatch says: "Charles G. Yelm, a traveling man of this city, while in Davenport, Ia., this week, received an 1804 dollar from a hotel clerk in settling his bill. The clerk was ignorant of the value of the coin, but Yelm was not. He has just disposed of it to the cashier of the First National Bank of Chicago for $855. The coin is one of four issued by the Government, and has long been unaccounted for."

# QUERIES.

This Department is open to all the readers of The Numismatist. A nom de plume may be used if desired in either the asking or answering queries.

A saying we here commend to you
Ye learned. ye wise ye great ye small;
Far better to have aimed and missed,
Than never to have fired at all.

25—What members of the A. N. A. collect war medals? I have to exchange Afghanistan, Kandahar, Abyissinia, Persia, Ghuzni, Burma, Seringapatam (copper), Hyderabad, Central India, Suakin and Suakin-Topek.

MAJ. ADAM SMITH, Poona, India.

26—Please give me the value of this coin. F. B. S.

Ans.—The coin is a denarius of Severus Alexander (A. D. 193—211) is accompanied by one of Robt. Morris' elaborate readings, with price marked up into the dollars. It was evidently one of those distributed by him about twenty years ago. It is described as follows: Obv., Laureated head of emperor, to right, SEVERUS AVG PART MAX, Severus the conqueror of the Paritians. Rev., The Emperor worshipping. RESTITVTOR VRBIS. The Emperor standing before an altar to the left, in his right hand the sacred dish, his left supported by a headless spear. "The restorer of the city (Rome)." The emperors were always high priests of the nation and thus led the way in the great religious festivals. This piece can be purchased in good condition for about fifty cents.

27—What are Tesseræ? I often see them mentioned in sale catalogues.

S. C. Jr., Cleveland.

Ans.—Pieces of metal, wood, bone or ivory used in ancient Rome much as tokens have been used in these days. Many are being dug up in Pompeii and those that have come under our notice have been of small lead, nearly all round or oval, and impressed with a variety of rude designs. They have no artistic or historic value and their only claim to the attention of numismatists is their novelty.

28—I have two small brass pieces that I should be glad to know more about if you or your readers can give me further information. P. R. D.

No. 1—Obverse: Head of Louis XIV to right; inscription, LVD XIIII D. G. FR ET NA REX; in front of bust LAG surmounted by crown. Reverse: Three lilies of France in field, 1 PISTOU W in three lines, thick, size 12.

No. 2—Obverse: Three-masted ship in beaded circle; inscription surrounding, TRAVAUX DU CANAL DE SUEZ EGYPTE. Reverse: • BON JOUR • 50 CENTIMES, inside beaded circle: inscription surrounding, BOREL LEVALLEX ET COMPNIE, 1865; size 12.

29—How can coins best be sent to the United States? A. S.

Ans.—There is no duty on coins for collections in this country. The best way to send them is by parcel post, registered. Comply with the local laws governing postage from the country sent and no interference or delay need be feared in the United States.

30—Will you please tell me how to clean proof coins? Mine turn black.
LOTHROP.

Ans.—It would perhaps be a more interesting matter to know the influences that cause your proofs to turn black. This correspondent is referred to Mr. Heaton's article "On the Preservation of Coins," to be published in our August issue.

10 and 14—Thos. D. McGarry writes: "I have always understood that the 1804 dollars were sent to pay our navy who were fighting in Tripoli, and found their way in shore and into the interior, where they were melted up into bracelets, armlets, etc., by the natives." This is an old theory and as unreliable as it is unreasonable.—EDITOR.

---

During a series of experiments for the royal society's committee on researches upon alloys, Capt. Hunt has made a discovery that will probably be utilized in the coinage of money. His alloy consists of seventy eight parts of gold to twenty-two parts of aluminum. These proportions, moreover, are the only ones in which these two metals alloy perfectly.

The product, it is said, is of a beautiful purple color, with ruby reflections, and cannot be imitated. Besides, as gold is 7.7 times heavier than aluminum, the same weight of the latter will be 7.7 times greater in bulk than the former.—Scientific American.

---

"The safeguards adopted by the Bank of England to prevent that institution being robbed are about as thorough and complete as human ingenuity and mechanism can devise," said Mervin O. Todd, of Manchester, Eng. "Its outer doors are so finely balanced that a clerk by pressing a knob under his desk can close them instantly, and they cannot be opened again except by special process. The bullion department is nightly submerged in several feet of water by the action of machinery, and in some of the banks the bullion department is connected with the managers sleeping apartments, so that an entrance cannot be effected without setting off an alarm near this person's head. If a dishonest official during the day or night should take even one from a pile of a thousand sovereigns, the whole pile would instantly sink, and a pool of water take its place, besides letting every one in the office know of the theft.—St. Louis Globe-Democrat.

# THE WORLD OF FAD.

Nine letters of John Lothrop Motley to Prince Bismark lately sold for $300.

The collector of postage stamps is said to be the most persistent and perniciously active of the *genus* collector.

Earl Roseberry has a fad for collecting razors. He has thirty that he uses habitually, one for each day of the month.

The latest hobby among literary folk is the collecting of sets of "annuals" so popular fifty to seventy-five years ago, before the magazine era.

Eugene Field, the brilliant writer but erratic collector, has quit collecting axes, after securing Gladstone's and many of the political kind, and gone to collecting inkstands which have been used by literary and other celebrities.

One of the oddest fancies brought to our attention is that of a young lady who has taken up the collection of wish bones. These she has arranged about her room and in boxes. They arrange from that of the diminutive humming bird to that of the ostrich.

The late C. P. Leland, of the L. S. & M. S. railroad, all his life collected souvenirs of various events in which he was interested, and had a fine collection of railroad curios, anceint freight bills and passenger tickets. It is said to be the largest and most complete collection of the kind extant.

The herbarium of the late Isaac C. Martindale, of Philadelphia, comprising more than 200,000 different plants and ferns gathered from every country in the world, has lately been presented to the Philadelphia College of Pharmacy, having lately been purchased from the estate for $10,000 by friends of that institution.

H. H. Gatty, of Chicago, has probably the largest collection of idols from India in this country, if not in the world. The Gunning collection, also of Chicago, has over 500 specimens of idols from all parts of the world: India, China, Japan, Central America, Africa, etc. It is probable that these two collections, together with the Gunther collection of idols, may go to the Field Museum, in which case the collection will far exceed anything of the kind ever known.

Miss Joanna Farnham lately died in Milton, N. H. She left behind 89 dresses of the finest silk, satin, velvet, and other expensive dress goods, 103 skirts of every texture and fabric, 114 pairs of silk hose, 19 rich and costly shawls, and yet she had always been "too poor" to wear any of them, always wearing the cheapest clothing. $7,000 in securities and on deposit were found after her burial, and other valuables sold at auction netted over $10,000 more, much less than their actual value.

ROOM AT THE TOP.—Some one has lately been studying the capacity of Heaven and taking Revelations xxi, "And he measured the city of Jerusalem with a rod 12,000 furlongs: the length, the breadth and the height are equal," as a guide, he comes to the following satisfactory conclusion. That if the world lasts 100 centuries and that if there should be 100 worlds with the same population as this, Heaven would be large enough to hold the collection of 297,000,000,000,000 souls and give each soul 100 rooms each 16 feet square.

SOME RARE AUTOGRAPHS.—Some autograph letters and documents with royal sign manuals, of great interest and rarity, were yesterday sold at Sotherby's, fetching varied prices. A document on paper, with manual in monogram of Richard III, dated from "Our Castel of Notyngham the IX day of Octobr (1483-4)," brought £20 10s; while one signed by his conqueror and successor, Henry VII, only fetched two guineas; another one of Henry VII, accounts of the royal household corrected by the king, £3 18s; a very neat specimen, dated May 1, 1570, signed "Elizabeth R.," fetched £6 10s; a letter of Lord Byron's to Sig. Alberghetti sold for £5 7s 6d; two letters from John Evelyn to Samuel Pepys, both indorsed with Pepy's autograph, brought £8 10s and £8 respectively: and a long letter from George Washington to his nephew Howel Lewis, giving minute instructions on some agricultural matter, went for £20.—London Standard.

## Shekels Came Down.

Some twenty-five years ago a peasant dug up, near Jericho, a pot full of silver shekels; they were Maccabaean shekels, and of the scarcest kind. They were, I believe, 120 of them. About five-and-twenty were secured by a friend of mine, who sent them to me with a request that I would take them to the museum, where they would be examined, valued and kept. This I did. Shekels—Maccabaean shekels—before this find, were worth about ten guineas apiece.

When I poured out the contents of my bag on the table of the numismatic chief, then my old friend W. S. W. Vaux, he called out to his two assistants:

"Here's a misfortune: come here quickly. What a misfortune! Shekels! All these are shekels!"

Then they all three laid their heads upon the table and wailed aloud—for the value of the shekels, had gone down at that one stroke by about one-half, and those that had shekels in their collections could no longer brag and boast of their value.

What became of this particular lot of shekels I know not. But the moral of the story is that the discovery of buried treasure is not a thing always to be prayed for, because it might, in some cases, prove highly destructive to property.—Walter Besant, in the Queen.

# WITH THE EDITOR.

As we come near to our annual convention it is important to know who will be present and we would be glad to publish the names of all such in our August issue who will receive proxies. The August NUMISMATIST with proxy blanks will go out promptly by August 1st.

To the list of papers to be read at our Detroit Convention, may be added: "The Coins of Venice, 1400—1600," by Ph. Whiteway, of England; "The Paper Money of the Confederacy," by Luther B. Tuthill, of North Carolina;" and "Cutch Coinage," by Major Adam Smith, Poona, India.

The Detroit Numismatic Club invite any or all the members of the A. N. A. to become associate members of their club, also any other collectors of coin who may be so inclined. Such associate members who may visit in Detroit and make themselves known will always find an "open sesame" to as congenial a set of fellows as any city of this country can afford. As these privileges are invitingly extended to all and no expenses attached or questions asked, it is quite probable that the D. N. C. might just as well get its umbrella up, for it is going to rain. Address the secretary, Geo. W. Rice, 186 east High St.

Every arrangement has been made for the security and care of all coins intrusted to the Association during our Convention and Exhibition. The Committee on Exhibition is composed of reliable men who know the value of good coins and how to care for them, and we feel perfectly safe in assuring any of our members that their treasures will be just as safe and secure in their care as if in their own cabinets or safes at home. All consignments should have the name of the owner outside and be sent to Geo. W. Rice, care of The Preston Safety Deposit Vaults, Detroit, Mich., there to remain until called for by the owner or used for exhibitive purposes by the committee. All expenses for carriage, storage, etc., will be borne by the Association. The matter will now be in the hands of the committee and it is hoped the members will see that this feature of the Convention will be a success. It is best that all applications for space be made as early as possible so that sufficient accommodations may be provided.

The gold medal to be presented to President Eliot of Harvard at commencement in commemoration of his completing twenty-five years in his office is to cost $2,000. It will bear on one side his face in profile and on the other an inscription.

# Wants, to exchange, etc.

This department gratis to all our readers.

Wanted.—Early issues of Rhode Island paper currency. Geo. C. Barton, Box 163, Providence, R. I.

To Exchange.—Foreign coins for numismatic literature or U. S. money (paper or metalic) medals or tokens. W. H. Taylor, North Wales, Pa.

The signature of Sir James Outram, K. C. B., the Bayard of India, for American coins. Also Asiatic stamps, coins and war medals. Major Adam Smith, Poona, India.

To Exchange.—Flint lock muskets, cannon balls from Bennington battle ground, old pistols, axes and swords, for cash or old coins. All letters answered. A. Oatman, Shaftsbury, Vt.

Wanted.—Scotts Coin Journal for 1884-5-6, or either, loose or bound. Liberal exchange offered in foreign silver and copper (some choice oriental) or part cash. F. C. Browne, Framingham, Mass.

To Exchange.—Half dollars, quarter dollars, dimes, half dimes and three cent silver pieces, old cents and half cents, for the same not in my collection. Arthur B. Stewart, 813 6th Av. Beaver Falls, Pa.

For Exchange.—Nice cabinet specimens of sulphur, calcite (dog tooth crystals), barite crystals, barite and sulphur in trachyte; all of this locality, for as good specimens of other localities. Write first. Dr. George F. Heath, Monroe, Mich.

Bunch of 10 Indian arrows (genuine) brought from the field of Little Big Horn, the scene of the Custer massacre, to exchange for 1856 Eagle cent, 1799 cent, 1811 half cent or dimes 1809 -11 -22 -23 -28, 3c. nickles 1877 -85 -86 -87 -89. Value of arrows $6. J. B. Goldsmith, 53 Hale St., Beverly, Mass.

TYPES OF EXTINCT CIVILIZATION · MORE HISTORIC THAN WRITTEN HISTORY

THE

# NUMISMATIST

## August, 1894.

An Illustrated Monthly devoted to the Science of Numismatics.

GEO. F HEATH, M.D. Monroe, Mich.

Vol. 7. No. 8.

PRESS STEAM PTG. CO., WATERLOO, IND.

## CONTENTS:




# The Numismatist:

A MONTHLY JOURNAL FOR COIN COLLECTORS,
AND OFFICIAL BULLETIN OF

## THE AMERICAN NUMISMATIC ASSOCIATION:

ONE DOLLAR A YEAR.

Editorial and publication office. Monroe, Mich.

THE NUMISMATIST is the only Illustrated Monthly Journal devoted to coin and their collecting published on the American continent.

ADVERTISING RATES very reasonable. Made known on application.

SUBSCRIPTION. $1.00 per annum, post free to any portion of the civilized world. Remittances may be made by money order. postal note, registered letter, or, when these are not obtainable. in unused postage stamps of low denominations.

Entered at Monroe, Mich., Postoffice, as second class matter.

J. A. Brahm

# The Numismatist.

VOL. VII. MONROE, MICH., AUGUST, 1894. NO. 8.

## THE PRESERVATION OF COINS.

*A paper read at the Third Annual Convention of the American Numismatic Association at Chicago, Ill., Aug. 21, 1893.*

[A. G. HEATON.]

All persons attracted to coins will recognize the importance of so keeping those in high condition that no injurious changes shall occur.

The numismatist is, strictly speaking, a student of the history, art and science of coins who does not necessarily own or retain many of them after acquiring needed information.

The average collector, however, often accumulates coins simply for the pleasure of their possession in great number, variety or rarity (as indicated by the lists of dealers or the writings of numismatists), and he generally takes pride in steadily improving his collection and retaining it through life. If the collection changes hands its best pieces are gained by other collectors and so, unless destroyed by accident, become a part of the numismatic reserve of the world. Consequently the collector should not only know and gather fine coins for his own gratification, but, in addition, should feel under the obligation of knowing how to keep them that he may bestow as full value upon the future as he has received from the past. Unless he has this finer feeling of being one of a series of custodians of the coinage of his own and of other lands for the interest and instruction of generations to come, he is but little more than a banker or speculator in a new field and loses a collector's highest dignity—save that of gathering to bestow upon educational institutions.

The best specimens in modern cabinets of not only the coins of existing nations but of the ancients, are those that owe their high condition to the care of collectors in the past or to selection for deposit in tombs, corner stones and other secure and enduring receptacles, with practically the same result.

The old Egyptian, Greek or Roman who involuntarily became the possessor of a collection of coins after death, often took much better care of it, despite some danger from dampness, than do one class of modern collectors. These not merely leave their pieces at times in damp or dusty drawers, in soiled wrapping paper, or in the poisonous cigar box and handle them with dirty and perspiring fingers, but there are a number who try to clean coins with acids or other dangerous agents, to brush or rub them to the last degree with bristles, skins and powders, to re-engrave worn parts of the design, and even to apply the heroic treatment of a battery. Of such are the heathen in the world of Numisma whose hearts may perhaps be right, but whose darkened minds need the earliest attention of our missionaries.

Such collectors are but elementary. The collector of another and higher class proceeds very differently. As his pieces grow in number, he wishes to give them an installation worthy of their cost and rarity. He buys a fine, strong, steel, air-tight, fire-proof. He orders a set of walnut drawers, or of any wood he may prefer, to fit the interior. These he has lined with velvet of some dark or rich color to show his pieces to advantage, and on the velvet narrow strips of wood are nailed or glued to separate the rows of coins. according to their size, that each shallow drawer is to hold. Then there are somewhat deeper drawers for perhaps his "proofs" or certain excessively fine or very rare silver pieces or gold and for the lustrous or sharp uncirculated cents he has acquired by such daring extravagance. These are nestled in little new pasteboard boxes, clean and fresh from the manufactures, upon beds of fleecy cotton batting procured at the nearest dry goods store. Little labels are carefully written out and appropriately pasted on the boxes or divisions that separate rows of coins. Duplicate pieces are wrapped up in soft white paper direct from the stationer, each package secured by gum bands or some pretty colored twine. There are yet deeper drawers also for catalogues, letters, the leather cases of medals, a few mementoes perhaps, and all seems complete. The collector, after communion with his choice pieces, shuts the heavy, finely fitted, steel door of his safe and goes to bed or to his business, delighting in their security. They may be secure from robbery or fire, but we will cause surprise by asserting that their condition is greatly imperiled and that, in no long time, their value will be much increased by injurious change of aspect.

In approaching the cause let us take some simple illustrations. If your servant brings a ham and a piece of beef from market in the same basket, you will detect it at the table, If two different kinds of crackers are put in the same tin box each will lose its palatableness. If you take a sulphur bath and leave your jewelry exposed to the air of the bath room, its blackening influence will soon be evident. How much more sensitive is the silver proof on the uncirculated copper cent upon which a sort of pallor spreads at the most careful touch of the fingers. If we then ask a chemist to give us evidence of the effect of injurious influences in a close atmosphere upon these pieces, we shall be astonished at the destructive work of apparently trifling agents and better prepared for further investigation.

Let us consider the pernicious agents which the collector we have last referred to shuts up in his air-tight, fire-proof with his treasures. Wood is rarely perfectly seasoned and the handsome drawers contain in their fibre a quantity of dampness and sap which simple scientific processes would make astonishingly evident. The glue used at the mortices and in attaching the division strips and the velvet is a second peril in the air. The dyes of the velvet itself are a third and always blacken proof coins displayed upon it. A fourth danger lies in the paste-board boxes holding the original dampness of the pulp, and the souring of the paste used in their manufacture. A fifth lurks in the cotton which, unless of the quality prepared for jewellers, always contains here and there minute seeds or fragments which hold oil euough to deface a coin permanently if in contact with it. The chemicals in the ink on the labels, the coloring matter of paper or twine, the sulphur of the rubber bands, the dyes of the leather cases, and every morcel of animal, vegetable and some mineral matters enclosed in that limited and unchanged mass of air, are steadily adding their currupting intluence for transmission to the lustrous surfaces of copper, silver and even of gold which the safe confines. Now need we wonder longer that fine coins blacken and tarnish and become irridescent and corroded, and suffer from every ill that metal is heir to, when we realize as a chemist does the extent of our mismanagement. Surely, if we are to transmit uncirculated pieces and proofs to future collectors in the condition they have come to us, there must be a general reform in our care of them.

And what shall these reforms be? First, if wood is used at all for drawers or cabinets, it must be that of clean old furniture, seasoned to the last degree, or must be long dried near fire to drive out all possible dampness. But we would abolish wood altogether for an ideal cabinent and have the interior of a safe fitted with slides and drawers of metal and trays of glass or porcelain. To guard against friction we would cover these trays with old white satin or silk, oven dried. We would abolish from the fire-proof paste-board, paper and all other articles previously mentioned as dangerous, and, if paper were in some cases more convenient, should insist upon its being white, thin, unglazed and dried also in an oven before use. The safe should be kept in a dry room and one that is heated in cool or damp weather. It should be opened at times to change the air within but only on dry days and when there is no dust. Lustrous coins should of course be handled as little as possible and then after the hands are washed and thoroughly dried. Hands should be clean in more than appearance, for not only invisible staining particles may adhere to them but the natural oil and dampness of the skin are dangerous. The best plan is to have the thumb and forefinger tips of an old glove cut off, washed clean, and always ready to draw on at need. It is hardly necessary to add that coins should be taken up only by the rim. Inexperienced persons should never be permitted to touch a collector's best pieces. To make this less easy, a pane of glass should cover the contents of every tray or drawer, raised slightly above the coins and removeable when desired. This is a good precaution for another cause rarely considered. Men are very apt to put their hands to their hair, mustache or beard while bending over a tray of numismatic treasures and the unnoticeable flakes of semi-oily dandruff thus often cast in a little shower upon the coins, are very disastrous, not to speak of the added grease and impurities which the hands gather.

Tobacco ashes and smoke and all other fumes and gases are harmful, as well as acids, salt air and sea water or spray.

The cleaning of coins is too distinct and broad a subject to be mentioned in this paper except in one particular. We do not believe in touching fine pieces in any manner with a view to improving them, but, if they are soiled or greasy, they need to be washed carefully with water and castile soap to avert further injury to them or contamination of the safe atmosphere, and should then be dried near a fire. The methods we suggest for preserving high class coins will not seem excessive when the causes of injury are so many and so apparent upon full consideration.

The old woman who has her keepsakes wrapped with a silk handkerchief in a warm and ventilated chimney corner, may indulge in far greater hopes of transmitting them in original state to her children's children than the collector of ample means who, with more zeal than judgement, imprisons proofs or uncirculated coins with any vegetable, animal or with many mineral substances in a small air tight compartment. Let us then keep our pieces as free from infections as we would our bodies and the result will reward all our pains.

## LATE ADDITIONS TO THE MINT CABINET.

[PHILADELPHIA TELEGRAPH.]

The Government Museum of rare coins and medals, on the second floor of the Mint, has had added to it by Curator R. A. McClure a number of ancient pieces and several American coins, all very difficult to obtain and valuable, from the numismatist's point of view. The Museum has been further enriched by the introduction of a new case containing a collection of the current moneys of the world, which lack but a few specimens to be perfect.

These additions go far towards making the Philadelphia Museum one of the most complete, if not the most extensive, to be found anywhere. It would be idle to compare the meagre 8,000 pieces on view in this city with the hundreds of thousands in the British Museum: yet the new specimens are of so much importance in filling series that contained gaps, and they perform this office so satisfactorily, that the Mint's collection is now surpassed, in essential respects, by the English one alone.

Although purchased some time ago, the permant introduction of several of the coins the Mint's cases has been delayed from time to time, because of the research necessary for their positive identification; indeed, one of the oldest remains a problem that still knits the brows of the Curator and his assistants. All, however, have been at last exposed to public view, and ejacuatory throngs during visiting hours testify to the interest they awaken. It has come to be a rule with the conductors to desert each party as it enters the Museum; even a Government cicerone can't afford to lose an hour at the end of every tour of the establishment.

### Choice Specimens.

It is safe to say that, under present conditions, the Philadelphia collection will always look up to the British Museum with awe and reverence: it will never wage war of rivalry, for the sinews are lacking. The great United States has provided, for the acquisition of rare and valuable coins for the Museum at the Philadelphia Mint, the munificent annual appropriation of $300. "Willful waste," says the Government, "apart from pensions and the tariff, makes woful want;" and it is very chary of its money where numismatics are concerned.

Every year this widow's mite of $300 is doled out to Curator McClure, for expenditure according to utmost caution and his best judgement. Every year, having got this $300 in his pocket, Curator McClure consults his twenty-five years' knowledge of coins, and feels like a boy with a nice new cent who would like to buy a watch, a rifle, a fishing-rod, and a penny whistle. Circumstances generally point toward the whistle; but occasionally he gets a bargain.

Thus, Curator McClure went to the World's Fair last July, the Governments coin exhibit in his charge and the Government's niggardly $300 burning a hole in his pocket. At the Fair, behind several trays of coins, he one day descried a grave and dignified Turk. They exchange names, the Turk's appellation sounding like a volley from a Gatling gun—Dikran G. Kelekian. The Turk showed Mr. McClure the contents of his trays, which were sufficiently unprofitable. Perceiving his customer was really an expert, the Turk opened his safe and produced several rarer coins. At sight of them Mr. McClure's little $300 moved uneasily in his pocket and tried to jump out. But he assumed the countenance of Sylvain Pons before the fan of Mme. de Pompadour, and looked contempt. At that the Turk became eloquent and gesticulatory. Mr. McClure remained unimpressed. The Turk offered his treasures at a thumping price, and declaimed. Lowered the price and elevated his voice. Failed to make an impression, and dropped another 10 per cent. Begged and pleaded, and threw off dollar after dollar, until he swore he was ruined. Then Mr. McClure bought some of the coins at one-eight of their value and departed, feeling he had served his government and had taught his impetuous $300 a lesson in caution. So effective was his cheapening that he secured a couple of very rare specimens of Greek art for $6 apiece.

### A Gem.

Of these gems, now formally installed in the collection at the Mint, one of the choicest is a very rare but much worn medallion, in silver, dating from the days when warlike Antony lay enervate in the embrace of Egypt's Queen. It contains 215¼ grains of silver, and its denomination is equivalent to something less than two double denarii—about 53 cents. The piece probably served as current coin, and may have been part of the money Cleopatra brought for the pay of her lover's army when he lay awaiting her at the Fort of White Hair, between Berytus and Sidon, after his expedition against the Parthians.

On the obverse of the medallion is the head of Cleopatra, fairly accurate in the die, but worn in passage from the rough hand of the legionary to the itching palm of the publican, to his wife, to her sandal-maker, to the rival publican, to some sailor who fought at Actium, to his slayer who clutched the purse from his belt and spat upon the fair silver face in resentment for the wrongs of discardad Octavia—and so down the ages, nimble by the hour here, dormant for centuries there, until at last it comes to be wondered at and gazed upon by faces fairer far than the royal one it has borne since Cæsar's rival cried: "This. Eros, was greatly done," and plunged into his vitals the sword on which the servant had found death.

For, indeed, the countenance stamped upon the disc by the minter's heavy mallet is far from beautiful. The eyes, that looked deceitful love, and the lips that won the dagger from the murderous hand of Haggard's royal Harmachis, could not have compared for sweetness and tenderness with those of humble Charmian. And Gautier's Meiamoun, the son of Mandouschopsch, of the land of Kemi, must have been dazzled by the light that beats around a throne when he dived through the vaulted arch of the canal leading to her bath, that he might play Actæon to her Diana and twelve short hours thereafter be dead and spurned by her Roman lover, rushing to her arms.

Nor does Antony's head, on the reverse of the coin, appear to better advantage. It bears mute witness against the hyperbole of Avon's grandiloquent bard, when he bids Cleopatra murmur:—

> "His face was as the heavens; and therein stuck
> A sun and moon, which kept their course, and lighted
> The little O, the earth."

His face is much rather as a certain other place, in its passion, its dominance, and its fierce cruel strength. And yet, Antony's is the more interesting countenance, for it has character in it; his mistress, on the medal, has but a calm unscrupulousness to redeem her from the insane.

## A Coin of Augustus.

Strangely enough, another rare coin that enters the collection now, that has been cheek by jowl with the imperious visage of the self-styled decendant of Hercules, and has pressed stern, metallic lips against the harsher lips of Egypt's royal courtesan, all in the vest pocket of a complacent nineteenth century Curator, is a medallion of that Augustus Cæsar who, as Octavius, crushed at a blow his sister's recreant spouse, and supplied food for discussion among diligent historians as to whether Octavia's detested rival escaped the conquerer's grasp by poison of man or serpent. The piece is a medallion, the size of an American half dollar, and contains 186 grains of silver. It is a fine specimen, nobly minted, and perfect in every detail. The reverse is the Goddess of Peace, standing, and holding the cista, or basket, and the caduceus, or rod of Mercury, the whole surrounded by a laurel wreath. The one ungraceful feature of this side of the coin is the figure of Peace, who displays a marked resemblance to a clothes-pin. So little attention to the charms of peace is not, however, to be wondered at among the Romans; before the time of Augustus, the temple of Janus had its doors closed but twice in seven centuries.

The obverse of the medallion is a remarkably fine imprint of the face of Rome's first Emperor. The inscription, "Cæsar Imperator, defender of the liberties of the Roman People," reads like an unblushing sarcasm, until the recollection comes of tnat advice which Macenas opposed to Agrippa's, "Rome can exist no longer without a monarch," and of the consequent resolution of Ovid's banisher to leave to the republic its form of government, while intrenching himself with its substance.

### A Piece of Art.

One of the most artistic pieces, and a very rare one, too, is a coin of Syracuse, minted about 415 B. C. This coin belongs to the time known among numismatists as "the period of finest art," extending from the siege of Syracuse to the accession of Alexander the Great. The art of engraving coins reached then the highest point of excellence it has ever attained, either in ancient or modern times. The types are characterized by intensity of action, perfect symmetry of proportion, elegance of composition, finish of execution, and richness of ornamentation. The triumph of art may be appreciated when the visitor remembers that all these coins were moulded first into the form of a bullet, and then placed between two dies and pounded into shape by hand.

The specimen at the Mint bears on the obverse the head of Arethusa, beloved of Alpheus, grandly struck in high relief, and surrounded by a dotted circle. Modern artists, in marble or in oil, might strive for years and accomplish nothing so severely beautiful, so proudly chaste, so grandly calm. The reverse is a Mars, bearded and helmeted. The piece contains about as much silver as a half dollar and has a strange and significant mark. Some keen, heavy weapon, swung by a powerful arm, has struck the edge and shorn the thick silver through, as if it were softest lead. The Curator can give no explanation of the cut: it is indiscreet, discourteous even, to inquire the history of a coin. Meum and tuum is less respected among numismatists than among bibliophiles, surreptitious appropriation being much less difficult. For all Mr. McClure knows, that mighty stroke may have been dealt ere the tyrant Dionysius fled from Syracuse to Corinth, there to instruct scoffing schoolboys and win in Athens his fatal prize of poetry at the feast of Bacchus. Or the sword of the soldier of Marcellus, as it struck down Archimedes ere he could finish his problem, at the taking of the city a century afterwards, may have bitten into the coin before the murder snatched it up, dripping with his victim's blood. The Curator of the Museum attempts no explanation. "See for yourself," says he, "and form your own opinion."

The coin that has puzzled all the Mint experts is a gold piece, worth intrinsically about $5. They believe it is a Bactrian piece, for the inscription corresponds exactly to that of a coin described in Mionnet's Description de Medailles Antiques, Grecques et Romainec. The annoying thing about it is that the inscription is perfectly plain, and yet cannot be read. Mionnet, who is an authority, gives a fac-simile of this very legend in his work, and dubs it "an uncertain language." One of today's visitors, unhampered by numismatic shibboleths, pronounced it bastard Greek, from the formation of the letters. This opinion may very well be correct, since Bactria, now Bokhara or Cabul, was a remote Greek colony, founded about B. C. 250, by a secession from the great Syro-Persian Empire.

As a coin and as a specimen of Greek art, the piece bears evidence of having been struck about 180 B. C. The purely mechanical portion is far better than that of the Syracusan piece; but from an artistic view-point, the Royal head which the obverse bears indicates at least over a century of decadence from high ideals. The reverse is a standing figure, facing and pointing to the left.

MODERN SPECIMENS.

The other additions to the collection include these:—

An American quarter of 1823; price, $25. It was obtained from a lady amateur in Kansas, who accepted $25 for it. It is a coin very difficult to obtain, and is to be found in no other public museum. Its value is low, because it is so much worn; were it perfect it would be worth $200.

A half-eagle of 1798; price, $50.

A half-eagle of 1795; price, $50. The 1795 half eagle is of two varieties, one having a small eagle on the reverse, the other a heraldic eagle. The latter is the rarer, and the Mint's acquisition is of this class.

An eagle of 1797, having four stars on the front of the face; price, $52.50.

The case of current coins, now shown to the public, stands to the left of the museum door, opposite the Curator's desk. The collection is incomplete as yet in a few respects, lacking noticeably the coins struck by the Austrian Government under its new system. It contains the current coins of nearly all the rest of the world, alphabetically arranged. Spain, however, is represented by but one piece, and Portugal not at all. When the United States Ministers applied for complete sets, regrets were returned instead, that no complete sets were in the possession of these Governments. But a promise was given to furnish them as soon as possible. All the other coinages are fully represented, from the Jubilee moneys of Queen Victoria to the Chinese silver and gold pieces, arranged on United States standards, that have replaced the old copper cash, which proved as cumbersome as the brittle iron pieces wherewith Lycurgus drove effeminancy out of Sparta.

A discovery of much interest to antiquarians, and especially to numismatists, is reported from Matabeleland. Eight coins, all in a fair state of preservation, were discovered a few months ago by a Mashona native in the neighborhood of the famous ruins tt Zimbabye. A local collector has now come into possession of the coins, which are undoubtedly Roman. On the obverse of two of them is the head of a woman with the words "Helena Augusta," and on the reverse the figure of a woman can also be made out. Four of the coins bear on the obverse the figure of a man with the words "Constantius Cæs." One bears on the reverse figures which appear to represent Romulus and Remus being suckled by the wolf. The coins will probably be sent to England for fuller examination.—New York Evening Post.

## JOHN ANDREW BRUDIN.

The subject of this sketch is a native of Sweden and was born May 2, 1846. He studied in Gothenburg and graduated there as mechanical engineer in 1871. Between 1872 and 1883 he managed a cotton mill in his native country, where American cotton was mainly used. On his retirement from this position he was presented by his fellow workmen with an elegant drinking horn of antique style. He married in 1876. For three years previous to coming to New York City in 1886, he conducted an electrical business in Gothenburg.

But it is as a collector and writer on Oriental coins that Mr. Brudin is best known, not only in America but on the continent as well. When a school boy he collected botanical specimens, insects, books, stamps, etc., and at the age of seventeen took up the collecting and study of copper coins of all nations, and had at one time about 6,000 specimens in his cabinet. In 1883 he sold his Swedish collection in Stockholm. and the balance of his collection, excepting his coins of eastern Asia, were later sold in Berlin. Since this time Mr. Brudin has given his whole time as a collector and student to oriental coinage, and it is probable that his collection and knowledge in this field of numismatic research is unequalled on this side of the water.

Mr. Brudin has been and is associated with the following associations: The Swedish Numismatic Association and The Swedish Archæological Association of Stockholm. The Polytechnical Society and "Gnistan" Society of Science and Art, of Gothenburg, Sweden. He has been a member of the American Numismatic Association since its organization, and has never been found wanting in any duty imposed upon him. G. F. H.

## THE MONEY METALS, AN EDITORIAL COMPILATION.

### NO. 1.—GOLD.

Gold has ever been the money of the banker, the broker and the useror. It is estimated that throughout the world from $65,000,000 to $80,000,000 in gold is used in the arts and dentistry. A cubic foot of pure gold is worth $362,600. All the gold in the world circulating as money would make a cube measuring twenty-one and a half feet on an edge, valued at $3,600,000,000. The more noted or historical accumulations of gold in ancient times were at Babylon under Sematies, at Jerusalem under Solomon, at Sardis under Croesus, at Babylon again under Darius, and at Alexandria under Alexander. Gold was used in Rome 300 B. C. in the dental art. Josephus says that at Jerusalem nothing could be bought or sold with silver in its earlier years for only gold was valued.

The Roman *solidus* was worth a half-eagle in gold. The Bank of England estimates the amount of gold in circulation in the world at 865 tons. Sixteen ounces of gold would suffice to gild a wire that would reach around the world. During 1893 the gold production of the United States was nearly thirty-six million dollars, an increase of over a mil lion and a half over 1892. South Africa promises a yield in gold the present year (1894) of $32,000,000. In 1888 this district was not recognized as gold producing. The bible first mentions gold in Genesis ii, 11-12: "And the gold of that land (Havilah) is good." "Abraham was very rich in silver and gold," Genesis xiii, 2. Jewelry and vessels of gold found in the Egyptian tombs give sufficient evidence of the perfection obtained in working this metal at a time antedating the government of Joseph. Gold was obtained from Arabia by the Hebrews. In Etruria excavations have brought to light the most beautiful ornaments of gold enriched with minute grains of the metal, the workmanship of which was unrivalled until Castellani studied and revived their methods. Solomon received gold from Hiram, King of Tyre, whose fleets brought him gold from Ophir. Gold is the one metal of yellow color, among them ranks first in beauty and value. The largest nugget found is the "Sarah Sands" found in Australia and weighing 233 lbs., 4 oz. Aaron prepared a golden calf for the people to worship. Large quantities of gold were used by Solomon in furnishing the temple. $120,000 worth of gold ornaments were taken from the bodies of the slain Midianites after their defeat by Moses. About $15,000,000 in gold was the ransom paid by Atahualfa, the Inca of Peru, for his deliverance. About this same amount Pyrrhus, the Lydian king, gave in gold to the Persian invader, Xerxes, to purchase imunity. Polybius in his time states that gold was so abundant in Rome (gotten from the mines near Apulia) that its value was reduced one-third. There is more gold held in solution by the waters of the oceans than ever has been extracted from the earth. The earliest gold coins were of electrum, (gold with from 20 to 40 per cent. of silver), rough nuggets on which were stamped images of animals. The early coins of Lydia were of electrum. Gold, next to iron, is the most widely distributed metal. Very ancient mines have been discovered by Linant Bey in the district known as Altaki, or Allaki, on the Red Sea, situated about 120 miles back from Ras Elba. These are probably the same mines that were described by Diodorus Seculus, and one of the oldest typographical maps known, a map or itinerary of the route to them from the Nile, is preserved in Turin. In the reign of Setee I, of the 19th dynasty, wells were opened along this route in order that the mines, that were then of great antiquity, might be re-opened. Similar gold mines of ancient working have been found recently, discovered by Burton in the land of Midian on the east coast of the Gulf of Akoba. The ancients refined gold by grinding and roasting, in this way the baser metals were eliminated and the gold uninjured. The darics of Persia and the gold coins of Philip and Alexander contained very little alloy. Pliny is the authority for the statement that gold was first coined in Rome during the war with Hannibal, about 207 B. C. The earliest gold coin in the British Museum is one of Miletus in Ionia. It is doubtful if any gold was coined in England up to the time of Edward III. The first gold coin struck in the United States, if not on the Western Continent, was the five dollar gold piece of which 774 were delivered by the Chief Coiner on July 31st, 1795. With the exception of some debased gold issued in B. C. 407, Athens struck no gold until the time of Alexander III. In 1000 ounces of our gold coinage there are 900 ounces of pure gold, 10 ounces of silver and 90 of copper. In the forty years preceding 1890, there were coined in the world's mints 9194 tons of gold. More gold was produced in 1893 than in any other year in the history of the world, over $150,000,000 being produced. The gold "talent" is variously computed at from $1,186.21 to $1,216.62. It is asserted that American dentists insert annually into the teeth of their patients over 1800 pounds of gold, worth over $450,000. With our increase of population and the continued deterioration of the human teeth, it is evident that in 100 years there will be more gold buried in our cemeteries than now exists in the country. The smallest coin ever issued is the gold one-sixteenth ducat of Nuremburg, weighing just two grains troy, or about one-half the size of the California gold quarter-dollar. The value of gold in any case can be readily determined by multiplying the number of ounces by 20.67. Gold was discovered in Australia in 1839 but the fact was hushed up by the governor for fear it would demoralize his convicts. The public announcement was not made until 1851. Gold coin is handled less than any other; it is usually kept in the banks for demands rarely made and for this reason the loss by abrasion is only about one-half of one per cent. in any twenty years. Gold can be beaten into a sheet less than one two hundred and fifty thousandths of an inch in thickness. In such cases it is of a beautiful green tint and almost transparent. During the month of April, 1894, gold to the amount of $10,184,000 was coined at the United States mints. One of the largest coins as well as one of the greatest in intrinsic value ever struck in America is the fifty-dollar gold piece struck in this country in 1851; it was octagonal in shape. Our gold dollar weighs 25.8 grains, of which 23.22 is pure gold. No charge has ever been made in the U. S. mint in the coinage of gold bullion. The only cost to the owner of the bullion is for the alloy used to give it the necessary hardness. Canada and Mexico have no gold coinage. The same is true of most of the South and Central American countries. Colorado claims to have over one billion dollars worth of low grade gold ore in sight. All the more important European countries have adopted a gold standard. In China gold is cast in long thin ingots and it is 20 carats fine. Absolutely pure gold is supposed to be 24 carats fine. Herodotus says Croesus was the first sovereign to make coins of gold. In 1237 the English coined gold pennies which passed for twenty pence; they weighed one one hundred twentieth of a pound. The largest and richest gold field in the world lies within the limits of Colorado, and extends from Boulder, Manhattan in Larimer county, and Halm's Peak southwest through the state.

The first forgery on the Bank of England was committed in 1758 by a lawyer's clerk named Richard Vaughan, who was detected and subsequently executed.

## EAST INDIA NOTES.

[MAJOR ADAM SMITH, POONA, INDIA.]

RODGER'S "COIN COLLECTING."—His Royal Highness the Duke of Connaught has been pleased to accept a copy of "Coin Collecting in Northern India," by Mr. Chas. J. Rodgers. His Royal Highness is a capital Hindustani scholar, and when he was at Amristar Mr. Rodgers had the honor of showing him a selection of Greek and Mogul Coins. He was especially delighted with the Greek ones, which took him quite by surprise, as having been found in India. His Excellency the Marquis of Dufferin and Ava has also been pleased to accept a copy of the same book. When his Excellency was in office in India he expressed a desire to be supplied with a copy of every work Mr. Rodgers wrote, and asked as a special favor that each should have in it the signature of the author "to add to its interest." His Excellency was an Eastern scholar of sound attainments, and appreciated Oriental learning. He gave Mr. Rodgers his own bronze medal, not only as a sign of personal appreciation of his labors, but to keep as a specimen of the greatest numismatic artist of the age. —Wyon.

ANCIENT GREEK COINS IN THE PUNJAB.—Most of the classical coins of Athens and the Greek colonies are figured in Smith's Classical Dictionary; the British Museum also publishes illustrated catalogues of coins. I have only Cassell's Illustrated Bible on my shelf. At page 255. Vol. II, there is a coin of Athens, also on page 977 are medallions of Alexander and Seleucus. The legend around the owl is ATHE AREPAOTONOX. I have heard of an Alexander's coin once purchased in these parts for thirty times its intrinsic metal value. This conqueror's helmet has ram's horns on the sides, for he claimed descent of Jupiter Ammon. There is a curious jingle or rude verse in the Punjab connecting "Sikander" with *Zu-ul-Karnien* or the *Sahib* or chief, with the two-horns; this is well-known in the Jhelum district, where Nikla and Bucephelæ are supposed to be built. This *Zu-ul-Karnien* is mentioned in the Koran, but the Arabic glossists attribute this name to the father of Job the patriarch. The legend about "Sikander" in Islamic Theology is somewhat mixed. I have mentioned the latter to excite interest, something more than the mere collection of coins.

OLD COINS.—The find of Roman denarii in Hazara is a much more interesting one than was at first supposed, says the Lahore paper. It was not all made public at once. Either coins were kept back or others have been found. New coins are at any rate coming to light. They are all, however, of the first emperor of Rome, and thus differ from the coins constantly being found in Madras and Mysore. Some little time back the Deputy Commissioner of Hazara secured five coins, four of which were new and not in the first find. Since then one denarius has been found of Hadrian, and now three other coins have been put forward. Each one is of the greatest interest. One has in a lined circle a portrait of Augustus. The reverse of this coin has a winged Victory standing on a globe and holding in her hand a wreath. The legend is *Cæsar Divi F.* The second coin has the head of Augustus, *Avgvstvs* to the left. On the reverse is the elevation of a temple of six pillars. To the left is *iovi*, to the right *olv.* The third coin has the head of a female with the hair bound by a ribbon, to the right is *bon event;* to the left *libo.* The reverse has a draped altar, on which are hung two lyres. Above is *Puteal,* below, *Scribon.* We might dilate on each one of these coins. It will be sufficient to state, however, that they were not in the first lot obtained for the Lahore Museum.

The discovery of the Greek-Roman coins in Aden, which we noted some time ago, has given an impetus to search for similar coins further east. The Honorary Numismatist to the Government of India has ascertained that coins of Roman Emperors with legends in Greek characters have been found, and are known, in the Punjab. He has lately examined coins of Claudius, Probus, Diocletian and Numeranius. He thinks he has also obtained one of Augustus. These coins are in bronze. On one side is the bust with the titles and name of the emperor. The reverse is occupied with some image and the year. The names and titles are in Greek. The titles are, as a rule, expressed by two letters *before* the name, A and K, meaning Autokrator and Kaisar, and the abbreviated form of Sebastos (Seb.) meaning Augustus, *after* the name. One coin of Probus was obtained in Kaithal, another from Rawalpindi. Two coins of Numerianus were found in the Amritsar bazaar, that of Claudius is in the collection of the late Dr. Stülpnagel. In all probability one of the coins examined is of Gordianus. These coins were struck in the eastern provinces of the Roman Empire. and as the language of Athens, Antioch and Alexandria was Greek, the coins, although of Roman emperors, were struck with Greek legends on them. Hitherto these Greek-Roman coins have not been noticed by any Indian collector. The fact that they have been found in India will perhaps stir collectors up, and make them examine their cabinets more carefully. A few months ago two gold coins of Caracalla were found in the Punjab. One has on it the title *Armeniacus.* This coin, it would seem is but little known in Europe, and it is not in the British Museum collection of Roman coins. We shall be glad to see the results of the Aden find, and hope that some of these coins will find their way into the museums of the Indian Empire. Students of Indian History will see that India in olden times continued to have transactions with the far West, and received for her products, then as now, payment in hard cash, gold silver, or copper.

## Coinage of the Mints.

Washington, June 1.—The monthly statement of the director of the mint shows that the total coinage of the mints of the United States during the month of May, 1894, was $9,120,450, of which $8,445,450 was gold and $675,000 was silver. The silver coining was entirely of half dollars and quarters.

## HOOPER'S RESTRIKES.

[JOSEPH HOOPER]

CONTINENTAL MONEY NOT REDEEMABLE.—During last month three batches of Continental currency were presented to the Treasury Department for redemption. The currency was, of course returned to the owners, as by law such currency, even if it was genuine, has no money value. At the close of the Revolutionary war, Continental currency was worth $1 in specie for $1,000 of Continental money. This money was extensively counterfeited by order of the British government, in its efforts to destroy the credit of the Continental government. One curious advertisement bearing on the subject, is among the archives of the Treasury department. It reads: "Persons going into other colonies may be supplied with any number of counterfeited Congress notes for the price of the paper per ream. They are so nearly and exactly executed that there is no risk in getting them off, it being almost impossible to discover that they are not genuine. This has been proved by bills of a very large amount which have been successfully circulated." The British government itself embarked in the business of counterfeiting Continental money, and General Howe, the British commander, it is recorded, "abetted and patronized those who were engaged in making and pushing spurious issues into circulation."

WOODEN MONEY IN ENGLAND.—Wooden money in the shape of exchequer tallies was, says an English exchange, prior to the establishment of the Bank of England, in 1694 current in this country. Tallies were the name given to the notched stocks formerly in use in England for keeping the accounts in the exchequer. They were square rods of hazel or willow, inscribed on one side with notches indicating the sum for which the tally was an acknowledgement, and on two other sides with the same sum in Roman characters. When the transaction was completed the tally recording it was split lengthwise, so that each section contained a half of each notch and one of the written sides. One half, called the tally or check, was given to the person for whose service it was intended; the other half, called the counter tally, was retained in the exchequer until its corresponding tally should be brought in by the person who had last given value for it. It thus became a current token representing cash. After the establishment of the Bank of England, government payments were made through its agency. The use of tallies in the exchequer was abolished by Statute 23 George III. The old tallies were, by the Act 4 and 5 William IV., ordered to be destroyed, and it was burning them that caused the conflagration by which the old Houses of Parliament were demolished.—Engineering and Mining Journal.

DEATH OF JOHN WINCHELL, THE COIN EXPERT.—John Winchell, the coin expert of the New York sub-treasury, died of pneumonia on December 26 after a short illness. Mr. Winchell was without doubt the most skillful detector of light weight and spurious coins in the country. His services to the government in the handling of gold coin have been invaluable. He entered the sub-treasury during Gen. Grant's administration and has been over twenty years in the government service. His reputation as an expert in handling gold coin was wide spread, and any coin that was ever questioned was invariably submitted to his decision, and his judgement was almost infalliable. Mr. Winchell, besides being an able official, was a most zealous and courteous one. Affable at all times, he was ever ready to contribute of his vast store of information to those who were in search of knowledge. He was modest in the expression of his opinion, but unerring in his judgement. His death was a shock to his associates, who honored and loved him. He was only about fifty years of age at the time of his heath, and it was hoped that he had many years of usefulness before him. The loss to the government which his death means is hardly to be repaired. Mr. Winchell was a veteran soldier and a prominent Mason.

---

EARLY COLONIAL MONEY.—The early settlers of this country brought with them from England a considerable amount of silver coin, and, following the practice of the mother country, expressed the values of commodities, and kept their accounts in pounds, shillings, pence and farthings. It is well known that the standard pound in England was originally a certain bar of silver, kept in the Tower, representing a pound in value, as it was divided into twenty parts, called shillings, the shillings being divided into twelve parts, called pence. As a pound in weight, it was divided into twelve parts called ounces, each being divided into twenty parts called pennyweights. A pennyweight was, therefore, both in value and in weight, 1-240 part of a pound. King Edward III., however, being pressed for means to pay his royal debts, directed that a pound of silver should be coined into twenty-two pieces, and declared by royal proclamation that each one of these pieces should be called a shilling, and should be accepted as such in payment of the debts of the Crown, as well as in the payment of private debts. In this way there accrued to the royal revenue, two shillings on every pound thus minted; and the royal counsellors imagined that they had discovered a very ingenious method by which a revenue could be obtained without taxation, and without defrauding anyone. But as silver, like other commodities, had a certain value of its own, the reduction of the weight of the shilling caused a corresponding increase of prices; and the subjects of the king, finding that through some mysterious agency, their property had apparently increased in value, made no complaint of the debasement of their coins. The successors of Edward III. repeated the robbery again and again, until Queen Elizabeth directed that fifty-eight pieces be coined from the pound sterling, or sixty-two pieces from a pound troy. By this time royalty had reduced the shilling to about one-third of its original value, and yet by edicts and proclamations had made each one of the same power in the payment of debts as the original piece. The shilling had now, however, become so small that the subjects of the Queen saw there was cheating somewhere about the board, and they put a stop to any further reduction of the coin. These shillings were the coins which the early settlers brought to this country.—Investment World.

## Closed to Silver.

| | Date | Population. |
|---|---|---|
| Great Britain closed its mints to silver and adopted tne gold standard in | 1816 | 50,000,000 |
| All its colonies have followed the example. | | |
| Germany closed its mints to silver in | 1871-3 | 42,000,000 |
| It called in $257,454,000 worth of silver thalers and sold 89,695,728 fine ounces of the melted silver at a loss of $23,000,000 to procure the necessary gold for coinage. | | |
| Norway, Sweden and Denmark, in a monetary treaty, demonetized silver and gold as sole legal tender standard in | 1872 | 10,000.000 |
| France closed its mints to silver in | 1874 | 38,000,000 |
| It has since filled up with gold. | | |
| Italy closed its mints to silver in | 1874 | 30,000,000 |
| It has since filled up with gold. | | |
| Belgium adopted gold standard in | 1883 | 6.000,000 |
| Switzerland and Greece adopted gold standard in | 1884 | 4,000,000 |
| Holland closed its mints to silver in | 1875 | 4,000,000 |
| In 1884 it authorized the sale of 25,000,000 silver florins whenever the state of the currency demanded it. | | |
| Russia stopped silver coinage in | 1876 | 100,000,000 |
| It is filling up with gold. | | |
| Austria-Hungary closed its mints to silver in | 1879 | 38,000,000 |
| It is filling up with gold. | | |
| Roumania adopted gold standard in | 1890 | 5,000,000 |
| It withdrew about $5,000,000 worth of silver coins from circulation, which were sold as bullion at a heavy loss. | | |
| British India closed its mints to silver in | 1893 | 280,000,000 |
| United States silver coinage was discontinued in | 1873 | 60,000,000 |
| It revived in 1878. | | |

The late action by British India leaves the United States and Mexico the only countries in the world that continue to purchase silver and coin it into legal-tender money.

## NUMISMATIC CHESTNUTS.

Little Harry—"Papa, is the tarriff bill a counterfeit?" Papa—"No." Little Harry—"Then why can't they pass it?"—New York Herald.

Preserving the Parity.—Binkerton—"Come over to the house, tonight, old man. We're going to celebrate our silver wedding."

Pilgarlic—"Your silver wedding? Ain't you a little previous? Why, you've only been married fifteen years."

Binkerton—"That's all, but silver is away below par now, you know."—[New York Daily News.]

### Our Mary Ann.

She sighs not for great riches, from further toil to stop her.
Her dream of bliss is satisfied, when fortune brings a "copper."

Mrs. Numisma—"Oh, John! John! What shall we do? Baby has swallowed that 1802 half dime."

Mr. N.—"Jementhy Christmas! Just paid $62 for it! Send for Dr. Knifem quick, and have him bring his operating case along."

### And Slim was Happy.

The banker said, with aspect grim,
  The while the daughter hung her head,
"You must get rid of that young slim,
He's an old coin crank up to the brim;
Next time he comes sit down on him."
  And when he came that night she did.

Two Chinamen robbed a bank messenger near Hong Kong, of 200 taels. They were caught and decapitated within forty-eight hours. "Taels you win, heads you lose," as the messenger remarked.

"How do you like your new neighbor, Mr. Numisma?" Mr. N.—"He's a most charming man and a delightful conversationalist. Why, last evening he listened to me for two whole hours while I expatiated on my collection of coins from Crœsus to Queen Lil, and didn't chip in a word."

Better than a Stomach Pump.—A small boy in a suburban town swallowed a penny. "Kitty," called his alarmed mother to her sister in the next room, "send for the doctor; Willie has swallowed a penny!" "No, mamma," interposed the terrified and frightened victim, "send for the minister." "Why?" faltered his mother. "Because papa says our minister can get money out of anybody."—[Christian Intelligencer.]

Reciprocity.—Clerk at the desk—"This is a bad half-dollar, sir."

Jones—That's all right. I had a bad dinner, too."—Life.

Very Busy.—Peddler—"Is Mr. Numisma in?"

Boy—"Yes, but he's got three A. N. A. fellers in there and they've got to talking about coins. Think you'd better drop in sometime next month."

She had several silver dollars,
  And she murmured with a smile:
"I'll hurry now and use them up
  Before they're out of style."—[American Industries.]

Rare Coins—Any of the American gold pieces.—Buffalo Times.

There must be something in the gold cure. Experience has proved that the silver remedy is of little efficacy when money's tight.—Philadelphia Times.

No Wonder.—Valet (entering chamber)—"I heard you yell, sir. Wot's the bloomin' row, sir?"

Algernon—"Come in, James. You'd better sit up with me till morning, James. I just had such a fwightful nightmare. Dweamt I had sold me coins at auction, James, and got me money all back on 'em."

## AUCTION ROOM ECHOES.

The following prices, realized at the Friesner sale, June 8, will be of especial interest to collectors of the United States series of Mint marks.

### New Orleans Mint.

| | | |
|---|---|---|
| 572 | Dollar, 1846, ex. fine | $ 4 10 |
| 573 | " 1850, very fine | 3 40 |
| 577 | " 1881, Standard uncirculated | 5 00 |
| 583 | Half Dollar, 1838, sharp dull proof surface | 113 00 |
| 584 | " 1839, o beneath bust, uncirculated | 1 85 |
| 585 | " 1840, uncirculated | 2 70 |
| 586 | " 1841, " | 2 80 |
| 598 | " 1852, extremely fine | 3 00 |
| 613 | Quarter Dollar, 1840, o to right of R, uncirculated | 2 70 |
| 614 | " 1840, o over R, uncirculated | 95 |
| 615 | " 1841, very fine | 2 20 |
| 619–625 | " 1842, small date, v. good; 1852, ex. fine | 2 00, 2 10 |
| 635 | Dime, 1838, Liberty seated; without stars, v. fine | 2 10 |
| 642 | " 1849, large O, very fine | 1 55 |
| 643 | " 1849, small o, fine | 1 50 |
| 652 | " 1860, o below wreath, fine | 4 00 |
| 656 | Half Dime, 1838, Liberty seated; without stars, fine | 2 50 |
| 658 | " 1840, without drapery, very fine | 2 00 |
| 664-658 | " 1849, 1852, very good and fine, each | 1 00 |

### San Francisco Mint.

| | | |
|---|---|---|
| 679 | Dollar, 1859, extremely fine | 5 30 |
| 680 | " 1872, good | 3 00 |
| 687-689 | Dollar, 1880, 1881, standard, uncirculated | 3 30, 2 40 |
| 691-692 | " 1887, 1889, " " ex. fine | 2 10, 2 90 |
| 697 | Half Dollar, 1856, sharp, uncirculated | 12 00 |
| 713 | " 1866, without motto, uncirculated | 31 00 |
| 731 | " 1878, proof surface, " | 7 70 |
| 736-737 | Quarter Dollars, 1860, 1861, fine | 2 40, 3 00 |
| 743-746 | " 1867, 1871, very good and very fine | 3 00, 2 00 |
| 765 | Dime, 1860, Liberty seated, 13 stars, uncirculated | 5 00 |
| 776-781 | Dime, 1874, 1884, Fine | 2 00, 1 35 |
| 792-793 | Half Dime, 1863, 1864, very fine and fine | 2 10, 1 00 |
| 794 | " " 1865 (5 over 3) fine | 2 00 |
| 796-7-8 | " " 1866-7-8, very fine | 2 10, 2 30, 1 25 |
| 800 | " " 1872, s within wreath, uncirculated | 2 30 |
| 801 | " " 1872, s below " " | 2 10 |

### Carson City Mint.

| | | |
|---|---|---|
| 803 | Dollars, 1870, fine | 4 40 |
| 804 | " 1872, uncirculated | 35 00 |

805 " 1873, pin scratches, very good,.............................. 9 25
806-7-8 " 1873-4-5, trade, fine................. .......... 4 60, 3 50, 3 00
810-11 " 1881, 1883, standard, uncirculated..................... 5 60, 3 00
828 Half Dollar, 1878, uncirculated.......................................... 2 90
829, 31 Quarter Dollars, 1870, very fair; 1873, arrows, good.......... 4 00, 5 00

UNITED STATES CENTS.

843 1793, chain, UNITED STATES OF AMERI, fine profile, date and reverse bold, very good, monograph no. 1.................................. 25 50
844 1793, chain, dot after LIBERTY and date, bust weak, monog. 2...... 7 10
845 1793, chain, UNITED STATES OF AMERICA, hair worn smooth around ear, olive, nearly fine, mon. 3.................................. 7 50
846 1793, wreath, very good impression, mon. 6.......................... 5 50
847 1793, wreath, stem between 7 and 9, good, mon. 8.................. 4 40
848 1793, wreath, lettered edge, very good, mon. 9........................ 7 60
849 1793, liberty cap, very good, dark, ex specimen, mon. 11............. 20 50
850 1794, olive color, ex. fine, Hays No. 23.............................. 6 00
853 1795, thin planchett, ONE CENT high in wreath, fine................. 15 25
854 1795, " " " " low " " " ................. 8 00
857 1797, broken die, bold impression, ex. fine.................... ...... 5 35
859 1798, small date, uncirculated............... ...................... 5 20
860 1799, knobbed 99, rusted over R T, v. good............................ 15 00
867 1804, perfect die, very good.......................... ............. 7 00
869 1806, fine bold impression two light pin scratches over the eye...... 4 00
873 1809, fine light impression, not perfectly centered.................. 5 70
930, 935, 937, 940 1850, 1855, 1856, 1857, proofs............. 2 50, 3 70, 5 50, 5 20

UNITED STATES HALF CENTS.

942 1793, very good, monograph 1........................................ 2 85
942 1794, very fine. " 3......................................... 15 20
946 1796, good for date.................................................. 17 25
949 1802, good.............................. ..................... 2 90
966 1831, obverse of 1831; reverse of 1849: large date, mint restrike...... 10 25
971 1840, original, proof ................................................ 20 00
972, 73, 74 1841-2-3, mint restrike, brilliant proofs.......... 10 25, 13 50, 13 75
975, 76, 77 1844-5-7, " " " " .......... 16 25, 16 50, 13 75
978 1848, original, sharp proof........................................... 21 00
979 1849, small date, original proof...................................... 22 00
981, 83, 86, 87, 88 1850-2-5-6-7, proofs................ 2 10, 9 25, 1 55, 1 90, 3 00

Jube Reynolds is dead! But the fife he played on during the revolutionary war, and with especial *eclat* at Yorktown when Cornwallis surrendered, is in the possession of Larkin R. Smith, of Danville, Va.

## THE AMERICAN NUMISMATIC ASSOCIATION.

BOARD OF OFFICERS:



### Secretary's Report.

TO THE PRESIDENT AND MEMBERS OF THE AMERICAN NUMISMATIC ASS'N.
GREETING:

The following report covers the period from June 20 to July 20:

In pursuance of a call for nominations to be voted upon the following have been reported:

For President: A. G. Heaton, Washington; Dr. Geo. F. Heath, Michigan.

For Vice-President: Joseph Hooper, Ontario; Geo. W. Rice, A. H. Griffith, Michigan.

For Secretary: O. W. Page, Massachusetts; Morgan H. Stafford, Michigan.

For Treasurer: Dr. A. L. Fisher, Indiana.

For Librarian and Curator: W. C. Stone, Massachusetts.

For Superintendent of Exchange: W. J. Luck, Michigan.

For Counterfeit Detector: S. H. Chapman, Pennsylvania.

Board of Trustees (five to be elected): J. A. Heckelman, Virginia; W. K. Hall, Ontario; C. W. Stutesman, Indiana; David Harlowe, Wisconsin; H. E. Deats, New Jersey; Geo. W. Rice, Michigan; W. F. Greany, California; Geo. W. Rode, Pennsylvania; Chas. S. Wilcox, Illinois.

The cash receipts during the month have been, for initiation fees $1.50, dues $7.00; total $8.50, turned over to the treasurer. Five certificates of membership have been issued. Expenses of office, (postage) 59 cents.

The following new members are received:

207 Albert Howver, Cambridge, N. Y.
208 Theron Y. Sebring, Kalamazoo, Mich.
209 A. B. Ragan, Monroe, Mich.
210 Dr. I. R. Bogue, 94 Michigan avenue, Detroit, Mich.
211 Chas. C. Deuel, 80 Sproat street, Detroit, Mich.

### Applications for Membership.

Daniel R. Kennedy, 59 Fifth avenue, New York City.
Vouchers: Messrs. Frossard and Page.

R. M. Rowley, Kalamazoo, Mich.
Vouchers: Messrs. Heath and Page.

W. Day, 46 Rue de France, Nice, France.
Vouchers: Messrs. Whiteway and ——.

Respectfully Submitted, O. W. PAGE, Secy.

## COMMUNICATION.

DR. GEORGE F. HEATH,

DEAR SIR:—In the May number of Numismatist I noticed a little article headed, "Once a Vast Fortune," wherein one Barker claims to have purchased eighty million dollars in Confederate notes.

This item first appeared in the Atlanta Constitution and Barker had copies struck off and sent out in his correspondence. What object he had in circulating such stuff is a mystery.

I have evidence sufficient to state that no such purchase was made; therefore the article is the more calculated to do harm to anyone dealing in the notes, and if the transaction really was effected, it would be good bye to high prices on scarce varieties for many years.

Barker claims to be a dealer and says that he is in the market to purchase more, in fact I have sold him, since his big purchase(?), several dollars worth of the commonest varieties; just think of it! "Four big dry goods boxes" full of the stuff and still hungry for more.

He says he is able to furnish every variety of C. S. A. notes; any collector can put the truth of his statements to a test. His address is Chas. D. Barker, 90 So. Forsythe St., Atlanta, Ga. Send for a few scarce issues or what varieties you want to fill in with and note your success.

July 18, 1894. LUTHER B. TUTHILL.

## AN IDEA OF DETROIT.

*For the Benefit of A. N. A. Visitors.*

Population, 300,000.

Bank Deposits amount to $56,331,457 a year.

One of the most beautiful cities in all America.

THEATERS: Lyceum, Detroit Opera House and Whitney's.

The Wholesale Trade of the city amounts to $40,000,000 annually.

Over five and a half millions were spent in new buildings in 1892.

In seven hundred manufacturing institutions alone 40,750 people are employed.

PLACES OF INTEREST: Museum of Art, Public Library, House of Correction, Belle Isle Park, Fort Wayne Garrison, Charitable Institutions, Cemeteries, Water Works and Public Buildings.

# WITH THE EDITOR.

[GEORGE F. HEATH, M. D., MONROE, MICH.]

Don't fail to make out your proxies and voting blanks immediately. Let there be no delay. We hope to see every one of them at the convention.

How would Washington, D. C., do for convention place in 1895? Of course providing Coxey's army has disbanded by that time. We don't want to get mixed up with them—or a tariff congress.

Ye editor notes his name again among the list of nominations for president of the Association. He is thankful for your consideration but when he respectfully declined the honor some time since, he meant every word. It is better for the Association to have a change in this office at least every two years. He believes in rotation in office. There are other and sufficient reasons why he asks to be relieved now. In this he shirks no responsibility or work. His voice will be still for war and the upbuilding of the A. N. A. As there is but one other name in nomination, and that a most excellent one, he has no hesitation in moving that the election of Mr A. G. Heaton be made unanimous.

We have the word of Eugene Field for it that the Field family, while all were noted collectors, some of them especially shone as numismatists. He says: "If as a family they have exhibited genius for any particular fad, that fad has been the collection of coins. True it is that not all of them have exhibited a genius for keeping what they have collected in this direction, but, not to be personal and to deal with more modest generalities, it is equally true that as a family the Fields have few equals and no superiors as numismatologists." We trust that Mr. Marshall Field will not forsake the family "fad" and will see that our science is as well endowed in the Columbian Museum as any other branch.

The following members of the Association will undoubtedly be present at the convention and proxies addressed to them will receive attention: George W. Rode, Havelwood avenue, Pittsburg, Pa.; W. J. Luck and Fred B. Stebbins, Adrian, Mich.; Geo. F. Heath, Monroe, Mich.; Dr. A. L. Fisher, Elkhart, Ind.; A. C. Gruhlke, Waterloo, Ind.; and the following from Detroit: Isaac M. Bates, 16 Oakley avenue; Dr. Joseph Lathrop, 271 Woodward avenue; George W. Rice, 186 east Hight street; H. B. Smith, 53 Gratiot avenue; A. H. Griffith, Museum of Art; W. P. Manton, M. D., 32 Adams avenue, W.; Fred H. Seymour, 44 Fort street, W.; or any other of our Detroit members. Proxies, if sent early (say before 15th), may be sent to Secretary O. W. Page, Waltham, Mass., or secretary of the board of trustees, H. E. Deats, Flemington, N. J.

In relation to the researches of Capt. Hunt upon alloys published last month Secretary Page writes us as follows: "In relation to the new alloy of gold and aluminum discovered by Capt. Hunt, what I should like to see is a gold dollar made on this basis and let it take the place of the silver dollar, using silver only for halves, quarters and dimes. A dollar struck with only a dollar's worth of gold and this over 22 carats fine in its make up, is altogether too small for convenience, but with the above alloy it would have some size and become a very popular coin, be much more convenient than either the silver or gold dollar as heretofore coined. Counterfeiters would have a barrier that would baffle their skill and there are certain peculiarities in aluminum that gold also possesses which is in favor of the union of these two metals in coinage."

Our friend Whiteway is getting to be quite a globe-trotter. His favors come to us with such a happy regularity and are liable to come from any portion of the globe. Algiers, Egypt, Switzerland, New Zealand, France and his last from Merrie England; a veritable Flying Dutchman: where next, whether Abyssinia or Japan, we wat not. Our lightning reporter and snap shot fiend lately caught him on the fly in the south of France. Mr. W. has had considerable experience as a numismatic editor and publisher and always puts in a good word for the NUMISMATIST wherever he goes, so we are getting quite well acquainted in the dark corners of the earth. Mr. W. said to our reporter, "What marvelous progress your NUMISMATIST is making; each number surpasses its predecessor in interest and"—here he heard a click, the concealed camera had done the rest. Mr. Whiteway fled but our reporter went over to England and looked up the family records. Next month we'll tell it all.

Secretary Page enjoys a joke, especially when it "points to a moral or adorns a tale;" and this he tells on his friend, Mr. Westwood. Mr. Westwood lately had occasion to visit Portland, Maine, and to reach his destination with the least exertion possible boarded an electric car at one of the terminals. As it was some minutes before his car started, he utilized a portion of the spare time by paying his fare (five cents) with a bright half-dollar. The conductor examined it eagerly and in such a curious manner that Mr. Westwood began to fear that he had imposed a counterfeit on him, still it looked too bright and sharp for that, but the conductor's curiosity not seeming to abate he asked him what the matter was with it—"if it was good?"

"Oh yes," the conductor responded, "it is good but it is a date I seldom see."

My friend W. got interested and inquired the date and found it to be 1852. Of course he was no more surprised at this than if it had been 1877, however he thought it over and on returning to Waltham asked me, "What is an 1852 half-dollar in bang up fine condition worth?"

I told him that his five cent car ride had cost him from $5.00 to $8.00, and you should have seen his eyes "bung out." Of course I put it on strong just to convince him that it paid to keep posted.

Ye editor has no means of knowing as yet who will exhibit numismatic specimens at our convention. A full report will follow in our next issue. We have this much to say, however, it will be the best thing of the kind ever seen in the West. We feel that we can say as much for our literary programme. Eighteen papers are on the list or promised. We shall deeply miss some who aided us last year. These papers, as a rule, will be shorter than last year's, and they will cover a wide field, as a glance at their titles will show. We hope all papers will be in our hands early, and they can be sent us up to Aug. 20, at Monroe, Mich.; Fred H. Seymour, 44 Fort St. W., or Joseph Lathrop, 271 Woodward avenue, or Dr. W. P. Manton, 32 Adams avenue, W., Detroit, Mich., who are the committee on arrangements.

Several inquiries have been received regarding hotels in Detroit, we take pleasure in recommending the following:

Hotel Normandie, Congress street, between Woodward and Bates.
Six squares from museum of Art Building; $2.00 to $3.00 a day.

Hotel St. Claire, corner Randolph and Monroe.
Nine squares from the Museum; $2.50 to $3.50.

Hotel Cadillac. Michigan Avenue, corner Washington.
Eleven squares from Art Museum; $3.00 to $5.00.

Franklin House, corner Bates and Larned.
Five squares from Art building: $1.50.

Tacoma, Woodward and Cadillac.
Nine squares from Art Building: 1.50.

The former hotel, which is centrally located, we think will be found in many ways preferable.

At no time does the president of the Association feel the responsibility of his place as on the eve of our annual convention. Its success or failure means so much to our Association that he could not be human and feel otherwise. There are two things that seem essential to the maintenance of our body. First and foremost, an official journal; second, an annual convention. Regarding the first, for three years we tried to find an official organ worthy of the Association; this year we have transposed matters and are trying to make the Association worthy the official journal. Regarding conventions, we must admit that from the first we have been skeptical; scattered as we are and bound down by business and professional cares, it is difficult for us to get together in good numbers on these occasions. We were overruled but went ahead to make them a success as far as possible and so far have had no reasons for regret. At Chicago last year we had a successful convention and have every reason to expect success in Detroit this month. There is too much tendency to put this preparatory work almost entirely in the hands of the executive. This is not right. He may be able to bear the burden during the year but he cannot hold a convention or exhibition by himself. At this time he must have the aid of the membership, and there are three ways he has the right to expect you to aid him to bear this responsibility: First, by your presence when at the convention; second, by contributing papers for the convention; third, by aiding in the exhibition. Certainly each member can do something in at least one of these lines, and that duty fulfilled the lines of the president's life will have fallen in a pleasant place.

# NUMISMATIC NOTES.

The Bank of England was two centuries old last month and the anniversary was duly celebrated.

The purchasing power of money in the days of the Roman Emperors was about ten times what it is now.

The British Mint has coined gold and silver to the value of upwards of $2,000,000,000, during Victoria's reign.

F. R. Kimball is up in the New Hampshire hills; and J. B. Aldrich in the Granite state enjoying their vacations.

The bank of Japan has a capital of twenty million yens. The value of a yen is about the same as one of our silver dollars.

Geo. W. Preston, of Detroit, has, among other gems in his collection, a silver coin of Afghanistan, Indosassanian period—about 300 A. D.

When the elephant Jumbo was dissected, a pint and a half of gold, silver, copper and bronze coins was found in his stomach. In the lot were coins of three kingdoms, five dukedoms, two principalities and one dependency.

The nickel three-cent pieces, minted from 1865 to 1890, are rarely seen nowadays. Three million of them are yet unaccounted for, Of 4,500,000 bronze two-cent pieces issued from 1864 to 1873, 3,000,000 remain outstanding; yet they are rarely seen in circulation.

There is no doubt but that bears and wolves had very much to do in the circulation of the old Pine and Oak tree shillings of 1652. In 1663 the bounty on a dead bear or wolf was enough to send, in each case, fifteen of those shillings on its circulating career in Massachusetts.

"I content myself with informing young persons who are desirous to study history in all its events, that the knowledge of medals is absolutely necessary to that kind of learning. For history is not to be learned in books only, which do not always tell the whole or the truth of things."—ROLLIN.

Brother Wismer suggests that something be done at our convention recommending that Congress take some action regarding the use of Aluminum as a metal for the minor coins. He thinks a little agitation of the matter and bringing it before members of Congress would ere long bring about the desired change.

It is estimated that there are 14,000,000 dolllars in our old fractional currency held today by collectors and private parties. Many persons have put away a few specimens of this currency for curiosities. The hard times has had a tendency to return more of this currency for redemption, lately. A short time ago a handkerchief full of it arrived, consisting of the earlier issues, in fine condition, each note being signed by General Spinner's own hand. The collection was worth far above face value if the owner had known it.

# THE WORLD OF FAD.

The postage stamp oldest in use and still used is the five pence of New South Wales.

The desk upon which President Lincoln wrote the Emancipation Proclamation is now the property of Senator Morgan.

The largest collection of cat and dog skulls in the world is owned by Martin Schluderhorn, of Newark. It is said to cover every known species of caninity and felinity.

Mr. J. J. Fernsler, of Pattsville, Pa., possesses the original scalp of his grandfather among other heir looms. An Indian got it first, and he bartered with the Indian for it.

Mrs. Sallie H. Redd, of Ridgeway, Va., has the very clay pipe with which Powhatan smoked the treaty of peace with Capt. John Smith. As it looks and smells very old it is probably strictly authentic.

During a recent trip through Southern Europe Marion Harland collected a large number of rosaries composed of amber shell, glass, olive seeds, carved wood, mother-of-pearl, ivory, lava, silver and pebbles, all fashioned into Christian or Mohammedan rosaries and chaplets.

"NAPOLEONIANA."—The present prevailing fad for collecting "Napoleoniana" in its various divisions of books, portraits, prints and relics is due to the fact that it is just 100 years since the great Corsican made his first definite appearance on the stage of Europe. The finest contemporary portraits of him, displayed in Chestnut and Walnut street print stores, bring high prices, and even coarsely engraved likenesses, if contemporary, possess considerable selling value. Philadelphia holds one of the rarest of Napoleonic relics—the duplicate in bronze of the death mask taken at St. Helena—in the library of the Academy of the Fine Arts.—Philadelphia Record.

VALUABLE EGGS.—Two more eggs of the great auk have been discovered in England and were sold last week at auction, one bringing $875 and the other $1,500. There was a slight flaw in each egg, which considerably lowered its value. They were found in a collection of fossils and eggs which a young collector bought for $9 at a sale of old household goods in the country three or four weeks ago. The collector recognized one of the eggs in the collection as a great auk's egg before he bid on the lot, but did not discover the second until he got home with his prize.

The value of the eggs was unknown to the seller. There was also sold at the same auction with the two great auk eggs, an egg of the long extinct roc, made famous in the "Arabian Nights." This was found in Madagascar, and it sold $255. A stuffed specimen of the great auk and a perfect egg were sold in London recently for $3,000.

# QUERIES.

This Department is open to all the readers of The Numismatist. A *non de plume* may be used if desired in either the asking or answering queries.

A saying we here commend to you
Ye learned, ye wise ye great ye small;
Far better to have aimed and missed,
Than never to have fired at all.

31—I would like information regarding a token that I have:

Obv: "Roxbury coaches."

Rev. "New Line, 1837." nickel.

I notice it listed in Steigerwalt's last sale, and he quotes it as RARE. My specimen is nearly uncirculated. What of its value, or scarcity?

J. B. GOLDSMITH.

32—I see in a late NUMISMATIST a letter offering a C. S. A. half dollar of 1861 for $3,000. Is this a joke or actuality? I have one and shall be glad to take much less for it. H. HERMAN, London, Eng.

Ans.—Quoted from the "Collector:" "In February 1861, the New Orleans mint fell into the hands of the Confederates and among its contents was the die for the new half dollar which had been sent from Washington some months before. The government, then in session at Montgomery, ordered the preparation of a die for a silver coin. Mr. Memoninger, the secretary of the Confederate Treasury, called for designs in April; this one was selected. Four coins only were struck. One was sent to the Government, one to Prof. Riddell of the University of Louisiana; one to Dr. C. Ames, of New Orleans; and one was kept by Dr. B. F. Taylor, the chief coiner of the C. S. A. There wasn't enough silver to be had to warrant circulation of coinage, however, and the mint was closed."

One of these pieces was in New York City a short time since; one was found on the person of Jeff Davis on his capture, but its whereabouts and the other two remaining ones are unknown. A few years since a New York dealer had an obverse *fac simile* die made and struck off 500 copies. For the reverse he used the back of half dollars of the 1861 issue which he smoothed down. These were sold at $2 each. The original obverse die is now in possession of S. H. Chapman, of Philadelphia, Pa.

33—What members of the A. N. A. are collecting coins of 1 Netherland Indies, 2 Indo Portugese, 3 Mysore, 4 Ceylon, 5 Bahmanie Kingdom, 6 East India Company, 7 the Moguls, 8 Guzrat, 9 Nizam(the Deccan). 10 Southern India, 11 Afghanistan, 12 Persia, 13 Kashmere, 14 Budhistic, 15 Burmese, 16 Ancient India, 17 Parthian, 18 Indo-Bactrian, 19 Sassanian, 20 Cutch. If they will state the numbers as given above and give address, and you will print replies I may be able to help them. ADAM SMITH, India.

We will gladly do so.—ED.

34—How many V nickels of 1883 were coined, and what is the premium on them? PERCY M.

About two million. No premium in ordinary condition.

35—What prices did the "pu" and "knife" cash bring in the Kingman sale? A. N. A.

Considering the prices usually asked and sold for, and the prices charged for these coins in China, they sold exceedingly cheap, ranging from 25 to 80 cents each. Some of the choicer single specimens brought from one dollar upwards. The bridge money sold from three to five and seven dollars. It is plainly evident that American collectors are not educated up to the value of ancient Chinese money for their owner would have gotten much better prices if he had taken them back with him to China.

---

BOOK-PLATE COLLECTING.—Philately, or postage-stamp collecting, has now reached the dimensions of an industry, but in the race for popularity the comparatively new department of artistic research dealing with "Ex Libris," or the collection of book-plates, bids fair to run it very hard. It has a society to itself and the literature around it increases very rapidly. Artistically a collection of "Ex Libris" is much more interesting than an agglomeration of postage-stamps. The latter are seldom or never works of art but are useful as an incentive to geographical research; while book-plates are, as a rule, high-class specimens of the engraver's skill and a collection of them really forms a study of history—an epitome of the rise and fall of historic families. In Germany much greater care is bestowed on book-plates than in this country, although several English artists have turned out work not unworthy of comparison with anything produced on the continent.—London Daily News.

---

THE LATEST WHOPPER.—Savannah, N. Y., July 29.—While Edward Carey, the superintendent of the Sibley nurseries at Fox Ridge, was excavating on Bluff Point, Thursday, the workmen unearthed a rich find in Indian relics. This place has long been a bonanza for relic hunters and many valuable Indian trinkets have been found. In this recent discovery by Mr. Carey a mound which was plowed up revealed several human bones which were deposited in a vault built of stone. Inside this roughly erected burial place were found several specimens of stone and copper knives, hatchets, pipes, heads, arrow heads, kettles and many copper coins, some bearing the date 1440. The pieces of money are square, with the Indian head upon one side and the date and bow and arrow on the other. The bluff is evidently an ancient burial place. The coins are evidences of the presence of Jesuits, who were known to be in this vicinity very early. These relics were probably deposited upon this bluff from 200 to 300 years ago by the Seneca and Cayuga tribes of Indians. They were probably not put there at the end of the Fifteenth Century as an exchange suggests, because even Jamestown wasn't settled till 1607, but the relics are evidently of great age.

# Wants, to exchange, etc.

This department gratis to all our readers.

Wanted.—Early issues of Rhode I land paper currency. Geo. C. Barton, Box 163, Providence, R. I.

To Exchange.—Foreign coins for numismatic literature or U. S. money (paper or metalic) medals or tokens. W. H. Taylor, North Wales, Pa.

The signature of Sir James Outram, K. C. B., the Bayard of India, for American coins. Also Asiatic stamps, coins and war medals. Major Adam Smith, Poona, India.

To Exchange.—Flint lock musket cannon balls from Bennington batt ground, old pistols, axes and swor for cash or old coins. All letters an wered. A. Oatman, Shaftsbury, V

Copper cents nearly all dates to exchange for dimes of 1800,-01-02 03-04-09 -11-22-28-44-63-64-65-67, Half cents 1793-94-95-96-97 1802-11: Fine 1801 cent. J. B. Goldsmith, 53 Hale St., Beverly, Mass.

Wanted.- Scotts Coin Journal for 1884-5-6, or either, loose or bound. Liberal exchange offered in foreign silver and copper (some choice oriental) or part cash. F. C. Browne, Framingham, Mass.

To Exchange.—Half dollars, quarter dollars, dimes, half dimes and three cent silver pieces, old cents and half cents, for the same not in my collection. Arthur B. Stewart, 813 6th Av. Beaver Falls, Pa.

For Exchange.—Nice cabinet specimens of sulphur, calcite (dog tooth crystals), barite crystals, barite and sulphur in trachyte; all of this locality, for as good specimens of other localities. Write first. Dr. George F. Heath, Monroe, Mich.

Bunch of 10 Indian arrows (genuine) brought from the field of Little Big Horn, the scene of the Custer massacre, to exchange for 1856 Eagle cent, 1799 cent, 1811 half cent or dimes 1809 -11 -22 -23 -28, 3c. nickles 1877 -85 -86 -87 -89. Value of arrows $5. J. B. Goldsmith, 53 Hale St., Beverly, Mass.

TYPES OF EXTINCT CIVILIZATION : MORE HISTORIC THAN WRITTEN HISTORY :

# THE NUMISMATIST

September, 1894.

An Illustrated Monthly devoted to the Science of Numismatics.

GEO. F HEATH, M. D. Monroe, Mich..

Vol. 7. No. 9.

PRESS STEAM PTG. CO., WATERLOO, IND.

## CONTENTS:




# The Numismatist:

A MONTHLY JOURNAL FOR COIN COLLECTORS,
AND OFFICIAL BULLETIN OF

## THE AMERICAN NUMISMATIC ASSOCIATION:

ONE DOLLAR A YEAR.

Editorial and publication office, Monroe, Mich.

THE NUMISMATIST is the only Illustrated Monthly Journal devoted to c and their collecting published on the American continent.

ADVERTISING RATES very reasonable. Made known on application.

SUBSCRIPTION $1.00 per annum, post free to any portion of the civilized world. Remittances may be made by money order, postal note, registered letter, or, when these are not obtainable, in unused postage stamps of low denominations.

Entered at Monroe, Mich., Postoffice, as second class matter.

# IMPORTANT NOTICE!

We want to place the NUMISMATIST in the hands of every coin collector in the world who reads the English language if we have to GIVE IT AWAY.

We will therefore, during July, August, and September ONLY,

**GIVE AWAY!**

With every subscription to the NUMISMATIST for one year, which is prepaid and received in this time, either:

**1 Set of Ten Beautiful World's Fair Tickets, worth - - - $1.00**
**1 Copy of "Mint Marks," by A. G. Heaton, worth - - - - $1.00**
**Foreign Coins, our selection, by Scott's catalogue, worth $1 00**
**One-half incn advertisement in Numismatist, 12 issues.**

Besides these premiums, the editor and publisher proposes to give you a magazine that will be worth your subscription price, not only today, but at any time in the future, should you desire to dispose of it. THE COMPLETE VOLUMES WILL NEVER BE WORTH LESS THAN $1.00 EACH. We could quote you from hundreds of letters and newspaper notices in its praise, but the magazine shall always be its own best spokesman.

Remember this offer is positively for THREE MONTHS only, and for new subscriptions. Postage extra on premiums to foreign countries. Address,

DR. GEO. F. HEATH, Monroe, Mich., U. S. A.

Philip Whiteway.

# The Numismatist.

VOL. VII. MONROE, MICH., SEPTEMBER, 1894. NO. 9.

## CHINESE TSIEN.

*A paper read at the Third Annual Convention of the American Numismatic Association at Chicago, Ill., Aug. 21, 1893.*

[J. A. BRUDIN.]

錢 Tsien, Tchen, or Chien is composed of the radicals kin, gold, metal and two ko's, spears; denoting property, wealth, bronze brass or iron formed into a coin, to exchange for commodities or money. This was formerly expressed by Chuen, signifying a spring or fountain in reference to its sending forth its stream in every direction to all parts.

The Japanese use the same character for SEN or similar money; the Coreans the same for MUN: the Annamese also for their DONG and the Siamese for SALUNG.

Tsien may be divided into two classes:

I. That used for money, called *Yuen pa*, issued by legal rulers and rebels and generally bearing only characters, numbers, nail marks and dots.

II. These used for other purposes, as medals, charms, amulets, etc. This paper will refer to the first class only.

These Tsien have a whole in the center for convenience in carrying. They are strung together by hundreds and in this state look something like strings of sausages. Most of them have also raised borders around the hole and on the circumference. They have been cast or struck in the following denominations: 1, 2, 3, 5, 10, 20, 30, 40, 50, 100, 200, 500, and 1000 tsien. There is no record of any half tsien ever having been issued.

1000 cash is usually equal to one Liang tael of fine silver, but this value be-

# ON CHINESE TSIEN

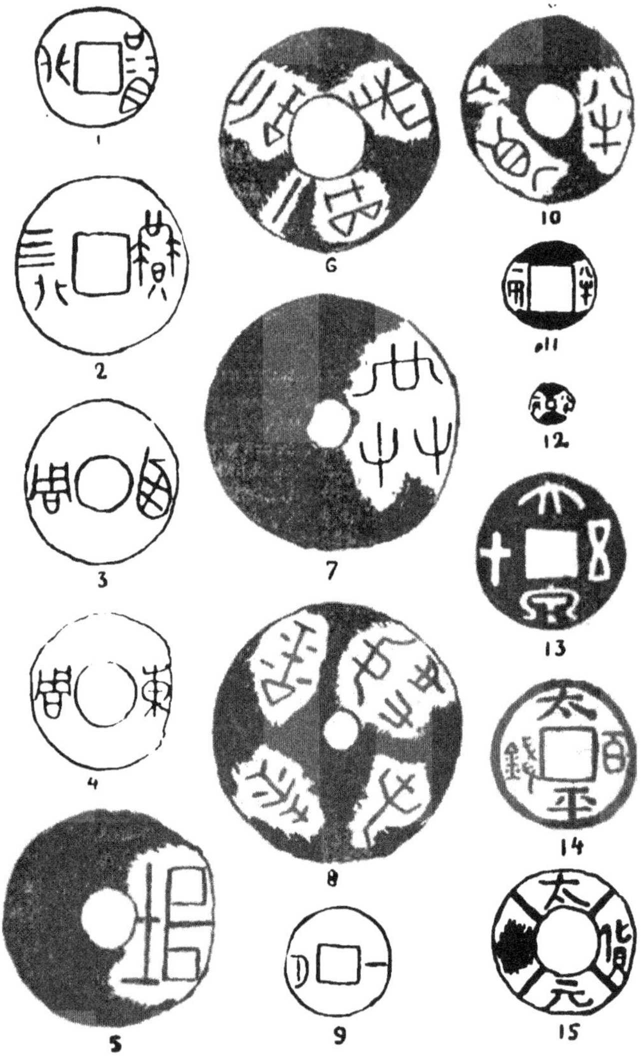

tween tsien and silver varies; sometimes 800 cash equaling a liang, again a fine silver liang being worth as much as 1600 cash.

To Read Chinese Coins: If the field above the hole is called 1, at the bottom below the hole 2, that to the right (same place as III on the clock) 3, and to the left 4, then the reading order of the characters would be as follows:

Coins with two characters 3-4, rarely 4-3 or 1-2.

Coins with four characters 1-2-3-4 or 1-3-2-4.

Coins are struck in many mints throughout the whole empire.

Chinese Measures of Lengths. One grain is called *Yih*; 10 Yih = one Fen; 10 Fen = one Chih; 10 Chih = one Chang; 10 Chang = one Yin. One Chih is equal to 35.812 centimeters. This computation is used in the custom houses and in trade with foreigners.

Chinese Money Weights: I. One Liang = 24 Chu = 240 Tsan = 2400 *Shu* = 37 17931 metric grammes.

II. One 兩 Liang (Tael) is equal to:

10 錢 Tsien (Mas or Mace), or

100 分 Fen (Condorin or Candareen), or

1000 厘 Li (Cash).

The monetary unit is one Liang fine silver.

One kin equals 1600 Liangs which equals 33¼ pounds averdupois. The names in parenthesis are the names given the coin by Europeans.

Whitney, on the "Chinese and Chinese Question," writes: "They adapted the decimal system for measures of quantity, weight and value, centuries before the French legislators recognized its utility or French scientists formulated its application to the traffic of Europe. Their unit of volume and leangth were literally native to the soil, for the one is the cubic contents of a hundred of the grains of the *Kow leang* or high millet, the *holcus sorgnum* of the botanists, and the latter, for the purposes of the artisan, the linear space occupied by a certain number of the same grains. For the measurements of distances the adopted standard is equally indigenous to the land. This was the Li, about two fifths of a mile the distance to which a man's voice, in shrill halloo, can be heard on a clear and windless day on the level fields of HoNan".

### Chinese Numismatical Terms.

面 Mien. Face or frontside, obverse.

背 Pei. Backside, ——reverse.

肉 Juh. Body or the main part of the coin.

好 HAOU. The hole in the centre.

郭 KWO. The raised edges or borders.

上 CHANG. The field above the hole.

下 HIA. The field below the hole.

右 YU. The field to the right.

左 TSO. The field to the left.

序 TSE. The characters.

文 WAN. The legend or inscription.

重 CHUNG. The weight.

— KING. The Diameter.

### DENOMINATIONS AND CHRONOLOGY.

We have no authority that round money (tsien) were used in China previous to the middle of the Chou Dynasty (1121-255 B. C.). The emperors Ping Wang 770-719 B. C., and King Wang are said to have issued round money with inscriptions. At this period China consisted of many small states. I give a list of the coins as given by Ku Chum Hui.

Pao Ho. Many varieties with square hole in the center. Table No. 1 represents one of them.

Pao 4 Ho. Table No. 2. Pao 6 Ho; both with square holes.

Si Chou, Table No. 3.

Tung Chou, Table No. 4.

Yuen, Table No. 5.

Chang Yuen Yih Kin Ho, Table No. 6.

Kung, Table No. 7.

Kung Hwuy Kin Ho.

Kung Shun Chih Kin, Table No. 8.

Tse Yin, with and without inscription. All these with round holes.

Ming Tao or Ming Yue.

Ming 4.

Yh Tao, Table No. 9, and Yh Tao, with negative characters, will turn right when seen in a mirror.

The coins of the Tsien Dynasty 255-202 B. C., are similar to those of the Chou Dynasty, and the more remarkable are:

Pan Liang. Half of a Liang or 12 Chús, sizes varying from 29 to 35 millimeters. They were issued by Emperor Chin Shih Huang 246-209 B. C.

Liang Tze, 6 Chús. Also several other varieties with square and round holes. Table No. 10 illustrates one inscribed with Pan Yean.

### Si Han Dynasty 202 B. C.,-6 A. D.

Emperor Kao ti, 202-194 B. C., issued Pan Liang coins in sizes from 7 to 14 millimetres. They were very small and thin and were called "leaf coins." Table No. 11 and 12 exhibits drawings of two of them, the last being the smallest known Chinese coin. Coins were also issued without inscriptions.

The Empress Lin Shih Kao Hou, 187-180 B. C., also issued Pan Liang coins with a weight of 8 chús.

Wen ti, 179-156 B. C., issued similar Pan Liang money in iron and bronze of the weight of 8 and 4 chús. Two of these iron coins were equal to one bronze.

Wu ti, 140-86 B. C. also issued Pan Liangs.

Wu Chús, 5 Chús and 3 Chús coins. Mythical coins from this dynasty are the Wu Feng and the Tortoise, Horse and Dragon coins, for descriptions of which see Dye's Coin Encyclopedia.

[TO BE CONTINUED.]

## WANTED TO USE PLATINUM AS MONEY.

"Once upon a time," said Mr. C. O. Baker Jr. of New York, who is connected with the on'y platinum refining plant in the United States, "Russia concluded to try the experiment of using platinum as a money metal. There is really little of that article found anywhere else on the globe except in the Ural Mountains, in the Czar's dominions, and having a monopoly of the precious stuff, the idea of using it as a coin seemed plausible. But it didn't prove a glittering success, and I have never seen any coin made of platinum by that government dated later that 1844.

"Here is one of the samples of the Russian experiment," said Mr. Baker, taking from his pocket a piece about the size of a silver quarter. It bore the date 1830 and had some Russian characters on it signifying it to be of the value of six rubles or about $4.75 in American money.

"I gave $11 for it, however," said Mr. Baker, "and its intrinsic value is worth nearly that amount. Of course, no other nation would go in with Russia and take platinum for money, seeing that no other country produced any of it to speak of, which may be a tip to some of our silver friends. Platinum is lower than it was two years ago, being worth now $10.50 an ounce, though a while back it was worth $17 an ounce. At its present price it is just about half as valuable as gold. It is the heaviest of metals, its specific gravity exceeding that of gold about 5 per cent, and so ductile that it can be drawn into a thread 1-1000 of an inch in diameter."

## PHILIP WHITEWAY.

*Fellow of the Imperial Institute of Great Britain and Ireland, Member of the A. N. A. and N. A. (Eng.) etc., etc.*

[FROM OUR SPECIAL CORRESPONDENT.]

Philip Whiteway was born at Weston, Cheshire, England, March 3, 1869. He comes from an ancient family who have been seated in Devonshire for several centuries—his ancestor Sir Walter Whiteway was created a banneret on the battle field of Bosworth, by King Henry VII. Another Philip Whiteway, grandfather of the present bearer of the name, was chairman of the Board of Magistrates for Cheshire, and was one of the most popular men in that country.

After the death of his father in 1873 Mr. Whiteway spent several years of travel on the continent, wandering in his years of early boyhood amid the marvels of Italy, ruins, pictures and museums; which left an impression on the plastic mind never to be effaced.

At the age of thirteen he spent a winter in Rome, and here a fine collection of Roman coins was presented him by a relative, which formed the basis of his present collection. And from that day to this he has never ceased accumulating coins and antiques. During these years of traveling, Italy, Austria, Germany, France, and Switzerland were visited.

The period from his 13th to his 18th year was devoted to school in the town of Bedford. But even then the vacations were spent in travel, and all his spare time given to the study of numismatics, the history and antiquities of Greece and Rome, and that of remoter periods—the Stone and Bronze ages.

The winter of 1887 found Mr. Whiteway in Nice, France; here he experienced a severe earthquake, which destroyed several towns and many hundred persons. In the spring of 1888 a tour through the wonderful island of Sicily was undertaken, and here his first article was written—"The Coins of Tauromenium," this was printed in The Numismatic Magazine; he has contributed to this magazine ever since.

On his return to England laden with numismatic spoils, he conceived the idea of producing a coin magazine, to be run on new and popular lines. The "Coin Collector's Herald" duly made bow to the public, and had a short but successful career. In the winter of 1888, Mr. Whiteway left home for an extended tour abroad, and did not see his way to carry on the paper from a distance. With his family, he spent five months in Egypt, including a three month's trip up the Nile as far as the first cataract in the spring of 1889. During this period spent among the wonders of this Morning Land of history he was studying its storied ruins and adding to his collections. Here he became acquainted with such men as Prof. Sayce, Zebehr Pasha, Brugsch Bey, Director of the Egyptian National museum, and other men of learning.

In the autumn of this year his first story, and journal of travel were published: "An Adventure in Egypt," and "Wanderings in the East." In addition to several coin articles. the summer was spent amid the ice and snow of the Engadine. He made an effort to arouse up English collectors to form a numismatic society, but the project was unsuccessful.

The winter of 1889-90 again found Mr. Whiteway in Egypt of which three months were spent in the "shadows of the pyramids," studying and exploring. He also excavated near the pyramid of Maydoom, and found a number of mummies, etc. (See "Digging for Mummies.") From Egypt he proceeded to the Holy Land—Jerusalem, the Dead Sea, Jordan, Damascus, etc.; and even here he managed to pick up a few goods coins and then returned to England for the summer via Italy and France after an absence of two years.

In the autumn of 1890 he returned to Egypt, and a large number of coins and antiques were added to his collection. A vast quantity of coins both Greek and Roman are found in Egypt, and as the Arabs know little of their value, they can be bought very cheap. In the spring two and a half months were spent camping at the foot of the Pyramids. The summer was devoted to exploring the Swiss Alpine resorts.

The queen city of the South—Nice—was his home during the winter of 1891-92. He was the center of a constant whirl of gayety, balls, parties, picnics, etc. Nice is indeed the home of pleasure. Even here some good coins were purchased. In the spring of 1892 he visited Algiers and spent three months, then another month at Nice, a driving tour through Provence and Dauphiné was undertaken, and then home to England for the summer.

In 1891, he again made efforts to arouse English numismatists and successfully launched the Numismatic Association of England.

Mr. Whiteway returned to Nice for the winter of 1892-3 which was again a whirl of gayety, intermixed with amateur theatrical and lawn tennis. From Nice he proceeded through Italy to Egypt; some rare coins were again added to his cabinets. Then on again, via. Suez Canal, the Red Sea, Indian Ocean, Ceylon to Australia. South Australia, Victoria, Tasmania and New Zealand were visited. At the latter colony he spent the winter and later returned to his old and favorite haunts in the south of France; and at this writing is at Nice.

In whatever part of the world he finds himself, he keeps his eyes open for the acquisition of coins and curios; and makes it a rule never to buy a dear coin, and in the course of his wanderings has managed to procure a quantity of rare pieces at wonderfully low prices. He has written a number of papers on antiquarian and travel subjects; also several popular stories of the kind now termed novels with a purpose, considerable newspaper work and upwards of thirty articles on numismatic subjects:

He collects Roman, Greek and Mediæval Italian coins. These are arranged in two fine cabinets and include many varieties. His collections of antiquities are considerable—Stone age, Bronze age, Egyptian, Greek, and Roman. The Egyptian is the most complete series. Among its rarities are inscribed casing stones from the Great Pyramid, a statue life sized, of the age of the Pyramid builders, and a scarab of the sixth dynasty, King Nefer-Ka-Ra (B. C. 3613). This latter is probably unique.

Mr. Whiteway is 6 ft. in height and weighs about 190 pounds. His constitution is of the cast iron order. He is a member of the Church of England, a staunch teetotaller, in politics of the old conservative party, an enthusiastic tennis and foot ball player, an ardent amateur actor, and a firm believer in athletics.

# 4th ANNUAL CONVENTION

## OF THE AMERICAN NUMISMATIC ASSOCIATION.

## Detroit, Mich., Aug. 23-24, 1894.

### PRESIDENT'S ADDRESS.

*"THE UTILITY OF HOBBIES."*

[GEO. F. HEATH, M. D.]

It was Artemus Ward that once said that this world contained "about thirteen hundred millions of people, mostly fools."

It was a celebrated neurologist that made the statement that "over half the people were cranky or insane on some one subject or another."

It was another writer who said there were two distinct classes of people in the world, to-wit., "Those who have hobbies, and those without," and added that the former greatly outnumbered the latter.

That these three statements from three different fields of literature are to a great extent true, I fully believe. The fools, the cranks, and the hobby riders comprise the bulk or large majority of humanity, and this fact needs no demonstration or argument from me.

Ever since God in his infinite wisdom created the earth and sent it spinning amidst the stars in space; ever since He made its rocky ribs, divided its waters from the land, clothed it in living green, and hung up its greater and lesser lights in the firmament; ever since He created the myriads of animal forms and his crowning work, man, and pronounced it good; ever since He planted the gold, the bdellium and the onyx in the land of Havilah, and the tress which were pleasant to the sight in Eden; ever since He brought forth the living of all kinds before Adam for a name and implanted in the human breast the desire for knowledge, not only of himself and the things by which he was surrounded, but of the author and finisher of all these wonderful things he had made—I say, ever since this time there has been from necessity collectors on the face of the earth. For as man alone of all God's creation is an admirer of the beautiful in nature and art, it is not therefore to be doubted but that his first thoughts were turned to meditative contemplation of the many beautiful things by which he was surrounded. For has not the wisest preacher said: "He hath made everything beautiful in His time," and farther on, "Wherefore I perceive that there is nothing better that a man should rejoice in his own works; for that is his portion; for who shall bring him to see what shall be after him?" Man is here but for a brief time, a time we have "to be born, a time to weep, a time to laugh, a time to love, a time to get, a time to cast away, a time to mourn, and a time to die." Between and during this time is the brief span of life. How to best use this time to the glory of our Maker and the happiness of ourselves and those around us is the end of all wisdom, the beginning and end of our existence.

When man first indulged his collecting instinct, to get, to keep, to cast away, to have hobbies, we may not definitely know, but I have no doubt that it was coeval with that time when he first viewed with wonder and admiration the works of his Creator, and began to cherish the things he himself had made.

The term "crank" is often derisively given to those who, in the exuberance of their enthusiasm, have gone beyond the bounds prescribed by an old, conservative world in its customs of the day. And so we have, and ever will have, religious, political, professional, mechanical, scientific and other varieties of cranks in the world, and our science is no exception to the rule. We have—to the credit of our association—possibly a few numismatic cranks enrolled on our books.

It is a remarkable fact that both religious and profane history records with minuteness the works and deeds of cranks, but it is mysteriously silent in most instances regard their assailants. I have no doubt but that when Noah, the first great collector, gathered together by twos the animals into the ark, a curious and unnamed crowd that didn't know enough to get in out of the rain gathered around and called him a crank. I have no doubt when Joseph gathered the products of the seven years of plenty into the granaries of Egypt, but that a wise and knowing but unnamed crowd gazed on in a sympathizing way at the young fellow who had "wheels in his head." The names that shine out in history with the greatest effulgence are those who, living and possessed of knowledge in advance of their day and generation, have been considered cranks. This is true from the time when "He who spake as never man spake," was scourged and crucified on Calvary as a religious heretic or crank at the hands of a rabble, down past St. Paul, Chrystostom, Galileo, Servitus, Luther, Gough, Garrison and John Brown.

Worcester defines "hobby" as "a favorite object, pursuit, or plaything." It is an old and trite saying that "All work and no play makes Jack a dull boy." As man is but a boy of larger growth, it is fully as important that the man have a favorite pursuit or plaything as the boy. To be sure, he will not, perhaps, delight in the simple plays, toys or pursuits that delighted his boyhood days, but in a larger and more extended field he may find full scope for his developed faculties. But whether it be athletic or field sports, music, painting, china, numismatics, geology, anthropology, stamps, or what not, it matters not so much, providing it proves a rest for the tired mind or body.

The physician, above all others, sees this necessity for physical and mental rest. The truly American type is fast becoming a bundle of nerves. The waiting rooms of our more fashionable prescribers for the ailments of mankind are haunted by nervous wrecks, and the terms "nervous dyspepsia," nervous debility" and "nervous prostration" are getting frightfully common in the vocabulary of both patient and physician. All this is greatly due to our manner of living. We live in the age of the telegraph and telephone, the age of electricity and steam. Better, it may be said, fifty years of today than a cycle of the days of the old stage coach or canal boat, but better than all, to live today without being a martyr to all these fashionable ailments.

In no other land on the face of the earth is there such a mad rush for wealth as in our own. It gives prestige in all the phases of life, whether in the political, social, mercantile or professional field; it is too often the measure of the man in the eyes of the community. It is therefore no wonder that humanity rushes forward in a mad scramble after that which gives them power, honor and standing, much the same as the moth is attracted to the brilliant flame, and in most instances with the same result. Tired, bruised, discouraged, the great masses fall by the wayside. Some die, a few only grasp the glittering bauble.

We see these physical wrecks grow old before their time on every hand. They throng our offices, they are found in our hospitals, and our asylums are overcrowded with them.

## The Remedy: A Hobby.

If I did not believe that the profession of medicine was the grandest of all, I would leave it. If I did not believe there was a balm in Gilead that would cure, or at least mitigate these ills of the human mind and body, I would not be before you today advocating the remedy. This remedy is no nauseous dose to torture the stomach, but one that charms through the senses into quietness and rest—it is simply a "hobby." It may be a simple or complex one, but let it be a hobby, and this remedy, like many another, should be applied early to get the best results. The good book says that "those who are filthy they will be filthy still;" the same with those who are bound down by their own ways, excesses and indulgences, they will be bound still; there is no hope of success after disease becomes confirmed, no more than there is in the ills that affect the body after they become chronic.

The hobby must be left to each individual taste. I would not have all become collectors or students of coinage, it would tend to demoralize values. Variety is the life of collecting as well as the spice of life, and so, whether it be butterflies, minerals, coins, Florentine mosaics, paintings, autographs, or some other object, pursuit or plaything, it matters not so much providing it keeps one out of the ruts of life's roadway or brings a rest or change from the monotonous daily grind—or something that will be a change from routine work—something in which mind and body may be able to forget for the time work and worry—something that will at the same time entertain, elevate and instruct.

I would develop this latest talent in the child; let him begin, if he pleases, with stamps, bugs or birds' eggs. Much can be learned from them and the germ under proper cultivation will lead to something higher and better. There are many persons who exist with no definite object ahead as far as they or others can perceive. To such the hobby is a divine gift; astride this Pegasus they can banish *ennui* and fly to the Isles of the Blest, to fields Elysian and pluck the golden apples of the Hesperides.

A hobby is always desirable. Unfortunate is he who has not the taste or inclination to indulge in one. It is a grave question to such whether life is worth living.

Dr. Beale has said, "A hobby, if not overridden, is also desirable—everyone can take up some subject of study; there are enough to suit all tastes and occupations. Enough in anyone for a long life. A well trained mind can never be satiated."

Change is the great law of nature. It is the law that governs our being. Man is an intellectual as well as social animal, and the healthy human mind demands something upon which to feed and grow, something it does not find in the ordinary rounds of life. It tires of forever doing the same thing, no matter what it is, and becomes apathetic. It is this longing for something outside of our environments, this something beyond, this desire implanted in the human breast, that distinguishes us from the brute and lifts us out of the dust of the earth to lean on the infinite.

The hobby need not be grand or expensive. It need not be in art, statuary or paintings. You can find it in your garden with your roses, chrysanthemums or dahlias, or in your green-house with your orchids. You can find it in your sports—lawn tennis, base ball; hunting or fishing, travel, or any voluntary or benevolent occupation—in your books, cabinet, music, any science or branch of literature; no matter what the taste, there is a field for its indulgence.

They tend to health, happiness, and long life. Medical men universally recognize the value of hobbies. A famous New York city physician used to say that it was not his passion for medical science that made his success, but his passion for fishing. One of the greatest pathologists of this age slips off between times collecting birds' eggs, Indian relics, and fishing or hunting, and he is successful in his hobbies as in his professional work.

Every one should have some resource for his hours of leisure, some hobby on which to lean or rest; not so as to absorb so much attention as to interfere with the regular occupation by which a livelihood is gained, but something to which you can retire after the worry of the day to rest from your labors and become refreshed; to begin anew your work with renewed vigor and interest.

It may be simply a coincidence, but in looking up the biographies of our great men and women, they are found to have their hobbies or diversions. Some of them seem to us quite puerile. Imagine Cardinal Richelieu diverting himself by jumping over his furniture and, with his servant, trying to see who could kick the highest; or Dean Swift, harnessing up his servants with cords and driving them up and down stairs about the house; or Sam Johnson touching every post on Fleet st, and if he missed one went back to touch it; or Shelley, sailing paper boats upon the Serpentine or Hyde Park; Jacques Rousseau used to pack large stones up the cliffs to dash them down into the waves below; Dante enjoyed his pet cat, Cowper his horses; Walter Scott and Washington their hounds, Peter the Great enjoyed being carted around in a wheelbarrow; John Bright loved his rod and gun, and Paley wouldn't have his portrait painted without the artist put his fishing rod in his hand; Byron enjoyed shooting at a mark, Henry V. loved tennis, while Bacon, Cowley, Addison, Buffon and Evelyn delighted to walk in their gardens; Henry Clay enjoyed a game of cards; Daniel Webster had quite a reputation as a fisherman and snipe shooter around Marshfield; Prescott and Hawthorne enjoyed long walks alone, and Lincoln delighted in a good story, particularly to relate one; Gladstone's diversion is with his ax in the Hawarden forests, and we all know that President Cleveland enjoys both hunting and fishing; but probably few of you know that ex-President Harrison has a collection of ancient coins at his home in Indianapolis. But there is no end to this, for of course "we all have our hobbies," and that is one of the best thing about hobbies, we all can have them. No one, however rich or poor, high or low, wise or foolish, old or young, or of whatever occupation, but what can find one suited to his taste or needs.

The farmer can have his blooded stock, races, fairs, granges, alliances, etc. The merchant, the banker, the professional man may go to the fields, the mountains, the seashore or abroad, or indulge in any of the sciences. The artisan, the day toiler, the railroad man, demanding the same rest, change or diversion, and without realizing the necessities of the case through any mental process of his own, gives vent to what he cannot control, and goes on a general holiday if he has to strike and demoralize the industries of a continent in doing it.

It will be well when the people of this land awaken to the necessities of diversion, when the laws that govern our beings shall be recognized. Other nations have learned this lesson, and the nervous American must halt in the race for wealth. glory and honor long enough to listen to the demands of his physical and mental being ere we become a nation of nervous, hypochondriacal and hysterical wrecks.

We gather here today in the interest of one of the most fascinating hobbies or studies of the time, a study that has occupied the time and attention of some of the noblest minds this world has produced. A year ago it was my pleasure so give to you the testimony of many of those in support of our science. We come together as numismatists, or students of coinage—not coin collectors *per se*, as we are sometimes called—for we hope we are not merely collectors of coin, for we take higher ground, and hope by intelligent, methodical collecting in certain lines of research and study to deserve the name of students of coinage or numismatists. It is not the mere metal that we treasure—the silver in the tetradrachm of an Alexander the Great or Philip is no more to us than that in a trade or standard dollar. The stamp impressed on it and the history it tells is what gives it value to us.

In our exhibition in this gallery are shown hundreds of coins struck from one to 700 years before Christ came on the earth. Few great names or events in profane history but are not represented in these pieces. Many of them have served to make this history more authentic. Without some of them some history would not have been made or known to us. These coins, with their historic, artistic and religious stamp and design, reflect the intelligence of the people of those times. Because they are time-enduring they have come down to us witnesses to corroborate many things we could not otherwise know. Some were before Alexander the Great, most of them were before Julius Caesar, and any one of them Christ himself may have gazed upon.

Many, unacquainted with our science, look upon these old coins as suggestive of the grave where dankness and musty smells abound. The same might be said of yesterday's history. But the true numismatist only sees in them the patinated lustre or symbolistic glitter of kingly glory and great achievements. His mind dwells rather upon the coat of mail than the clay which it inclosed. To him the coin or medal does not record defeats or disappointments, but rather great events and victories. The past is ever present with him in all its actuality. In his diversion he dwells in intimate communion with kings, princes and the lords of earth: with Alexander he sighs for more worlds to conquer; with Tamerlane traverses the Indian plain; with Xerxes and Caesar crosses the Hellespont and Rubicon. He stands on Calvary while the temple is rent in twain, sees the streets of Jerusalem run with blood and Judea captive.

And finally, he thinks that of the collectings, the studies, the diversions, the sciences, the hobbies; that his own is a little the best, the most refining, the most moral, the most charming, entrancing and fascinating of them all—in fact, he knows it.

Monroe, Mich.

## ADDRESS OF WELCOME.

[Dr. Joseph Lathrop, President of the Detroit Numismatic Club.]

Mr. President, and Gentlemen of the American Numismatic Assoc'n:

It becomes my pleasure and duty as president of the Detroit Numismatic Club to extend to you in behalf of its members a warm and happy greeting to our City of the Straits.

As a club we represent the youngest child of your Association—a baby scarcely four months old, and we extend our arms to you expecting you to take us to your bosom and nurse us through the teething period. We ask you to suspend the traditionary "dollar of our daddies" around our necks, to enable us to properly cut our eye teeth. We feel that we are legitimate children, that we belong to you, for we have the same tastes that are transmitted by heredity, and while you remain with us we hope to fill our brains so full of numismatic love that our pockets may ever after be filled with old coins.

We are glad that we were born, even at this late hour, so youug in fact that some of us still retain memories of our ante-natal existence.

As evidence of this I refer you to the collection of our worthy secretary, Mr Geo. W. Rice, and other members of our club, which you will have the privilege of examining during your sojourn with us.

We take pride in having you with us on the fourth annual meeting of your Association, and while we cannot offer you the same attractions that Chicago presented to you last year, still we invite you to look over our city of homes, our beautiful Belle Isle Park, our river, the grandest God ever made, whose clear blue waters are both pleasant to the eye and palate.

We invite you to a ride on its surface to Lake St. Clair, thence through the ship canal to the Flats, "our little Venice," where our citizens have built their summer homes and clubs for fishing and hunting, to partake of a fish supper at "Rushmere."

If any of you enjoy fishing, I extend to you the privileges of the North Channel Club, where you can spend a few days very pleasantly angling for black bass, pickerel, perch, etc.

Gentlemen, we feel honored in having you with us and we hope that your presence here will stimulate our local society, and will result in developing a taste in the young for the study of numismatics. Every man should have a "hobby" that will furnish him diversion and recreation from the cares and worries of a business life, where he can spend his leisure moments with pleasure and profit. We feel that ours is profitable in many ways; as an educator of ancient and modern history it has no superior.

The coins and medals we study are records none can question. Their study leads to a spirit of investigation in other directions, and can only result in the elevation of its students.

We sincerely hope you will have an enjoyable and profitable meeting, and as this is the first effort at an exhibition at your annual meeting, a feature which I trust will be continued in the future, as it must be of special interest to the members and will be the means of attracting the attention of the public to us, and ought to become a permanent feature of this Association.

Gentlemen, I again welcome you to Detroit.

## RESPONSE TO ADDRESS OF WELCOME.

[JOSEPH HOOPER, VICE PRES. OF A. N. A.]

DR. LATHROP, DETROIT NUMISMATIC CLUB, GENTLEMEN:

In response to your very cordial welcome, allow me on behalf of the American Numismatic Association to tender you their sincere thanks for the very kind reception given them on this their first visit as an association to this beautiful City of the Straits, the historic city of Detroit, whose original founders under the "FLEUR DE LIS" landed with Cadillac on the eventful 24th of July, 1701. We also thank you for the thoughtful provision you have made in securing the use of such suitable accommodation for the holding of our Fourth Annual Convention in so appropriate and magnificent building as "the Detroit Museum of Art." We trust the occasion of our visit will be of great mutual interest and benefit to every true student of the "Science of Numisma," an art so continuous in sequence and broad in extent, the energy of whose devotees has produced such copious literature for our instructive inception and guidance, has given cause for the inauguration and placement on a permanent basis this national association for a study so instructive, covering such a vast field for research into the history and progress of art of the past ages with its vital lessons and teachings, that which ever path we pursue in its study, vistas open on either side equally inviting, the strange face to face vestiges of vanished aeons bringing us into immediate contact with the life and history of the past as no mere book study can do. "Types of extinct civilization more historic than written history."

Through the skillful guidance and untiring zeal and en-rgy of our president, Dr. Geo. F. Heath, assisted by an efficient board of officers, this association has risen step by step until we have a membership of 200, represented by an illustrated monthly entirely devoted to the science of numismatics issued in very cre litable form and intellectuality of matter. Since our organization we have passed many shoals and breakers. We rejoice that we have passed into smoother waters, and today finds us through your kind generous hospitality (in prosperous circumstances) anchored safe in this arbor of your historic city.

Again thanking you, gentlemen, for your kind welcome, and trusting we shall be so mutually benefitted and edified by being for the time we are together brought into closer contact at this our Annual Convention, that at its close we shall with regard to our Association, say "DEI GRATIA PERPETUA."

## PRESIDENT'S REPORT.

FELLOW MEMBERS OF THE AMERICAN NUMISMATIC ASSOCIATION:

It is mypleasant privilege to report briefly to you on the work of our Association the past two years, during which time you have honored me as your presiding officer. It is now three years since our Association has become one of the powers in the numismatic world. From a membership of about sixty in 1891 we have gone steadily forward until our rolls bear upwards of two hundred names of collectors and students of coinage scattered from ocean to ocean, from gulf to lakes, and even beyond the confines of our own territory.

As near as I can ascertain we have in good standing today 191 members. They are distributed by sections as follows:

| | | | |
|---|---|---|---|
| New England, | 41 | Beyond the Mississippi, | 12 |
| Middle States, | 43 | Dominion of Canada, | 10 |
| Middle Western States, | 60 | Other Foreign, | 13 |
| Southern States, | 12 | Total, | 191 |

By states and countries we are divided as follows:

| | | | | | |
|---|---|---|---|---|---|
| Massachusetts, | 24 | Indiana, | 10 | Ohio, | 4 |
| Michigan, | 24 | Ontario, | 8 | Connecticut, | 4 |
| New York, | 20 | Rhode Island, | 7 | Iowa, | 3 |
| Pennsylvania, | 16 | New Jersey, | 7 | North Carolina, | 3 |
| Illinois, | 14 | Wisconsin, | 6 | New Hampshire, | 3 |
| Nebraska, | 5 | Virginia, | 3 | | |

California, District of Columbia, South Carolina, Vermont and Minnesota, each 2; Texas, Montana, Missouri, Maine, Tennessee, Florida and Oregon, each 1; England, 7; Ontario, 8; Brazil, Nova Scotia, New Brunswick, Japan, China and India, 1 each.

It would be interesting to know the occupation of our members, the average age, etc., but this must be left to our future historian. I only note here that all the professions and a great diversity in occupations are represented with us, and that the gray haired sire of upwards of sixty and the youth march along together. It is a matter of note that at our Chicago convention a year ago, many were present whose thinned locks and silvery crowns attested that they were well along the declivity of life's journey. It is a matter of gratification for us to know that advancing age fails to dim the flame, or declining powers quench the thirst from this fountain; that there is something as tangible and enduring in this science as in the metal itself, whose lessons can never be fully learned or told.

As an Association we have every reason to be thankful and go forward with renewed courage. The few of us who gathered in Chicago in convention in October, 1891, while fully realizing the necessities of an organization like this, little dreamed that we were laying the foundations of our present superstruction

We have had no frictions, no bickerings, no desertions of account. Of course some have grown weary, some have wearied us, three have been gathered by the great Maker and collector of all things to himself. Their names shall remain on the roll of the Association while we cherish their memory. Altogether by death, desertion and suspension we have lost in the past three years twenty one members.

A year ago we varied our program by requesting our members to contribute papers on subjects connected with our science to be read at our convention. Some of our members cheerfully responded. These papers have mostly been published and greatly added to the interest of our meeting and have done much to place us advantageously before the scientific world. This feature cannot and must not be dropped. I am very grateful to those who have so kindly co-operated with me in this part of our programme.

This year we inaugurate a new feature—an exhibit. This is to a great extent an experiment. I know it can be made successful and have no doubt but that it will be. I hope this will be the first of a brilliant series and that wherever we go the fame of our exhibitions may attract not only those who belong to our own and similar organizations, but the general public as well.

There has been too much tendency to leave too much of the work of the Association on the president or official board. It has been and is too much an official board association. The adding of so much new work at our conventions has thrown too much work and responsibility upon the few. This they should be relieved of and I shall make the following recommendations.

1st. That a committee of five be appointed as soon as practicable by the incoming president, whose duty shall be to provide for the literary portion of the coming convention.

2d. That a committee of five be appointed, by the incoming president, as soon as practicable to arrange for and take charge of the exhibition for 1894; this committee to be selected from the city in which the convention is to be held.

3d. That a committee of three be appointed by the retiring president, whose duties shall be to provide an address to students or others interested in our science, setting forth the advantages of belonging to this association; also to suggest some means whereby the influence and circulation of THE NUMISMATIST, the official organ of this Association, may be extended to the mutual benefit of both Association and Journal.

This address to be placed in the hands of every collector of coins and student of our science whose address can be obtained, and at as early a period as possible.

There are, I am sorry to state, a few members delinquent on our books. The Association has been very lenient with them, but it is not just and right for the paying members to provide the official organ gratis to those who do not appreciate the benefits of association sufficient to keep their records clear on our books. I shall therefore recommend that while our rules and regulations be interpreted liberally as regards suspending or dropping members, that at the discretion of the secretary the official journal be withheld from such as pay no attention to his demand for assessments due, until such have been paid.

I have had occasion to bring charges against but one member of this Association. These were based upon a newspaper account and not from any personal knowledge I had of the matter. This was placed into the hands of the board of trustees for investigation and will doubtless be incorporated in their report.

In conclusion I beg to express my thanks to this body which has twice conferred honor on me. On the whole the duties of office have been pleasant, the work genial, and in my association with officers and members and becoming better acquainted with them I have been led to have a more and more exalted idea of our science and its followers.

Religiously believing in rotation in office, especially where distinction or honor is conferred, I stand aside as a matter of duty that you man honor some other of our worthy sons; and my best wishes for him is that he may receive the same kind consideration you have ever extended to me. Again I thank you.

GEO. F. HEATH.

## SECRETARY'S REPORT, A. N. A.

TO THE PRESIDENT AND MEMBERS HERE ASSEMBLED, GREETING:

The yearly report of the secretary's office for the year beginning August 1st, 1893, is briefly stated in the following:

In the year given above, there was an increase in membership of 49 new members, or from Membership No. 162 to Membership No. 211, the exact membership being somewhat below the latter figure on account of resignations, non-payments, etc. Those resigning were: Chas. W. Kirk, No. 44; L. C. Whitney, No. 63; Robert Shiells, No. 109; and Edward Heusinger, No. 118.

The mail matter issued for the Association amounted to 454 pieces, of which 173 were statements, 36 were certificates of membership, remaining lots being letters and parcels, the entire mail matter calling for $8.40 in postage,

The unused property and supplies of office consist of 156 old constitutions and by-laws; 99 copies of the Numismatist for February, '94, containing new constitution and by-laws; 230 receipt blanks; 152 certificate blanks; 205 order blanks; stationery, etc.

Cash received, $151.00; turned over to treasurer, $141.00, of which $4.50 was turned over to Treas. Harlowe, balance of $136.50 turned over to Treas. Fisher; amount on hand, $10.00, which could not in any certainty be got in in time to enter treasurer's report, so that the same might correspond to my report.

The bonds of Dr. A. L. Fisher, treasurer, and W. J. Luck, superintendent of exchange, were received and referred to the board of trustees.

The orders drawn on the treasurer were:

| | | |
|---|---|---|
| No. 5, in favor of | Wm. C. Stone | $ 4 00 |
| No. 6, " | Geo. F. Heath, M. D. | 5 00 |
| No. 7, " | Wm. C. Stone, (Library fund) | 15 00 |
| | Total, | $24 00 |

Respectfully submitted,

WALTHAM, MASS., Aug. 18, 1894. O. W. PAGE, Secretary.

## TREASURER'S REPORT.

TO THE PRESIDENT AND MEMBERS OF THE AMERICAN NUMISMATIC ASS'N.

GENTLEMEN:

Allow me to submit the treasurer's report of receipts and expenditures from Oct. 1, 1893 to August 1, 1894:

| | REC'D. | PAID. |
|---|---|---|
| Ex-Treasurer Harlowe, his balance, | $ 138.47 | |
| Secy. O. W. Page, dues, | 122.00 | |
| Secy. O. W. Page, initiation fees, | 14.50 | |
| Geo. J. Bauer, dues to Oct. 1, '93, | 1.00 | |
| J. B. Goldsmith, dues to Oct. 1, '94, | 1.00 | |
| Vouchers 5, 6, and 7, | | $ 24.00 |
| *Balance on hand,* | | *252.97* |
| | $276.97 | $276.97 |

Owing to the unfortunate circumstance that I have never received the books of my predecessor in office, I am unable to make any statement in regard to those members who are in arrears. Respectfully submitted,

A. L. FISHER, Treasurer.

## LIBRARIAN'S REPORT.

GENTLEMEN OF THE A. N. A.

In submitting my second annual report I can report but a few additions to the library during the past year. The most important addition has been that of a copy of Breton's work on the coins and tokens of Canada which was denoted by the author. About forty catalogues and the same number of periodicals have been donated by our members in addition to what we receive regularly by subscription and exchange. Monographs by H. R. Storer on the "Medals of Natural Scientists" and by C. T. Tatman on the "Virginia Coinage" are among the donations. An autograph letter by James Ross Snowden, Director of the Philadelphia mint, dated Dec. 1, 1857, has been donated by B. H. Collins and contains much information regarding the pattern double-eagle designed by I. Goldsborough Bruff, of Washington.

The appropriation of $15 made at the last convention has been amply sufficient for the expenses of the library. Only one new periodical has been added to the list and but few of our members have availed themselves of the periodical circuit. There are numerous publications in French, German and Italian but the Librarian does not care to subscribe for them unless the members manifest some interest in the department and give their preferences as to what publications they would like added to the library. A good summary of the contents of the foreign papers is given each month in Spink & Son's Circular and if our members will state their preferences the librarian will be only too glad to send for the publications desired.

Of the appropriation of $15.00 the sum of $5.30 has been expended for periodicals, pamphlet cases and postage. There is a balance of $9.70 on hand. The librarian would recommend an appropriation of the same amount as last year as he would like to purchase priced catalogues on all auction sales to occur during the coming year. Respectfully Submitted,

SPRINGFIELD, MASS., Aug. 20, 1894. WM. C. STONE, Librarian.

## EXCHANGE SUPERINTENDENT'S REPORT.

DR. GEO. F. HEATH, PRES. A. N. A.

DEAR SIR:—Herewith find my report of the transactions of the Exchange Department from May 2, 1893 to Aug. 11, 1894.

The following members contributed coins and paper money, viz:

| | No. lots. | Priced at. | No. lots sold. | Amount. |
|---|---|---|---|---|
| E. B. Kimball, | 170 | $111.17 | 107 | $ 53.71 |
| Geo. F. Heath, | 164 | 59.77 | 36 | 9.39 |
| D. C. Wismer, | 20 | 25.50 | 8 | 11.75 |
| W. J. Luck, | 59 | 17.48 | 11 | 3 56 |
| C. H. Trask, | 14 | 5.90 | 1 | 05 |
| J. B. Goldsmith, | 57 | 3. 57 pap mny | 57 | 3 57 |
| Totals, | 484 | $223.39 | 220 | $ 82.03 |

Supt. commission on sales, 10 per cent....$8.20

| | |
|---|---|
| Amt. advanced by Supt. towards tin boxes for shipping coins, | $ 1 40 |
| Postage, | 84 |
| Express, | 2.20 |
| Total disbursments, | $ 4.44 |
| Receipts, supplies sold, | 1.60 |
| Total amount due Supt. Exch. Dept | $ 2.84 |

I have on hand books and supplies amounting to..................$ 16.33

With the exceptions of the amount advanced by the superintendent the department has no debts.

| | |
|---|---|
| Actual deficit in cash A. N. A. acc't after amount is paid; advanced by superintendent | 16.42 |
| Total deficit of department, | $ 32.75 |

Respectfully submitted,

W. J. LUCK, Supt. Exchange Dept.

## BOARD OF TRUSTEES REPORT.

MR. PRESIDENT, AND MEMBERS OF THE A. N. A.:

As secretary of the board of trustees of the American Numismatic Association, I have had little to do.

The bonds of the treasurer and exchange superintendent were forwarded to the board for approval. As neither of them were made out in legal form, we could not approve them, but accepted them as they were given as an evidence of good faith.

The case of Dr. James B. Breeding, of San Antonio, Texas, was discussed by the board and the majority were in favor of expelling him. Being uncertain of our authority to do so and it being such a short time before the convention, we decided to refer the matter to the Association in convention for final consideration. Section 9 of article 2 of the constitution provides that the member against whom charges are brought shall be notified in writing and that he shall have an opportunity to put in a defense. It seems to me in this case, (as

I understand he is already convicted of the crime with which he was charged) that he is not a proper person to continue a member of our Association and that it is not necessary for him to be notified if he is now in confinement.

I submit herewith a copv of what I consider a proper form of bond for the secretary, treasurer, and exchange superintendent. You will notice that this bond is given to the board of trustees, mentioning them by name, which I am informed by legal authority is the only proper form for an unincorporated association. All of which is respectfully submitted.

FLEMINGTON, N. J., Aug. 17, 1894. HIRAM E. DEATS, Sec. of Board.

## MINUTES OF THE 4th ANNUAL CONVENTION.

*Of the American Numismatic Association, held at Detroit Museum of Art, Thursday and Friday, August 23 and 24, 1894.*

FIRST SESSION, AUG. 23D, 1894.

The convention was called to order by President Heath at 10:10 a. m. Dr. Joseph Lathrop, president of the Detroit Numismatic Club, who was to deliver the address of welcome, being absent, it was read by Mr. A. H. Griffith. President Heath then introduced Vice-President Hooper, who replied on the part of the Association. Owing to the absence of Secretary Page, Mr. Geo. W. Rode was elected secretary protem. On motion, reading of the minutes of the last convention was dispensed with and they were approved as published in the official organ. The chair appointed the following standing committees:

Credentials: Messrs. Rode, Seymour, and Christopher.

Finance: Messrs. Rice, Newcomb, and Griffith.

Standing Rules: Messrs. Christopher, Rice, and Hooper.

Library and Cabinet: Messrs. Luck, Smith, and Rode.

Exchange Department: Messrs. Luck, Rice, and Deuel.

Official Organ: Messrs. Hooper, Manton, and Lathrop.

Constitution and By-Laws: Messrs. Deuel, Walker, Lathrop, and President Heath, ex-officio.

Owing to the absence of every member of the board of trustees, the committee on credentials was instructed to count the vote for the official board for the coming year.

President Heath read his report. which was referred to the committee on standing rules. The reports of the secretary and treasurer were read and referred to the committee on finance. The report of the librarian and curator was read and referred to the committee on library and cabinet. The superintendent of exchange read his report, which was referred to the committee on exchange department. The report of the board of trustees was read and referred to the committee on finance. Adjourned to meet at 2 o'clock.

SECOND SESSION, AUG. 23d, 1894.

President Heath called the convention to order at half past two.

Roll call showed the following members present:

| | | |
|---|---|---|
| Geo. F. Heath, M. D., | A. L. Fisher, M. D., | J. R. Christopher, |
| F. H. Seymour, | C. C. Deuel. | Howard Newcomb, |
| J. H. Valpey, | Dr. D. R. Bogue, | A. H. Griffith, |
| Geo. W. Rice, | W. J. Luck, | Joseph Hooper, |
| John Walker, | Geo. W. Rode. | |

The committee on credentials reported the following proxies:

Dr. Geo. F. Heath, 18 and 5 transferred by O. W. Page, (24 in all).
Geo. W. Rode, 3.
W. J. Luck, 1.

(Total present in proof; represented by proxy, 28.)

It also reported the following result of the annual election:

| | | | | |
|---|---|---|---|---|
| President: | A. G. Heaton, | 23 votes | Dr. Geo. F. Heath, | 14 votes |
| Vice President: | Joseph Hooper, | 31 | Geo. W. Rice, | 2 |
| | A. H. Griffith, | 2 | | |
| Secretary: | O. W. Page, | 36 | M. H. Stafford, | 1 |
| Treasurer: | Dr. A. L. Fisher, | 36 | | |
| Librarian: | W. C. Stone, | 35 | S. H. Chapman, | 1 |
| Supt. of Exchange: | W. J. Luck, | 36 | | |
| C'nt'rf't Detector: | S. H. Chapman, | 35 | Ed Frossard, | 2 |
| Board of Trustees: | J. A. Heckelman, | 28 | C. W. Stutesman, | 26 |
| | David Harlowe, | 23 | H. E. Deats, | 22 |
| | Geo. W. Rice, | 19 | W. K. Hall, | 18 |
| | Chas. S. Wilcox, | 10 | Scattering, | 21 |

Seventeen members preferred Washington, D. C., for the next Convention; a few scattering votes were cast, and the balance expressed no preference. On motion, the report was adopted. President Heath the declared the following duly elected to serve during the coming year, viz:

President: A. G. Heaton, 1618 17th St., Washington, D. C.

Vice President: Joseph Hooper, Port Hope, Ont.

Secretary: O. W. Page, Box 296, Waltham, Mass.

Treasurer: Dr. A. L. Fisher, Elkhart, Ind.

Librarian and Curator. W. C. Stone, 384 Union St., Springfield, Mass.

Superintendent of Exchange: W. J. Luck, Adrian, Mich.

Counterfeit Detector: S. H. Chapman, 1348 Pine St., Philadelphia, Pa.

Board of Trustees: J. A. Heckelman, Daggers, Va; David Harlowe, 3002 Mt. Vernon Ave., Milwaukee, Wis; C. W. Stutesman, 1730 Market St., Logansport, Ind; Geo. W. Rice, 186 E. High St., Detroit, Mich.; Hiram E. Deats, Flemington, N. J.

The committee on Standing Rules recommended that the rules of the last convention be adopted, and also that the recommendations in the President's report be approved. The report was adopted and the President's recommendations approved and referred to the President elect. The committee on Finance reported the reports of the Secretary and Treasurer correct; it also advised the adoption of the form of bond submitted by the board of trustees. On motion, the report was adopted. The committee on Library and Cabinet made the following recommendations, viz:

1st. That the request of the Librarian and Curator for an appropriation of $15 be granted.

2d. That the Librarian be authorized to exchange our official organ with other numismatic Journals, and that he subscribe for those with which he cannot arrange an exchange.

3d. That we should have current files of "The Numismatic Chronicle" and "Numismatic Magazine" in our library. On motion, the recommendations were approved. The committee on Exchange Department recommended the adoption of the Superintendent's report, which was done.

The Convention then took up the case of Dr. James B. Breeding, of San Antonio, Texas, (referred to it by the Board of Trustees.) A motion was made that he be expelled from the Association; this was amended to refer the case back to the Board of Trustees for action: after a full discussion, a vote was taken on the amendment and it was declared lost. The original motion was then put and carried, whereupon the President declared that James B. Breeding be expelled from the Association. A long discussion took place on the subject of a medal of membership, resulting in the passage of a motion that a committee of three be appointed to consider the subject of a Jeton and medal of membership, the committee to report through the official organ. The chair appointed Messrs. Hooper, Griffith, and Rode. Washington, D. C., was unanimously selected as the meeting place of the next convention. Superintendent of Exchange Luck, submitted additional rules for his department, which were referred to the committee on Constitution and By-Laws. On motion, it was resolved that when we adjourn, we adjourn to meet on Friday morning at nine o'clock. The president read an obituary of the late William M. Friesner. On motion, the chair was instructed to appoint a committee of three to prepare a suitable minute to be published in the official organ: the chair appointed Messrs. Fisher, Hooper, and Rice.

The following papers were then read:

"The Utility of Hobbies," Geo. F. Heath, M. D.

"A Few Coins of Syracuse," Ph. Whiteway.

On motion, adjourned.

THIRD SESSION, AUG. 24TH, 1894.

In the absence of President Heath (who was unavoidably detained by professional duties), the convention was called to order at 11 o'clock by Vice-President Hooper. Present at roll call: Messrs. Hooper, Seymour, Rice, Deuel, Christopher, Luck, Newcomb, Valpey, Fisher, Ragan, Lathrop, Griffith, and Rode. A long discussion took place regarding the exchange department, but as there was not a constitutional quorum present, no action was taken.

The following papers were then read:

"Aluminum for Minor Coins," D. C. Wismer.

"Confederate Treasury Notes," L. B. Tuthill.

"Restrikes of the United States Half Cents," Geo. W. Rice.

"The Coinage of the Jews," Joseph Hooper.

"A Novice Among the Coins," A. L. Fisher, M. D.

On motion, it was resolved to authorize the publication of the last paper in

some Detroit paper. On motion, the following papers were read, some of them by title, and ordered printed in the official organ, viz:
"Chinese Numismatic Bibliography," Henry Kingman.
"Auction Sales," A. G. Heaton.
"The Beginning of United States Coinage," Charles T. Tatamn.
"Porcelain Coins of Siam," J. A. Brudin, M. D.
"The Coins of Venice, 1400—1600, A. D.," Ph. Whiteway.
"Cutch Coinage," Maj. Adam Smith.
"The Denarii of Republican Rome," Geo. F. Heath, M. D.
"The Numismatic Library," W. C. Stone.
"Numismatic Treasures of Japan," W. C. Sakai.

Mr. Rice stated that the boat for St. Clair Flats (where the convention had been tendered a fish supper by the Detroit Numismatic Club) left at 3 o'clock sharp.

On motion, a vote of thanks was given to President Heath for his able efforts in behalf of the Association during the past year. On motion, a vote of thanks was given to the Detroit Museum of Art for the use of the room for the convention, tendered through its director, Mr. A. H. Griffith.

On motion, a rising vote of thanks was given to the Detroit Numismatic Club for the handsome entertainment of the visiting members, and also our congratulations on the magnificent display of coins and medals.

On motion, adjourned sine die, at one o'clock.

GEO. W. RODE, Secretary pro tem.

Which is at the same time the smallest coin and the coin of least value at present current in Europe? In the absence of a knowledge of any smaller and more worthless, I should be inclined (writes a correspondent) to award the palm to the Greek lepton, a specimen of which has recently come into my hands. It is about the same size as the Italian centesimo, and the way to get one is to buy something marked 4 lepta, give a pendara, or Greek halfpenny, and wait for the change.

The lepton is, according to the decimal monetary system current in countries belonging to the Latin union, the hundreth part of the drachma. Now, the Greek drachma is, while nominally the equivalent of the franc or the lira, at present worth rather less than 6d, the rate of exchange about a fortnight ago being 42.60 drachmas to an English sovereign. The lepton is therefore approximately worth about one-fifth of an English farthing. In nothing does the deplorable condition of Greek finances strike the casual observer more forcibly than the fact that at present Greece has no "money" but copper, and is obliged to issue bank notes for sums of sixpence upward, and a nastier little rag than the one-drachma note would be difficult to find. All travelers in Greece should provide themselves with a small pair of tongs to take them up by.—Westminster Gazette.

# OBITUARY.

## Prof. William M. Friesner.

It is related that an old Grecian philosopher upon being informed of the death of a beloved son, responded: "I know that I begat a mortal;" and so today on this anniversary occasion in the midst of our rejoicings we are again reminded by the grim courier of our mortality.

It is now my painful duty to inform you that our brother, Prof. Wm. M. Friesner, of Los Angeles, Cal., is no more. I read the following memorial published in the Los Angeles Daily Times, of Aug. 5, 1894.*

For some time had Mr. Friesner realized that his time with us was short. About a year since he resigned his life work and later his collection, one of the finest of the American series, to the Auction Room. He was getting his house in order for the summons. A few weeks since he writes me in a matter of fact way that one lung is two thirds and the other one third gone, but expected to live until the winter, possibly until spring. History tells us of martyrs for religion, for science, for country: but none ever went to the lions, the stake or the battle field with greater fortitude, than he, who with mental faculties acute, calmly sits down with death and bids the grim tyrant he can no longer defy to sup with him. GEO. F. HEATH.

### *WILLIAM M. FRIESNER.*

Member of the A. N. A., died at Los Angeles, Cal., Aug. 1, 1894.

The failing health of this lamented numismatist caused the recent sale of his collection of coins in New York and its extraordinary completeness as a collection of United States silver and minor coinage together with the fact of its being the first recorded sale of branch mint pieces properly classified and very full in every series, with the resultant establishment of a preliminary standard of prices in this fresh numismatic field, make Prof. Friesner's name memorable in our annals. The following extracts from an obituary in the Los Angeles Sunday Times will therefore be read with interest and pride by our fraternity.

Mr. Friesner was born in Fairfield Co., O., Jan. 24, 1851. When he was quite young his parents removed to Allen Co., O., near Lima. After the death of his mother when he was twelve years old he resided on a farm near Lancaster until he was 18 years of age. In the fall of 1869 he entered Fairfield Union Academy at Pleasantville, where he fitted for college and graduated in 1872, teaching country schools during the winter terms. During the year 1872-3 he was principal of the graded schools of Lithopolis, O. In September, 1873, he entered the junior class of the Ohio Wesleyan University, graduating with honor in 1875. He was employed as tutor during part of his college course. During his senior year he was Secretary of the Grand Chapter of Phi Kappa

*For abstract of same see Mr. Heaton's memorial.

Psi, then located at Ohio Alpha. From 1875 to 1879 he was principal of the High School at Portsmouth, O.; from 1879 to 1881 superintendent of the city school; from 1881 to 1885 superintendent of schools at Cedar Rapids, Ia., and from 1885 to 1893 superintendent of Public Schools at Los Angeles, when failing health admonished him that his working days were over.

Mr. Friesner was twice married. His second wife and an infant son survive him. The deceased as a public educator had a long and honorable career and his death will be deeply regretted here and elsewhere by both parents and children who had learned to respect him for his purity of character and his faithful conscientious work as a teacher. He was long a member of the Masonic fraternity, having reached the thirty-second degree, and was also a Knight Templar.

A. G. HEATON.

## *RESOLUTIONS OF RESPECT.*

*William M. Friesner.*

At the Fourth Annual Convention of the American Numismatic Association held in the Museum of Art, Detroit, Mich., U. S. A., Aug. 23 and 24, 1894, it was unanimously resolved as follows:

WHEREAS, the great Ruler of all events has seen fit in his Inscrutible Providence, Infinite and Divine Wisdom, to remove by death from our midst our Beloved and respected Brother and co-laborateur Prof. W. M. Friesner, of Los Angeles, Cal.; whereby this Association has lost an intelligent and zealous member, whose labors were highly appreciated and conducted with wisdom, whose exemplarity as a true and faithful student of the science of Numisma has caused his name to be held in respectful remembrance by the members of this Association; Therefore be it

RESOLVED: That the American Numismatic Association, now in convention do hereby unanimously and fraternally extend our sincere expressions of deep sorrow and heartfelt sympathy to his bereaved family in this their hour of tribulation. Awaiting the the Day dawn

"When the shadows flee,
And the mists are rolled away,"

And the great Collector of the Universe shall open his "Cabinet of Gems" and restore for a nobler placement those "not lost but gone before." It is also

RESOLVED: That this memorial be entered on the records of this Association and the secretary be instructed to forward to the deceased family a copy of the same.

GEO. W. RICE,
A. L. FISHER, } Committee.
JOSEPH HOOPER.

# Detroit Museum of Art.

## THE EXHIBITION.

The Exhibition, like everything else so far attempted by the Detroit Numismatic Club or American Numismatic Association, was a success. When it is stated that there were not less than 10000 coins on exhibition whose value was estimated at $75,000, one may gain some idea of its size and importance: but only those who were present and had the time to critically examine can have but little conception of the value, historic, fictitious and financial of this exhibit never attempted and never equaled heretofore in this country. Only its probable annual repetition by the Association can mitigate the great loss one would feel were this the last opportunity of the kind.

Six large portable cases, the property of the Association and manufactured especially for the purpose, filled the floor space of the large gallery of the Museum of Art building. There surrounded by master-pieces in painting and art they proved a gem in an appropriate setting—a picture to bring joy to the heart of any lover of the beautiful, the historic, the antique or the curious in coinage.

It would be impossible in our limited space to speak in particular of the many notable examples on exhibition, a volume could not do full justice to the subject.

The collector of the American series would naturally first turn to Mr. Geo. W. Rice's exhibit in which were some 3,000 pieces occupying about ninety square feet of space. This collection is considered one of the finest and most complete in the world containing as it does all the coins and mint varieties below the dollar with the single exception of the 1827 quarter, struck at our mints. A strictly fine perfect die 1804 cent valued at $75, and two of the $50 California gold slugs of 1852 attracted particular attention. He had also on exhibit his latest find, a large silver medal No. 6, one of twelve struck by the government for the twelve Indian chief, after the treaty of 1876. Mr. Rice is said to have bought this piece for the value in old silver.

Dr. Joseph Lathrop, president of the Detroit Numismatic Club, had on exhibition his large and valuable collection of early American gold coins, besides almost complete collections of the Jackson or "Hard Times" tokens; also a complete series of the U. S. mint medals in proof condition.

Fred Seymour had a fine series of old Roman coins in gold, silver, and bronze. Other Detroit collectors who exhibited were I. M. Bates, Miss Grace Rice and Henry B. Smith; Mr. Smith having some 3,000 varieties, mainly of modern coinage.

John Walker had on view his valuable collection of war medals. Decorations for distinguished service, comprising complete series of the Legion of Honor from the First Napoleon to the present Republic, Italy Papal; Belgium, Prussia, Russia, Turkey, Tonquin, Mexico, etc., in all over a hundred specimens besides a Tecumseh medal presented to this celebrated chief by George III. His exhibit of Columbian medals included over 200 varieties.

J. H. Valpey, of Detroit, exhibited some 800 pieces of ancient Roman and Greek bronze. He has an unique method of exhibiting his specimens. He either perforates the coin and attaches a small ring or solders an eye to the coin which is attached by staple on a narrow strip of covered wood, eight to twelve pieces being on the block depending upon the size of the coin. In this way both sides of the coin can be examined without handling the piece. Each coin had been plated or brushed with some bronze solution giving them a decidedly new and bright appearance. The arrangement was as pretty to the eye as it was unique. As the collection is solely intended for the amusement and instruction of himself and friends, and as he cares nothing for their after numismatic value, outside criticism is perhaps uncalled for.

From outside the city Mr. H. E. Morey, of Boston, had a beautiful set of medals of the French Kings whose exquisite design and workmanship made them envied by everyone.

Jas. A. Brudin sent in a fine series of Ming taos, Temple medals, large and small round coins of the Chinese empire. In the gallery, from the Brudin, Rice and Heath collections, were all together, over a hundred of these ancient Chinese Taos or razor cash ranging from 450 to 228 B. C.

Dr. A. L. Fisher, of Elkhart, Ind., and W. J. Luck, of Adrain, also had valuable exhibits. Dr. Heath, of Monroe, contributed 200 varieties of Roman Family or Consular denari, besides some 800 varieties of Roman First Brass, Greek

Roman, Persian, Bactrian, Parthian, Syrian silver, etc.

Besides these exhibits of hard money, there was paper currency galore. Luther B. Tuthill, of South Creek, N. C., had a magnificent and complete series of C. S. A. notes, two pieces a $1,000 and $500 bill being valued at 40 and 65 dollars respectively. Then there were hundreds of old Colonial and Continental currency, thousands of Broken Bank, "Wild cat" and Foreign paper money, Bonds, U. S. Script, Shin-plasters and others and curious notes of exchange. Here was a check on the Merchant's Bank, of New York City, dated 1802 for 15 dollars signed by Aaron Burr; a piece of military script for $50 of the Nicaraguan Republic 1857, signed by the noted Fillibuster, William Walker as president; a Hungarian Bond signed by Louis Kossuth and a Hong Kong and

THE STUDENT'S STAIRWAY.

DRAWN BY THEODORE SAUNDERS.

Shanghai Bank Note for five Mexican silver dollars sent in by member Major Adam Smith, of Poona, India.

The general public were invited to inspect this exhibit on Thursday evening (23d) from 7 to 10; Friday from 10 to 4 p. m.; and on Saturday (25th) from 9 to 4 p. m. The large attendance from among the more cultured and intelligent was very gratifying, the steady throng attesting beyond doubt the interest taken by the people in our science. The daily press showed great interest in our work by publishing extended accounts of the sessions, stories and histories of some of the more noted coins and some of the papers of special interest to the lay readers were published entire. The Illustrated American's special artist was on the ground and photographed the Convention and Exhibition for an early number of that estimable illustrated journal. It was remarkable the number of visitors who brought with them old and odd coins to find out from what country or their value. Most of these were comparatively common, but quite a few would have graced any collection. It is needless to state that all questions were correctly answered.

With all the pleasures of a successful exhibition it is unfortunate that regrets must follow—the writes regrets that the duties of Convention prevented him from giving the time to the exhibit he would have liked. This feeling must have prevailed with all. So much to see and so little time to see it in. Taking it all in all, Convention work, Papers, Exhibition and Excursion, three days could have been very profitably occupied. Again it was a matter of regret that more of our membership were not present to enjoy with us. Mr. Christopher came 300 miles, next year a thousand (D. V.) would not keep him away.

And again, the writer regrets that he cannot give you more regarding the personalia of the gathering, of the veteran newspaper man, Mr. James E. Scripps, one of the patron saints in the calendar of the Detroit Museum of Art; of its genial, whole souled Director, Prof. A. H. Griffith; of Mr. Henry Gillman who as U. S. Consul at Jerusalem for five years became filled with archæology and numismatology; of Joseph Hooper brim full of coin history and bubbling over all the time; of Dr. A. L. Fisher who is in a brown steady all the time wondering what those old worthies did when not fighting or making coins, or, of the members of the Detroit Numismatic Club, as genial a set of fellows as one can run across and enthusiasts to the core.

The Association builded better than it knew when it selected Detroit as a Convention place. The long roll of new applicants, and the prestige of one of the most successful and pleasurable gatherings of the kind on record, cannot fail to work to the glory of our science and Association.

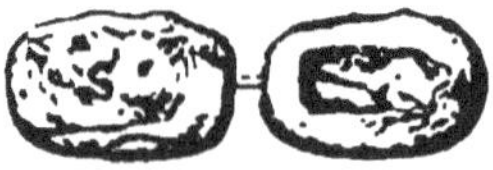

Rushmere.

## EXCURSION TO RUSHMERE.

One of the most enjoyable features of the Convention was the visit to Rushmere given to the members of the Association and their friends by the Detroit Numismatic Club. At half past two in the afternoon of Aug. 24th, the convention having adjourned, the following persons assembled in the hurricane deck of the elegant steamer Darius Cole for a trip to the St. Clair Flats about thirty miles away.

| | |
|---|---|
| Dr. and Mrs. A. L. Fisher, | Dr. and Mrs. Geo. F. Heath, |
| Mr. and Mrs. Geo. W. Rice, | Mr. and Mrs. I. M. Bates and baby, |
| Mr. and Mrs. D. R. Bogue. | F. I. Meryman, |

| | | |
|---|---|---|
| Fred Seymour. | J. H. Valpey, | Howard Newcomb, |
| Henry B. Smith, | H. L. Boyeau, | J. R. Christopher, |
| Geo. W. Rode, | Joseph Hooper, | Edwin B. Hill, |
| C. C. Deuel, | Joseph Lathrop, | Samuel Wilkins, |
| W. J. Luck, | Hon. Henry Gillman, | John Walker. |

The writer has been on most of the travelled waters this side the Rocky mountains, along the rocky shores of New England, up Long Island Sound and the romantic Hudson and Lake Champlain, along our inland rivers and great lakes, but if there is anything more enchanting or more beautiful than a trip between the waters of the Huron and Erie on a pleasant day in August he has failed to find it. It used to be said, "See Naples and die." It should be amended these days to "See this great water way and die." It's a poet's dream, an artists vision, and a glimpse of paradise commingled into one.

Up past Belle Isle, Detroit's great natural park, the most beautiful in the world, past Grosse Pointe and Peche Island; the former the summer homes of many of Detroit's Nabobs, the latter the island home of the Canadian distiller Hiram Walker, and Lake St. Clair spread out before us.

Lake St. Clair as is well known is a widening of the Detroit and St. Clair rivers, it is from 25 to 30 miles across at its widest and for the most part is quite shallow, the head of the lake being so marshy and shallow that the government has dredged out and keeps up at considerable expense a ship canal. Through this great highway passes more tonnage than goes through the Suez canal or enters the harbor of any city along our coasts.

Here near the mouth of the St. Clair river has been dredged and built up the Venice of America. Very many private club houses, residences have been built on made ground or piles and surrounded in most cases by beautiful grounds covered by the greenest of grass. For the discouragement of mosquitoes, trees or shrubbery is not generally encouraged.

Of all the delightful places in this city of the sea, Rushmere stands pre-eminent. Some of the best known people of Detroit belong to it and its home like appearance and general cheerfulness is particularly noticable. Here the guests spend the delightful hours of summer and enjoy themselves on the broad verandas or in sailing, fishing, yachting, private theatricals, card parties, concerts or dancing. Each day the boats bring up members from the city to spend a few hours. take supper, perhaps pass the night, or may be remain a few days amidst the bewitching breezes always abounding.

Here to this enchanting spot was transferred and entertained in a royal way for the time, the faithful few of the A. N. A. and their friends. Here for a while Rushmere was converted into a temple of Numisma, though numismatics seemed forgotton in the gastronomical discussion of fish, frog legs and other delicacies of the season and locality; and the gazing upon the amazing antics of Prof. Seymour's collection of trained bass. Here science was dropped out of sight. and for the nonce members assumed their usual characteristics of plain American citizens with the peculiarities usually accompanying such. Ye reporter does not propose to exhibit the worldly weaknesses of any to the vulgar gaze of the "stay at homes," even if he had the space which he has not; there were two things, however. that particularly struck the Rushmere people that he cannot forbear mentioning: First, that, for a person with dyspepsia and several other stomach disorders, Luck could dispose of a pretty fair meal and second, that all the matrons heaved sighs of relief of such unusual size that they could be heard clear across the water. when Christopher got on the boat to leave. Every one of them for three mortal hours had been in a state of nervous excitement and suspense for fear he would spright away some of their babies. And all the A. N. A. people couldn't help but note the fact that Rode who has developed into somewhat of a kicker of late years, on this occasion didn't kick a kick.

We came back on the steamer Greyhound. Here in a warm corner of the upper deck we gathered in a circle and by the light of the stars told stories in which Walker and Luck excelled, or listened to songs by the A. N. A. quartet accompanied by Mr. Seymour's orchestron. The songs of the nations proved attractive; at the close of each song representatives of the nations whose song was given acknowledged the compliment by gracefully rising and expressing their thanks. "God Save the Queen," brought up Messrs. Wilkins, Christopher and Hooper; the "Marseilles," Dr. Bogue; Mr. Rode got up after "Der Wacht und der Rheine" and acknowledged that he was a near descendent of state where England got her latest crop of kings, Hannover; "Wearing of the Green" brought up our personified windmill, Luck, who responded by singing a short Irish song, but after singing 29 of the 130 odd verses his audience begged off, and with hands clasped all joined in "Auld Lang Syne:"

Should auld Numisma be forgot,
This beloved friend of mine,
No, never! while this tongue can sing
For auld lang syne.

And when we meet again next year
In Washington so fine.
May this circle unbroken be,
For auld lang syne.

"And here's a hand my trusty friend,
"Give me a hand of thine,
"And we'll take a right good draught again
"For auld lang syne.

And then on the wharf we said "good bye," and the Fourth Annual Convention of the American Numismatic Association, with its profits, its pleasures, and kindly associations, became what it ever must remain, one of the most pleasant reminisences in the lives of these who were fortunate enough to have been present.

## WHAT'S IS THE MATTER WITH HEATON?

WASHINGTON, Sept. 2, 1894.

MY DEAR DR. HEATH:

You have doubtless been surprised at my silence in regard to numismatic events of such personal interest and flattering character as have lately occurred and I now "rise to explain."

When I went nearly a month ago to a camp in the mountains near Luray, Va., I directed my waiter to send me only letters, and hold other mail matter until my return. Consequently it was but yesterday that upon reaching home I found for the first time not only the newspapers you sent me announcing the proceedings of the Convention and my election to the Presidency of the Association for the coming year, but the August "Numismatist" containing your very courteous nomination of me. Had I seen the latter in time I should have again protested against being a candidate and urged the honor for any one of the officers of the Association whose faithful labors in its interest have so much more merited recognition.

## HE IS ALL RIGHT.

As it is, however, and the work of the Convention is all done, I can only thank the members most sincerely for the compliment that has so entirely surprised me and assure them that I shall study the preservation and growth of the Association as earnestly as that of my collection of coins, seeking with equal interest United States and Colonial additions of every denomination, and valuing the copper of right condition quite as much as gold. As I do not believe in brushing up or the use of acids, I shall leave all that to the efficient Treasurer, but I shall keep a sharp look out for counterfeits. One difference in treatment, however, suggests itself. While I believe in keeping coins dry, I hold that visiting members should be preserved, if not exactly wet, yet sufficiently damp to develop that beautiful irridescence of surface which lends a charm to perfect condition and tends to modify an excess of specific gravity. This theory I shall be eager to elucidate at the next meeting of the Association and the appointment of Washington for the Convention of 1895 is to me, therefore, especially gratifying. Brother Collins is not less hearty in his welcome, and with Brother Hays and others we intend to follow Detroit's honorable example and early organize a local numismatic society which will, in due time, emulate its hospitality. I remain fraternally yours,

A. G. HEATON.

## THE AMERICAN NUMISMATIC ASSOCIATION.

BOARD OF OFFICERS:

President: A. G. Heaton, 1618 17th St., Washington, D. C.
Vice President: Joseph Hooper, Port Hope, Ont.
Secretary: O. W. Page, Box 296, Waltham, Mass.
Treasurer: Dr. A. L. Fisher, Elkhart, Ind.
Librarian and Curator. W. C. Stone, 384 Union St., Springfield, Mass.
Superintendent of Exchange: W. J. Luck, Adrian, Mich,
Counterfeit Detector: S. H. Chapman, 1348 Pine St., Philadelphia, Pa.
Board of Trustees: J. A. Heckelman, Daggers, Va; David Harlowe, 3002 Mt. Vernon Ave., Milwaukee. Wis; C. W. Stutesman, 1730 Market St., Logansport, Ind; Geo. W. Rice, 186 E. High St., Detroit, Mich.; Hiram E. Deats, Flemington, N. J.

### Secretary's Report.

TO THE PRESIDENT AND MEMBERS OF THE AMERICAN NUMISMATIC ASS'N.

GENTLEMEN:

The report of my office from July 20 to Sept. 1 is as follows:

Certificates of membership issued, 8.
Cash receipts, dues and initiations,..................$4.50.
Expense of office (postage),..............................................$ .91.

The following became members on Sept. 1:

212 Daniel R. Kennedy, 59 Fifth Ave., New York, N. Y.
213 R. M. Rowley, Kalamazoo, Mich.
214 W. Day, 46 Rue de France, Nice, France.

### Applications for Membership.

R. M. Bateman, M. D., Pickering, Ontario.
Vouchers: Messrs. Ineson and Page.
John Walker, 47 Edmund Place, Detroit, Mich.
Vouchers: Messrs. Rice and Lathrop.
John F. Bateman, 14 Stevens St., Lowell, Mass.
Vouchers: Messrs. Morey and Page.
A. E. Doeherty, care Cass House, Saginaw, (E. S.) Mich.
R. Archer, Jr., 15 Prussia St., Dublin, Ireland.
Dr. Geo. W. Massamore, 334 N. Charles St., Baltimore, Md.
Vouchers: Messrs. Heath and Page.
Geo. Eavenson, Chief Mach. Cl'k, D. & R. G. Ry., Denver, Col.
Vouchers: Messrs. Heaton and Heath.
Fred I. Meryman, Port Huron, Mich.
John C. Johnson, Port Huron, Mich.
Vouchers: Messrs. Hooper and Heath.

Edwin B. Hill, 432 Fourth St., Detroit.
Vouchers: Messrs. Rice and Deuel.
Samuel Wilkins, 63 Elmwood Ave., London, Ont.
Vouchers: Messrs. Hooper & Walker.
Charles M. Klumpp, 15 Valpey Bl'k, Detroit, Mich.
Vouchers: Messrs. Bogue and Smith.
Howard Newcomb, 1145 Woodward Ave., Detroit.
Vouchers: Messrs. Bates and Lathrop.
W. H. Holden, 350 Meldrum St., Detroit.
Vouchers: Messrs. Hooper and Lathrop.
Fred N. Bonine, M. D., Miles, Mich.
Vouchers, Messrs. Stewart and Heath.

WALTHAM, MASS., Sept. 1. O. W. PAGE, Secy.

# WITH THE EDITOR.

This issue of THE NUMISMATIST may be considered our Convention number, being given over mainly to the detail and extra work of the Convention. This will be of special interest to the members of the Association and to all others who glory in the growth and upbuilding of our science. Considering the general depression of the times, the past year has been a most favorable one for us. The year has placed our own country at the head numerically of the nations, in the number of devotees to our science.

There are many reasons why the numismatic editor should be more in touch with all the classes of the numismatic world than any other. At the head of our great organization, he has felt the warm throbbing heart that tells of life and vitality and he has lately been within the temple and seen the fires burning from the alter of Numisma, and he brings you, individually and collectively, this greeting that was given to one of old, "to hold fast to that which is good," for a day and era cometh, and is now at hand, the like of which no man hath seen.

THE NUMISMATIST proposes to continue on the topmost wave and to become more and more indispensable to collectors and students of coin. Our October issue will conclude Mr. Brudin's paper on Chinese Tsien. Geo. J. Bauer will tell us something about arranging coins in cabinets. Mr. Ph. Whiteway's paper on A Few Coins of Syracuse will be published entire. Joseph Hooper will devote a few thoughts to that old German who demoralized him for the time by asking, "Vare ish de Monish en dis ting"? Major Smith will continue his India Notes. An Abstract on Early New England Currency will be furnished by Chas. H. Howes, and an interesting letter from Europe by Rev. Jeremiah Zimmerman will be a few of the good things to look forward to in next issue. The Departments crowded out this month will be resumed.

## A Much Needed Coin.

In these days of money discussions it is pertinent to call attention to a much needed coin. The denomination in mind is a 9-cent piece. Modern business ingenuity and enterprise have brought a fine discrimination in the matter of selling prices and instead of being satisfied with fixing their profits in decimals and demi-decimal denominations, find it to advantage to make the concession of a single penny on a $5, $10, or $15 sale. In values that are less than $5 it is almost as common to see 99 and 49 figures as it is those ending with 0 or 00.

Mr. Secretary of the Treasury, we submit that a 9-cent piece is now as necessary as a 10-cent piece. It is very pleasant to our feeling and desirable to our purses to enter a large store and purchase a 20-cent collar for 19 cents, but it transforms us into pestiferous and cranky individuals to be compelled to stand on one foot for 27 minutes and wait for the return of the penny due in change. The pennies we save in promiscuous buying would provide us with afternoon papers and postal cards, but the time lost in waiting for change would make an annual income sufficient for an African prince.—Chicago Times.

## Sale of Greek Coins.

On Wednesday Messrs. Sotheby, Wilkinson & Hodge sold at their rooms in London a collection of Greek coins in gold, silver and electrum, the property of Mr. Robert Carfrae, of Edinburgh. The highest prices obtained were the following: Pandosia, B. C. 500. This was described as one of the most exquisite productions of any Greek mint, and, after a spirited bidding, was disposed of for 185 pounds. Metapontum, B. C. 350-330, 75 pounds; Syracuse, B. C. 400-336, 51 pounds; Syracuse, B. C. 345-317. 54 pounds, 10 s.; Syracuse Hiers II., B. C. 275-216, 130 pounds; Amphipolsi B. C. 424-338, 56 pounds.—Lloyds Weekly.

# ADDITIONAL RULES

## ADOPTED FOR THE EXCHANGE DEPARTMENT.

I. Blanks will be furnished to members at cost. Room on each blank for 25 descriptions.

II. Classification must be correct and description right. Because a coin is rare does not alter its condition

III. All coins and other material must come to this department in some kind of an envelope, with date if any and description marked plainly.

IV. Coins will only be listed in journal once (but may remain in department several months). In ordering always give number.

V. Orders for coins, etc., must be accompanied by price and approximate transportation charges, as orders will always be sent on approval, charges to be prepaid by member ordering if returned. All balances to be settled promptly at close of the deal unless member has a running account with the department, in which case he must satisfy department that he is responsible.

VI. Members will receive full amount for coins as priced by themselves, the cost of selling being added to selling price. 10 per cent. will be deducted from all lots of coins returned to owners unsold to cover cost of printing the lists.

VII. This department reserves the right to notify members if coins are priced too high to sell, but in no case will department change prices without written order from owner.

VIII. If members want to leave prices open to judgement of department, so state, but preferred that members price them themselves.

IX. Members wishing to exchange will send lists on their own letter heads. Wants to be on a separate sheet. Department will file wants, and when possible will arrange so that members may exchange between themselves.

X. Remittances must be made in current funds, money orders, N. Y. drafts, or registered letter.

XI. All orders will be filled in turn as far as possible. Members not hearing from the department in 15 days may consider that what they want is not to be had. To insure getting goods, get in order as soon as possible. Correspondence should always be on separate letter heads from orders for coins.

ADRIAN, MICH. W. J. LUCK, Ex. Supt.

## *INVNICE NO. 1. Sept. 1, '94.*

| Lot | Description | Price |
|---|---|---|
| 1 | 1854 U. S. cent; v. fine | $ 55 |
| 2 | 1793 - 1 - soldi. good (selge) | 55 |
| 3 | Nova Scotia and New Brunswick success; ob. Britian seated R ship; good | 2 20 |
| 4 | 1873 New Foundland ½ dol. g'd. | 85 |
| 5 | 1873 U. S. 3c silver proof | 1 10 |
| 6 | 1825 " dime; good | 45 |
| 7 | 1860 " " no stars | 65 |
| 8 | 1821 " " ob. G. R. fine | 45 |
| 9 | 1846 " " V. G. | 1 10 |
| 10 | 1848 " " G. | 45 |
| 11 | 1840 " " G. sleeves | 55 |
| 12 | 1801 one-half dime; good | 3 30 |
| 13 | 1843 " " v. fine | 55 |
| 14 | 1843 " " good; two scratches on ob., large date | 55 |
| 15 | 1842 half-dime; uncirculated | 55 |
| 16 | 1868 " proof | 55 |
| 17 | 1808 U. S. half-dollar; fair | 85 |
| 18 | 1809 " " good | 95 |
| 19 | 1810 " " fair, with large o | 85 |
| 20 | 1810 U. S. half-dollar | 65 |
| 21 | 1812 " " cracked die; good | 85 |
| 22 | 1812 U. S. half-dollar; fair to g. | 65 |
| 23 | 1812 " " perfect die; good | 85 |
| 24 | 1813 U. S. half-dollar; good | 85 |
| 25 | 1817 " " fair | 60 |
| 26 | 1819 " " good | 85 |
| 27 | 1821 " " " | 85 |
| 28 | 1822 " " " | 95 |
| 29 | 1823 " " " | 80 |
| 30 | 1823 " " " | 90 |
| 31 | 1825 " " " | 80 |
| 32 | 1825 " " " | 90 |
| 33 | 1826 " " | 80 |
| 34 | 1827 " " fine: base 2, straight | 1 00 |
| 35 | 1827 ditto | 1 00 |
| 36 | 1828 U. S. half-dollar; good, large date | 70 |
| 37 | 1828 U. S. half-dollar; v. good, large date | 90 |
| 38 | 1828 U. S. half-dollar; good, large date | 80 |
| 39 | 1829 U. S. ½ dol.; v. fair | 70 |
| 40 | 1830 " " fine, large o | 1 00 |
| 41 | 1831 " " good | 70 |
| 42 | 1831 " " " | 70 |
| 43 | 1831 " " fine | 1 00 |
| 44 | 1832 " " " | 85 |
| 45 | 1833 " " good | 70 |
| 46 | 1833 " " v. fair | 65 |
| 47 | 1833 " " fine | 1 00 |
| 48 | 1834 " " fair, sm'l date | 65 |
| 49 | 1834 " " v. good, pierced, large date | 60 |
| 50 | 1835 U. S. ½ dol.; fine | 1 00 |
| 51 | 1836 " " g'd, let'r'd ed. | 70 |
| 52 | 1836 " " " " " | 75 |
| 53 | 1836 " " fine | 90 |
| 54 | 1837 " " g'd ob., f'r rev. | 70 |
| 55 | 1838 " " fine | 90 |
| 56 | 1838 " " v. fine | 1 00 |

# Wants, to exchange, etc.

This department gratis to all our readers.

Wanted.—Early issues of Rhode Island paper currency. Geo. C. Barton, Box 163, Providence, R. I.

Wanted.—Uncirculated U. S copper cents. Give date and price. Clayton C. Herr. Bloomington, Ill.

To Exchange.—Foreign coins for numismatic literature or U. S. money (paper or metallic) medals or tokens. W. H. Taylor, North Wales, Pa.

Wanted.—Cheap American sale catalogues, with plates and priced, also plates for Parmelees, and Woodward's 69 sale. R. Archer Jr., 15 Prussia St., Dublin, Ireland.

The signature of Sir James Outram, K. C. B., the Bayard of India, for American coins. Also Asiatic stamps, coins and war medals. Major Adam Smith, Poona, India.

To Exchange.—Flint lock muskets, cannon balls from Bennington battle ground, old pistols, axes and swords, for cash or old coins. All letters answered. A. Oatman, Shaftsbury, Vt.

Copper cents nearly all dates to exchange for dimes of 1800,-01-02-03-04-09-11-22-28-44-63-64-65-67. Half cents 1793-94-95-96-97 1802-11: Fine 1801 cent. J. B. Goldsmith, 53 Hale St., Beverly, Mass.

Wanted.—Scotts Coin Journal for 1884-5-6, or either, loose or bound. Liberal exchange offered in foreign silver and copper (some choice oriental) or part cash. F. C. Browne, Framingham, Mass.

To Exchange.—Half dollars, quarter dollars, dimes, half dimes and three cent silver pieces, old cents and half cents, for the same not in my collection. Arthur B. Stewart, 813 6th Av. Beaver Falls, Pa.

Wanted.—Irish medals, silver and copper, O'Connell, Gratton. Dr. Quinn, Charlemont, Thos. Ryder, Wm. Dean, Col. Talbot, Lord Perry, Bantry Garrison, Drumkeen Infantry, Fermoy Cavalry, Limerick Militia, Rathdown Cavalry, Cork Volunteers, Tyrone Militia, Wicklow Militia. Also wanted following small silver tokens: Alex Morton Armagh 3 pence 1736, Ben Bowen Dublin iii pence sterling, John Overend Portadown 3 pence 1736, Sam Mackie Richhill 3 pence 1736. Address R. Archer Jr., 15 Prussia St., Dublin, Ireland.

TYPES OF EXTINCT CIVILIZATION
MORE HISTORIC THAN WRITTEN HISTORY

# THE NUMISMATIST

**November, 1894.**

An Illustrated Monthly
devoted to the
Science of Numismatics.

GEO. F HEATH, M.D. Monroe, Mich.

Vol. 7. No. 11.

PRESS STEAM PTG. CO., WATERLOO, IND

# CONTENTS:




# The Numismatist:

A MONTHLY JOURNAL FOR COIN COLLECTORS,
AND OFFICIAL BULLETIN OF

## THE AMERICAN NUMISMATIC ASSOCIATION:

ONE DOLLAR A YEAR.

---

Editorial and publication office. Monroe, Mich.

---

THE NUMISMATIST is the only Illustrated Monthly Journal devoted to coins and their collecting published on the American continent.

ADVERTISING RATES very reasonable. Made known on application.

SUBSCRIPTION $1.00 per annum, post free to any portion of the civilized world. Remittances may be made by money order, postal note, registered letter, or, when these are not obtainable, in unused postage stamps of low denominations.

Entered at Monroe, Mich., Postoffice, as second class matter.

# ADDITIONAL RULES

### ADOPTED FOR THE EXCHANGE DEPARTMENT.

I. Blanks will be furnished to members at cost. Room on each blank for 25 descriptions.

II. Classification must be correct and description right. Because a coin is rare does not alter its condition

III. All coins and other material must come to this department in some kind of an envelope, with date if any and description marked plainly.

IV. Coins will only be listed in journal once (but may remain in department several months). In ordering always give number.

V. Orders for coins, etc., must be accompanied by price and approximate transportation charges, as orders will always be sent on approval, charges to be prepaid by member ordering if returned. All balances to be settled promptly at close of the deal unless member has a running account with the department, in which case he must satisfy department that he is responsible.

VI. Members will receive full amount for coins as priced by themselves, the cost of selling being added to selling price. 10 per cent. will be deducted from all lots of coins returned to owners unsold to cover cost of printing the lists.

VII. This department reserves the right to notify members if coins are priced too high to sell, but in no case will department change prices without written order from owner.

VIII. If members want to leave prices open to judgement of department, so state, but preferred that members price them themselves.

IX. Members wishing to exchange will send lists on their own letter heads. Wants to be on a separate sheet. Department will file wants, and when possible will arrange so that members may exchange between themselves.

X. Remittances must be made in current funds, money orders, N. Y. drafts, or registered letter.

XI. All orders will be filled in turn as far as possible. Members not hearing from the department in 15 days may consider that what they want is not to be had. To insure getting goods, get in order as soon as possible. Correspondence should always be on separate letter heads from orders for coins.

ADRIAN, MICH. W. J. LUCK, Ex. Supt.

### U. S. CENTS.

| *No.* | *Date* | *Price* | *Description* | *Condition* |
|---|---|---|---|---|
| 57 | 1793 | $10 [illegible] | Wreath lettered edge........ | fine |
| 58 | " | [illegible] | " " 3 punch marks on obverse................ | poor |
| 59 | 1794 | [illegible] | Hays No. 33................ | good |
| 60 | " | 40 | ........................ | very fair |
| 61 | " | [illegible] 00 | Hays No. 14 flaw in planchet. | fine |
| 62 | 1795 | 25 | Plain edge.................... | fair |
| 63 | 1808 | 1 00 | ................. | very good to fine |
| 64 | 1819 | 10 | Large date over 1888....... | good |
| 65 | 1835 | 75 | " stars and date..... | very fine |
| 66 | 1839 | 25 | Booby head................ | good |
| 67 | 1856 | 4 00 | Eagle cent......... | uncirculated |
| 68 | 1857 | 75 | Large date.......... | " |

### 3 CENT SILVER TRIMES.

| | | | | |
|---|---|---|---|---|
| 69 | 1853 | 10 | .............................. | fine |
| 70 | 1855 | 05 | .............................. | fair |
| 71 | 1860 | 05 | .............................. | fair |
| 72 | 1862 | 10 | .................... | uncirculated |
| 73 | 1863 | 75 | ........................... | proof |
| 74 | 1866 | Do. | | |
| 75 | 1867 | 60 | ........................... | proof |

### MISCELLANEOUS.

| | | | | |
|---|---|---|---|---|
| 76 | 1837 | 20 | Feutchwanger cent. | uncirculated |
| 77 | 1697 | 1 00 | Wm. III ½ crown ........ | good |
| 78 | 1834 | 90 | 8 Reals Mexican dollar...... | fine |
| 79 | 1843 | 1 25 | " Bolivia...... | uncirculated |
| 80 | 1835 | 1 25 | " Peru ......... | uncirculated |

**Wanted!** Descriptions of medals and tokens relating to Pittsburgh and Allegheny, Pa. If for sale, please state condition and price.

**GEO. W. RODE,**

*38 Hazelwood Ave.*

PITTSBURGH, - - PENN.

---

## C. H. BOARDMAN,

**BOX 223.**

**EAST HADDAM, CONN.**

U. S. Duplicate Coins for sale or exchange.

---

## AMERICAN CoINS

FRACTIONAL CURRENCY, ETC.,

**BOUGHT AND SOLD.**

Catalogue giving dates and premiums paid, 10c. Patronage solicited.

BOSTON COIN COMPANY.

26 Arnold Street, - - Boston, Mass.

---

## ISABELLA QUARTERS!

A few for sale at **$2** each, fine condition

Send me your want list in Canadian coins, medals and tokens. Wish to buy old stamps, in collections, parcels and duplicates and also Columbians, in any quantity. Write me.

W. KELSEY HALL, Vice pres. C. P. A., Peterborough, Ont.

---

## Geo. J. Bauer

Collector of and dealer in

U. S. AND FOREIGN

**COINS!**

Correspondence desired

P. O. BOX 302. , ROCHESTER, N. Y.

---

## CHARLES STEIGERWALT.

130 E. KING ST., LANASTER, PA

Dealer in

**Coins, Medals, Paper Money,**

Etc. Largest stock in U. S.—from $15,000 to $20,000 in value, always on hand. A stamp department has lately been added. Address all letters relating to stamps to Wm. R. Welchans, 404 N. Duke St., Lancaster, Pa.

---

## ED FROSSARD,

108 E. 14th St.,

New York City.

NUMISMATIST AND ARCHAEOLOGIST.

Collections of Coins, Medals, Antiquities, etc., Bought.

---

## LUTHER B. TUTHILL,

SOUTH CREEK, BEAUFORT CO., N. C.

Dealer in

CONFEDERATE TREASURY NOTES,

U. S. FRACTIONAL CURRENCY,

AND ALL ANTIQUATED PAPER MONEY. PRICELISTS SENT TO EVERYONE FREE

Lyman Haynes Low.

# The Numismatist.

VOL. VII. MONROE, MICH., DECEMBER, 1894. NO. 12.

## THE CENTENNIAL OF UNITED STATES COINAGE.

*In two parts. Part one.*

[GEORGE F. HEATH, M. D.]

Up to the close of, and for some years after, the American Revolution an endless variety of metallic money, good, bad and indifferent found ready circulation in this country. Foreign and American speculators found this the convenient dumping ground for much of their refuse copper and surplus silver, and short as it was in weight and base as some of it was in metal, by placing on the coin some of our national emblems, effigies or patriotic inscriptions and thus appealing to the patriotism of the people, the metal was taken in preference to the paper currency of the time so much depreciated in value.

This mixed state of monetary affairs early received the attention of Congress, and even before the treaty of peace was signed, steps had been taken for a national and uniform coinage. Several plans were proposed and discussed in the years following 1782, but it was not until the fifteenth of April, 1790, that Congress instructed Alexander Hamilton, then secretary of the Treasury to prepare plans for the establishment of a mint. His report was passed by both houses of Congress on the third day of March, 1791, and on April 2d, 1792 the law "establishing a mint and regulating the coins of the United States" was approved by Washington then president.

Previous to this, in 1787, the adoption of the Constitution had legislated out of existence all local issues and vested the sole right of coinage in the general government.

To make provision for the deficiency arising from the withdrawal from issue and circulation of this currency, the report of the Secretary of the Treasury provided for the striking of the following coins in the metals as stated:

Gold: Eagles of ten dollars and Half Eagles.

Silver: Dollars, Half Dollars, Quarter Dollars, Dimes, and Half Dimes.

Copper: Cent, or one hundredth of a dollar, and Half Cent.

The silver unit or Dollar was the first silver coin struck under authority by this government; the first deposit of silver bullion being made on July 18th, 1794 for the purposes of coinage by the Bank of Maryland. It was in the coins of France and amounted to $80,715.73½. The first return of silver dollars to the Treasury was made on Oct. 15, 1794, and comprised 1758 pieces: all that were struck that year.

Obv.—Head of Liberty facing right, hair flowing, fifteen stars, seven facing. Above the bust LIBERTY; beneath at the base, 1794.

Rev.—An eagle with upraised wings, crossed branches of laurel surrounding. Around the whole this inscription, UNITED STATES OF AMERICA. On the edge HUNDRED CENTS, ONE DOLLAR OR UNIT. Weight 416 grains; fineness 892.4.

Half Dollar. Same type and design as the dollar. The first delivery of half dollars was made to the Treasury on the first day of December, 1794, and consisted of 5,300 pieces. This was all that were coined in 1794. Same fineness and half the weight of the dollars. On the edge: FIFTY CENTS OR HALF A DOLLAR. Size 21.

Half Dime. Same type and design as the Dollar and Half Dollar but with fourteen stars, in place of fifteen in the higher values. Snowden in his Description of Ancient and Modern Coins in the United States Mint states; that this issue for 1794 were pattern pieces for the purpose of trying the dies and not regularly issued. Be this as it may very few were struck, and in good condition command a high premium with numismatists. They weigh 20.8 grains and in size 10.

Cent. This denomination was authorized to be coined in April 22, 1792, and was first struck in 1793: 112, 212 being issued. Of this date there were several distinct types and many die varieties The cent of 1794 was patterned after the last variety of the previous year and in general may be described as follows:

Obv.—Bust of Liberty facing right with liberty cap and pole. Above LIBERTY: beneath the bust the date 1794.

Rev.—ONE CENT within laurel wreath: UNITED STATES OF AMERICA surrounding the whole. On base at border $\frac{1}{100}$; on edge ONE HUNDRED FOR A DOLLAR. No coined 918,521: weight 208 grains.

Many dies were used for this date. Dr. Maris who first classified this issue found no less than forty-four varieties which he named as follows:

1 1793 Head.
2 Double chin.
3 Sans Milling.
4 Tilted 4.
5 Young head.
6 The Coquette.
7 Crooked 7.
8 "
9 "
10 Pyramidal head.
11 Many haired.
12 Scared Head.
13 Standless 4.
14 Abrupt hair.
15 Separated date.
16 " "
17 The Ornate.
18-19 Venus Marina.
20 Fallen 4.
21-22 Short bust.
23-24-25 Patagonian.
26-27 Amiable face.
28 Large planchette.
29-30 Marred field.
31 Distant 1.
32-33 Shielded hair.
34-35-36-37 The Plica.
38 Roman piece.
39 Head of 1795.
40 Variety of 11.
41 Egeria.
42 Trephined hair.
43 Crowned date.
44 Diana.

Several more varieties have been discovered since Dr. Maris' work was given to the press and have been incorporated in a monograph on "Varieties of the United States Cents of 1794", by Messrs. Frossard and Hays. This work issued in 1893 illustrates and describes fifty-six varieties, and yet makes no claims to being complete. Owing to the prominent edge given this issue, the body of the coin has been quite well protected, and many cents of this date are found in good condition, the price at which they can be purchased is very reasonable.

Half Cent. Like the cents this coin was first struck in 1793. The design is the same as that of the cent and six die varieties are mentioned. On the base of the reverse is the fraction $\frac{1}{200}$ and on the edge TWO HUNDRED FOR A DOLLAR. Weight 104 grains. Number struck 81,900. Like the cent they are often found in good condition and can be bought for $1.50.

## THE COINS OF VENICE. 1400-1600.

*A paper read at the Fourth Annual Convention of the American Numismatic Association at Detroit, Aug. 23-24, 1894.*

[CONTINUED FROM PAGE 248.]

[PHILIP WHITEWAY, F. I. INST., ETC.]

### Pietro Mocenigo, 1474-76.

*GOLD.*

SEQUIN. $R_3$.

*SILVER.*

LIRA. $R^2$. *Obv.*—PE - MOCENIGO - S - MARCVS - V. The Doge kneeling to the left. receiving the standard of St. Mark; along the spear DVX.

*Rev.*—GLORIA - TIBI - SOLI. The Saviour standing, holding a globe in his left hand. m. m. 39.

MARCELLO. R. *Obv.*—Similar to the one of Nicolo Marcello.

*Rev.*—GLORIA - TIBI - SOLI; at the side of the Redeemer, IC-XC.

### Andrea Vendramin, 1476-78.

*GOLD.*

GOLD. $R^2$.

*SILVER.*

MARCELLO. R.

*COPPER.*

¼ BAGATTINO. $R_3$. Similar to that of Moro, with the initials A-V-D-V.

### Giovanni Mocenigo, 1478-85.

*GOLD.*

SEQUIN. $R_2$.

*SILVER.*

MARCELLO. C.
MOCENIGO. R4. (Ven.)
SOLDINO. R2. Similar to that of Andrea Contárini.

*BILLON.*

QUATTRINO. C. *Obv.*—IOANES - MOCENIGO - DVX. The Doge kneeling, the standard of St. Mark in his hand.
*Rev.*—A lion standing. m. m. 18.

*COPPER.*

BAGATTINO. U. (Milan). With the bust of St. Mark.
½ BAGATTINO. U. (Ven). Similar to that of Moro, with the initials I-O-M-O.

### Marco Barbarigo, 1485-86. (Reigned 8 months 26 days.)

*GLOD.*

SEQUIN. R4. (Ven.)

*SILVER.*

MARCELLO. R3. *Obv.*—M - BARBARICO - —MA - —MARC.

### Agostino Barbarigo, 1486-1501.

*GOLD.*

SEQUIN. R.
MARCELLO. R.
MOCENIGO. C.
SOLDO. R4. (Ven). *Obv.*—AVG · BARBADICO - DVX. A cross.
*Rev.*—SANCTVS - MARCVS - V. A lion standing. Base silver. m. m. 14.
DO.—*Obv.*—AVG - BARBADICO - DVX. A floreated cross.
*Rev.*—SANCTVS - MARCVS - VENETI. A lion standing, facing to the left holding a standard in its paws. m. m. 18.
DO.—*Obv.*—AVGV - BARB - DICO - DVX. The Doge kneeling, looking to the left with the standard of St. Mark in his hand. At the sides: N—R.
*Rev.*—AVG - BARBADICO - DVX. A cross patent. m. m. 18.
BEZZO. R3. A new coin first struck in this reign.
*Obv.*—AVG - BARB - DVX. The doge holding a standard.
*Rev.*—S - M - VE—NETI. A half figure of St. Mark. m. m. 13.
SOLDINO. C. *Obv.*—AV - BAR - DVX - S - M - V. The doge kneeling, receiving the standard of St. Mark, looking to the left.
*Rev.*—LAVS - TIBI - SOLI. The Redeemer, a globe surmounted by a cross, in his hand. m. m. 13.
DO. C. *Obv.*—AVG - BARBADIC - D. A cross of lilies.
*Rev.*—S - MARCVS - VENETI. A lion in a small circle. m. m. 11.
DO. U. *Obv.*—AVG - BAR - DVX - S - M - V. St: Mark seated, consigning the standard to the kneeling doge.
*Rev.*—RESVRESIT. The Redeemer in the act of leaving the sepulchur. m. m. 13.
DO. Resembling that of Andrea Contarini.
½ SOLDO. *Obv.*—AVG - BARBADICO - DVX. A cross joined in the centre, but no outer circle.

*Rev.*—S - M - VENETI. A lion within a circle. m. m. 11.

*BILLON.*

QUATTRINO. *Obv.*—AVG - BARBADIC - DVX. A cross.

*Rev.*—S - MARCVS - VENETI. A lion. m. m. 16.

*COPPER.*

BAGATTINO. U. *Obv.*—The bust of St. Mark.

½ BAGATTINO. Similar to that of MORO, with the initials A—V—B—D.

## Leonardo Loredano, 1501-21.

*GOLD.*

SEQUIN. R².

½ SEQUIN. R⁴. (Ven). This coin was first struck in this reign.

*Obv.*—The same as that of the ordinary sequins.

*Rev.*—EGO - SVM - LVX - MVNDI. m. m. 19.

*SILVER.*

MARCELLO. C.

MOCENIGO. C.

OF 32. U. *Obv.*—LEON - LAVREDANO - S - M - VENET. A seated figure of St. Mark presenting the standard to the kneeling doge. Down the spear: DVX.

*Rev.*—GLORIA - IN - EXCELSIS - DEO. m. m. 32.

OF 16. R¹. LEONAR - LAVRED - DVX - S - M - VENETI. The Doge kneeling to left receiving the standard from St. Mark seated opposite.

*Rev.*—GLORIA - TIBI - SOLI. The Redeemer holding a globe surmounted by a crucifix. m. m. 30.

OF 8. R. *Obv.*—LEO - LAVREDANVS - S - M - VENETI. The doge kneeling in front of St. Mark, who presents him with the standard, down the flag staff: DVX.

*Rev.*—GLORIA - TIBI - SOLI. The Redeemer holding a globe. m. m. 24.

OF 4. R¹. *Obv.*—L - LAVRED - S - M - VENETI. The doge kneeling, receives the standard of the Republic, from a seated figure of St. Mark. In a vertical column: DVX.

*Rev.*—GLORIA - TIBI - SOLI. A half figure of the Redeemer, in the act of benediction at the side IX—XC. m. m. 21.

OF 4. R². *Rev.*—As above, and below the figure of the Redeemer three stars. The monogram is omitted. The above four new types of coins were struck in order to provide for a growing want of small change: but their similarity proved somewhat confusing. They were pieces of 32, 16, 8, and 4 soldi.

SOLDINO. Very common, worth about a penny.

SOLDO. R³. (Ven).

" R³. (Ven). *Obv.*—LEONAR - LAVREDA. The Doge holding the standard facing to the left: at his back disposed vertically: A - B - (Antonio Bembo, master of the mint 1526).

*Rev.*—S - MARCVS - VENETI. A lion with a square of dots. m. m. 15.

BEZZO. R³.

" R³. (Ven). *bv.*—LE - LAV - DVX. The doge kneeling to the

left, before a standing figure of the Virgin, with the infant Saviour in her arms.

*Rev.*—A lion standing in the exergue M - K -. m. m. 12.

*COPPER.*

QUATTRINO. R3. *Obv.*—L - LAVREDANO DVCE. The doge holding the standard kneeling, facing the left within a circle of dots.

*Rev.*—S - MARCVS. A lion within two circles one simple and one of dots. m. m. 13.

BAGATTINO, R2. With bust of St. Mark.

½ " R3. *Obv.*—L - L - DV— or L - DVX.

## Antonio Grimani, 1521-3.

*GOLD.*

SEQUIN. R1. (Ven.)

½ " , R4. (Ven.)

*SILVER.*

OF 16. R.

OF 8. R2.

OF 4. R3.

*COPPER.*

BAGATTINO. R4. With the head of St. Mark.

[TO BE CONTINUED.]

---

The feat of counting 2,000 silver dollars per minute is now being performed at the mint by a little machine invented by Sebastian Heines, the chief carpenter of the institution, and by its aid the work of counting the coin and weighing the silver bars can, it is thought, be completed soon. The slow process made in counting by hand led Mr. Heines to experiment, with the result, after the expenditure of much thought and time, of turning out a very successful machine. Mr. Morgan, of Mint Director Preston's office, was greatly interested in the experiments, and, upon witnessing the final successful test of the invention, he granted permission for its use in counting the great mass of silver dollars. The machine when worked to its limit easily disposes of two bags of coins, containing $2,000, in a minute. The machine consists of a hopper, into which the coins are dropped. A cogwheel, the teeth of which resemble those of a circular saw, carries the coins to the tubes, and from there they are forced out upon a little table, containing twenty grooves, each holding just fifty coins. A turn of the crank counts one thousand coins, which are immediately put into a bag, and a second thousand follows before the expiration of the minute.—Philadelphia Record.

# CUTCH COINAGE.

*A Paper read at the Fourth Annual Convention of the American Numismatic Association, at Detroit, Mich., Aug. 23-24, 1894.*

[MAJOR ADAM SMITH.]

Cutch (Kachh) is a Province in western India almost entirely cut off from the continent of India, on the north and east by the Runn of Cutch, on the south by the Gulf of Cutch, and on the west by the Arabian Sea and the eastern or Kori mouth of the Indus. The country is a belt of land about 160 miles from east to west, and from 35 to 70 miles from north to south, while at its narrowest it is only about 15 miles across. It is situated from 20° 47′ to 24° north latitude and 68° 26′ to 71° 10′ east longitude. From its isolated position the special characters of its people, their peculiar dialet, and their strong feeling of attachment and personal loyalty to their Ruler, whose title is the "Rao", and of attachment for their country, the province of Cutch has more of the elements of a distinct nationality than any other of the dependencies of the Bombay government. The population of the province is according to the last census taken in February, 1891:

| | |
|---|---|
| Males | 276,899. |
| Females | 278,916. |
| Total | 555,815. |

This small State has a coinage of its own and also a mint at which gold, silver and copper coins are turned out, silver and copper being met with in general circulation. The unit of Cutch currency is the silver "Kori", value about four annas. The following are the coins minted:

| GOLD COINS. | VALUE. |
|---|---|
| Raosai Mohur | 100 Silver Koris |
| Half Mohur | 50 " " |
| Golden Kori | 26¼ " " |
| **SILVER COINS.** | |
| Panchia | 5 " " |
| Ardh-Panchia | 2½ " " |
| Kori | ¼ Indian rupee |
| Half-Kori | 2 annas. |
| **COPPER COINS.** | |
| Dhabu | 1-8th Kori. |
| Dhingla | 1-16th " |
| Dokeda | 1-24th " |
| Trambhia | 1-48th " |

In the early days of the British connection with Cutch the rate of exchange of the Kori was fixed at 379 Koris, equal to 100 Imperial rupees, and at this rate the State subsidy was paid. Since 1887 the rate of exchange has touched 400 Koris, varying about 398 to 401 according to the time of the year and state of the markets. The loss sustained by exchange called for an assay of the

Cutch currency, which was carried out at the Bombay mint in the early part of 1889. The Mint Master, in his letter No. $\frac{B}{10067}$ of the 29th of June, 1889 to the Secretary to the Government of Bombay in the Political department, reported as follows:

"The coins consist of Koris and Panchias, the latter being nominally worth 5 Koris. Of Koris there are four kinds, and of Panchias two. The average result of their intrinsic value was:—

| Description of Coins. | Number tested. | Averag wt. in grains. | Average wt. in grains | | Value pr 100 in rupees | Value in Koris per 100 rupees Brit. currency. |
|---|---|---|---|---|---|---|
| | | | Silver | Copper | | |
| Bharasai Koris......... | 100 | 70.53 | 42.36 | 28.17 | 25.67 | 389.51 |
| Desalsai Koris......... | 100 | 71.58 | 43.29 | 28.29 | 26.24 | 381.15 |
| Pragsai Koris.......... | 100 | 71.83 | 43.32 | 28.51 | 26.25 | 380.88 |
| Khengarsai Koris...... | 100 | 72.21 | 44.22 | 27.99 | 26.80 | 373.13 |
| Pragsai Panchia....... | 10 | 214.56 | 203.01 | 11.55 | 123.03 | 81.27 |
| Khengarsai Panchai... | 10 | 214.74 | 203.28 | 11.46 | 123.20 | 81.16 |

In weight the coins were found fairly regular, but in bnsiness they varied a good deal owing to inferior manufacture. Assayist considered it questionable whether enough coin had been tested to obtain a trustworthy value.

The Accountant General, Bombay, in a report to the Political Agent of Cutch, stated, that after examining 15,000 Koris and 3,000 Panchias, taken from the Treasury at random, he found the following varieties of coins:

2,080, Bharasai Koris.
9,265, Desalsai Koris.
3,462, Pragsai Koris.
193, Khengarsai Koris.
88, Pragsai Panchias.
2,912, Khengarsai Panchias.

Up to the death of Rao Desalji II in 1860 these coins had on one side the name of the Emperor of Delhi in Persian, and on the other side the name of the Rao in Devnajare characters. Since that year the name of the Queen Empress Victoria has been substituted for that of the Delhi Emperor. In appearance the coinage is of a very rough and irregular manufacture, more especially in the case of copper coinage, but the later issues of Panchias are much more uniform.

The subsidy to the British Imperial Government is now paid at the rate of exchange of 400 silver Koris per 100 British Indian rupees.

Up to 1889 the British garrison in Cutch was paid in Koris at the rate of 379 Koris per 100 British Indian rupees. Imperial coinage being only issued to the amount certified as required for post office money orders, but since that date the British troops quartered at Bhuj, the capital of Cutch, have been paid in Imperial currency.

POONA, INDIA.

## A MISINTERPRETATION.

I have a friend who likes a joke
And knows my taste for copper coin.
One day we met and, with a poke,
He said "Come, Harry, wont you join

A fellow at his lunch today?
I go where little need be spent,
And, if you'll meet me, I'll repay
You with a fine light olive cent."

Although the weather was too hot
To warrant one an appetite,
The promise drew me to the spot
Where sat my friend with visage bright.

A plump mulatto maiden brought
The food in such perspiring haste
That, as she hovered 'round, I thought
Her odor rather spoiled its taste.

And, pushing by my plate, I said
"Come now, my boy, I want to see
That fine light olive coin instead
Which you this morning promised me."

As Susan to the kitchen went,
The scamp replied "Coin? not a bit,
I promised a light olive *scent*
And there goes all you'll have of it."

—[A. G. HEATON.

# HOOPER'S RESTRIKES.

[JOSEPH HOOPER]

The Bank of England was 200 years old last July.

In all the World there is in coin $3,582,605,000 of gold; and $4,042,700,000 of silver.

Nearly a million and a half dollars remain unclaimed in the New York savings banks.

The highest price paid for a single coin was of the reign of Charles II, England, being $2,500.

Some Chinese and many Africans use the ear as a pocket to carry coins and other small articles.

The largest collection of coins, 125,000 in number, is in the cabinet of antiquities, Vienna. 50,000 are Greek and Roman.

The Society for the Abolition of the Slave Trade, have the following device for their seal—a negro naked, bound with fetters and kneeling in a supplicating posture—the motto. "Am I not a man, and a Brother."—London Chronicle March, 1788.

It is worth noting that the Bank of England has fewer notes in circulation than it had fifteen years ago and the total active note circulation of England is hardly greater than when the act of 1844 was passed. Bank notes are much less used in business than formerly, other means of exchange having taken their place.

The Philadelphia mint is about to issue a new index of collection; the following rarities will be disclosed: Gold half-sovereign, England, struck during the reign of Henry VIII, very rare; Gold half-sovereign, England, reign of Edward VI, still rarer. John Brown bronze medal, very rare, struck in facsimile of Gold medal made in Paris commemorative of his death and presented to his widow: medal of Cortez.

A Vase of Gold.—Athenaeum: The department of Greek and Roman antiquities, British museum, has quite recently secured by purchase one of the choicest examples of ancient art in solid gold which even that great collection possesses. It is a vase of this metal in its purest condition, without sculptures, measuring nearly eight inches in height, about four inches in diameter, and in shape most like a police when deprived of its handles. It is of Roman origin, perhaps of the period of Augustus. An inscription on the bottom of the vessel indicates that its weight nearly corresponds to two pounds troy of the modern scale. It was lately found by a sponge diver in the sea off the Island of Samos, and may be all that remains of a wreck which occurred nearly 2,000 years ago.

The oldest known coin comes from China. It is brass or copper, is a block nearly cubical, and weighs about a pound.

The sweepings of the Denver mint, which have been accumulating for years, were washed recently and yielded $3,000 worth of gold.

A NAIL MARK ON COINS.—A curious feature of Chinese coins, the nail-mark, appears to have originated in an accident very characteristic of China. In the time of Queen Wentek a model in wax of a proposed coin was brought for her Majesty's inspection. In taking hold of it she left on it the impression of one nail, and the impression has in consequence been a marked characteristic of Chinese coins for hundreds of years.

The inscription on a guinea is too well known to need more than an allusion, and is probably the best illustration of the modern style of abbreviation as applied to coins. A less familiar but not less striking illustration is the inscription on the famous medal issued by Queen Elizabeth to commemorate the dispersion of the Spanish Armada. Amplified to its proper dimensions this reads, "Afflvat Deus et dissipantur:" "The breath of God has issued and they are dispersed."

LARGE CHECKS.—Concerning large checks London Tid-Bits says: "The Great Indian Peninsular Railway Company, it is reported, recently drew a check on the London and County Back for £1,250,000. This might well be thought the largest ever drawn, but such is said not to be the case, as at the Clearing house checks for equal, if not larger sums are occasionally seen. In 1879 a check for over £3,000,000 was paid through the Clearing House. It was drawn on Messrs. Glyn & Co., and was paid to the Bank of England."

The first American cent was "struck off" and put in circulation just 101 years ago, in 1793. Previous to that date several "pattern pieces" had been made, but they were experiments only and were never put in circulation. The so-called "Washington cents," which existed previous to the date above given, were not issued by the government and were, therefore, only medals. The cent of 1793 was very similar to the large copper cents of later date, with the exception that the face of "Liberty" was turned to the right, and the legend, "One Cent" was inclosed in a chain of 13 links.

GOLD PRODUCTION LARGE. The output of gold in 1894, in a revised estimate of the Director of the Mint, is put at $174,000,000, or nearly $20,000,000 more than in 1893. Of this increase the United States supplies $7,000,000, Australia $2,000,000, and South Africa $10,000,000. The gold product of 1894 will exceed in value the combined output of silver and gold in the years from 1861 to 1865. From 1865 to 1873 the average value of both the silver and gold produced annually was about $190,000,000, which will probably be equaled by the gold production of 1895. These figures indicate that there is no likelihood of a gold famine. Prices of commodities are fixed by the law of supply and demand, but even if they were low on account of an inadequate supply of gold they should now go up. The banks are abundantly supplied with gold in Europe and in this country and the supply is being rapidly increased.

British Systems of Currency.—Within the British Empire the following systems of currency are now in use; (1) The British gold standard (£ s d) in the British Island, the Australian Colonies, New Zealand, South Africa, and a number of small scattered colonies. (2) Foreign gold standards: Canada and many West India Islands using the United States gold dollar; Gibraltar, Spanish gold and silver; Cyprus, French and Turkish gold and silver; and Newfound land a gold standard of its own, the double dollar. (3) Modifications of the silver dollar, the Mexican dollar being current in Hongkong and the Straits Settlements, the Guatemalan dollar in Honduras, and French silver on the west coast of Africa. (4) The rupee in India, Ceylon and Mauritius. It is proposed in the Asiatic Quarterly to do away with this confusion by adopting as common unit for all these currencies the British silver double florin, which is very nearly the equivalent of the silver dollar of the United States and of Central and South America, of the French five-franc piece, of two rupees, and of half the Newfoundland double dollar, and to adopt the familiar term dollar as the name of the coin instead of florin.

## WITH THE DEALERS.

The American Stamp and Coin Company is a new coin dealing organization located in Philadelphia, Pa., in a store on Chestnut St. It has a moderate stock thus far but is fortified by certain prominent local collectors, apparently, who find an open market in the Quaker city desirable.

From the Messrs. L. & L. Hamburger, Frankfort on the Main, Germany, we have received an extensive catalogue of ancient mediæval and modern coins which they will sell on January 7th and the following days. The catalogue is particularly rich in mediæval and modern German coins and medals. 4013 lots with plate.

S. H. & H. Chapman sold on Dec. 3 and 4 the gold, silver and copper coins of the United States belonging to Mr. W. H. Spedding, of St. Louis, Mo. The collection contained many of the rarer colonial, including Somers Island Shilling, and Carolina half-penny (elephant) and an unusually fine and complete line of U. S. coins and medals. 1316 lots.

The United States Coin and Stamp Exchange, 1130 Masonic Temple, Chicago, have issued a Manual and Premium Coin Catalogue of about forty pages. It contains prices they will pay for American and foreign gold, silver, and copper coins, fractional currency, old bank bills, etc., besides much general information for collectors of coin. The price is twenty-five cents and may be obtained at above address.

The following prices were realized at Frossard's 129th sale of Nov. 16, 1894:

| | | |
|---|---|---|
| 97 | U. S. Dollar 1799, six stars facing, uncirculated | $ 4 25 |
| 107 | " 1853, bold impression, extremely fine | 3 50 |
| 108 | " 1854, sharp, uncirculated | 15 25 |
| 109 | " 1855, mint luster, uncirculated | 12 00 |
| 110 | " 1856, two fine scratches in field, very fine | 3 50 |
| 121 | Half Dollar, 1795, almost uncirculated, two cuts on shoulder | 5 10 |
| 122 | " 1802, small almost invisible defect in field, sharp, very fine | 15 00 |
| 125 | " 1815, beautiful impression, extra fine | 8 60 |
| 137 | " 1836, reeded edge, extra fine | 3 50 |
| 141 | " 1856, S. very fine | 6 10 |
| 144 | " 1861, S. uncirculated | 2 95 |
| 152 | Quarter Dol. 1820, sharp, almost equal to proof | 8 60 |
| 153 | " 1821, extremely fine | 2 60 |
| 154 | " 1825, sharp, uncirculated | 2 85 |
| 176 | Dime 1814, large date, fine | 1 45 |
| 177 | " 1821, " " sharp, uncirculated, | 1 35 |
| 178 | " 1821, small date, nearly as good as 177 | 2 50 |
| 179 | " 1824 over '22, sharp, uncirculated, dull mint lustre | 20 25 |
| 180 | " 1828, small date, sharp, extra fine | 2 05 |
| 224 | Massachusetts shilling, 1652, small tree, fine, evenly centered | 8 40 |
| 231 | U. S. A. "Bar Cent," uncirculated, original, | 8 40 |
| 250 | Columbian Half Dollar, 1893, uncirculated | 75 |
| 254 | " Quarter " 1893, " | 1 30 |
| 280 | Cent 1809, dark, good | 2 00 |
| 302 | " 1856, nickel, uncirculated | 4 50 |
| 303 | " " " " | 4 00 |
| 307 | Half Cent. 1793, good | 2 10 |
| 366 | Annam, circular dollar, fiery dragon, extra fine | 4 00 |
| 437 | England. Eadgar (958-75) silver penny, small cross in circular, EADGAR REX; Rev: IVE ON RN, very fine, | 2 85 |
| 439 | " Edward III.(1327-77)gold half rose noble, king in ship; Rev: cross in arched circle, crowned leopards in angles, fine | 8 10 |
| 440 | " Henry VII, gold angel, St. George and dragon cross over shield on ship. H to left; v fine | 10 00 |
| 441 | " Same as 440 but different punctuation. v fine, | 11 00 |
| 442 | " Elizabeth, sovereign, queen crowned seated holding a scepter and globe, ELIZABETH D : G : ANG : FRA : ET ; HIB : REGINA: v. fine | 32 00 |
| 444 | " Charles II, 1673.5 Guineas, bust laureate in flowing hair; Rev: four crowned shields, equal to proof | 52 50 |
| 446 | " George III. Guinea, 1782, uncirculated | 7 00 |
| 447 | " " " spade Guinea, 1790, uncirculated | 7 25 |
| 453 | California, 1852, octagonal $50, fine | 86 50 |
| 465 | Judæa Maccabaeus, shekel usual type year 2, fine | 23 50 |
| 466 | " " half shekel " " " 2, " | 21 50 |

## THE AMERICAN NUMISMATIC ASSOCIATION.

BOARD OF OFFICERS:

President: A. G. Heaton, 1618 17th St., Washington, D. C.
Vice President: Joseph Hooper, Port Hope, Ont.
Secretary: O. W. Page, Box 296, Waltham, Mass.
Treasurer: Dr. A. L. Fisher, Elkhart, Ind.
Librarian and Curator. W. C. Stone, 384 Union St., Springfield, Mass.
Superintendent of Exchange: W. J. Luck, Adrian, Mich,
Counterfeit Detector: S. H. Chapman, 1348 Pine St., Philadelphia, Pa.
Board of Trustees: J. A. Heckelman, Columbus, Va: David Harlowe, 3002 Mt. Vernon Ave., Milwaukee, Wis C. W. Stutesman, Peru, Ind; Geo. W. Rice, 186 E. High St., Detroit, Mich.: Hiram E. Deats, Flemington, N. J.

### Secretary's Report.

TO THE PRESIDENT AND MEMBERS OF THE AMERICAN NUMISMATIC ASS'N.

GENTLEMEN:

The report of my office for the month of November is as follows:

Total cash receipts, dues and fees....................$11.00
Cash turned over to treasurer,........................ 15.50
Cash now in my hands.............................. 16.00
Expense of office (postage)........................................$ .52.

### New Members.

233 E. B. Stevens, Parsons, Kan.

### Applications for Membership.

Dr Edwin P. Robinson, 102 Flower St., Newport, R. I.
Vouchers: Messrs. Sisson and Storer.

R. W. Geary, Pinkerton, Ontario.
Vouchers: Messrs. Bateman and Ineson.

Charles B. Brodrick, Elkhart, Ind.
Vouchers: Messrs. Kavanagh and Fisher.

WALTHAM, MASS., Dec. 1, 1894. O. W. PAGE, Secy.

## DETROIT NUMISMATIC CLUB.

Notwithstanding the inclement weather there was a good attendance at the regular monthly meeting of the Detroit Numismatic Club at the office of Dr. Joseph Lathrop, Wednesday, Nov. 7th.

The proceedings were as usual, for the most part informal. The coins shown and compared were mostly United States. A dozen or more Copper Cents of 1851 over 1881 were shown and resulted in finding two varieties; they all, with one exception show what appears to be the left curve of the lower half of a figure 8, between the 8 and 5, and in addition show a slight defect in the die producing a small spur from the right side of the last 1, about two thirds down from the top. A single specimen belonging to Dr. Lathrop clearly shows the 5 cut exactly over another figure, the upright being connected with knob of lower part.

Mr. Rice exhibited half dollars of 1838-40 to show that the half dollar of 1840 catalogued with large letters on reverse really had the reverse used on the 1838 and 39 with head of Liberty. In 1839 with the adoption of the Liberty seated obverse for half dollar appeared a new reverse with smaller letters and a different eagle, in fact every detail differing, but both these reverses were used on the Philadelphia Coinage of 1840.

The quarter dollar with Liberty seated which appeared in 1838 had on the reverse the eagle used on the half dollar of 1838-39-40 only, and this eagle was continued on the quarter dollar coinage to 1891 but the dollar which appeared in 1840 had the eagle found for the first time on the 1839 Liberty seated half-dollar and this eagle continued on the dollars till their coinage was discontinued in 1873.

Mr. Rice read a paper on The Errors and Discrepancies in the U. S. mint records, written with the view of giving a possible explanation for the same. The paper was thought by the Club to be of sufficient interest to offer to THE NUMISMATIST.

DETROIT, Nov. 7, 1894. GEO. W. RICE, Sec'y.

## AMERICAN NUMISMATIC AND ARCHÆOLOGICAL SOCIETY

**17 West 43d. St., New York, N. Y.**

Regular meeting held Nov. 19, 1894; President Andrew L. Zabriskie presiding. The Executive Committee reported that the proposition for resident membership of Daniel R. Kennedy and Victor David Brenner, also for corresponding membership of Charles H Huberich, of San Antonio, Texas, have been received and approved. Attention was called to the decease of Permanent Corresponding members Matthew Adam Stickney and William Fewsmith. The resignation of William Austin was received and accepted.

The Librarian reported donations since the last meeting of 116 bound volumes, 333 pamphlets, 151 periodicals and 746 catalogues; a total of 1,346. Special mention was made to the gifts of 71 bound volumes from Daniel Parrish jr.

L.

and five handsome volumes from Samuel P. Avery. Attention was called to a large and handsome oak pamphlet case containing 85 drawers presented by Daniel Parrish jr., Andrew C. Zabriskie, John M. Dodd, jr.; Wm. R. Weeks, John A. Hadden, Charles H, Wright, Charles Pryer, Herbert Valentine, H. Russell Drowne and Bauman L. Belden.

The Curator reported donations of 226 coins, medals, etc., and called particular attention to 16 beautiful medals of Pope Leo XIII presented by the most Reverend Archbishop Corrigan, also to two unpublished tokens, not mentioned in Boyne's work on the 17th Century Tokens, from William Fenwick. On motion a special vote of thanks was tendered to these two donors. Through the kindness of Samuel P. Avery, there was exhibited a large case of beautiful medallions by the celebrated sculptor M. Roby of Paris, containing many examples of exquisite workmanship. A special vote of thanks was tendered Mr. Avery for the loan and the request made that the case remain on exhibition as long as practicable.

An interesting letter was read from corresponding member George McArthur, of Malden Victoria, giving an account of the early mining and electoral rights of Australia, which was accompanied by a number of early original documents. On motion, the thanks of the Society was extended to Mr. McArthur for the donation, as well as for the kindly expressions of good will.

On motion adjourned. H. Russell Drowne, Secy.

## What Dollar Bills Weigh.

Several customers were chatting in a Lafayette avenue grocery store one evening recently when the grocer pointed to a half barrel of small beans and asked how many of them it would require to make a bushel.

Various estimates were offered. One man recklessly put the number down at 50,000, which occasioned a laugh from all the others who had guessed a much lesser quantity, ranging all the way from 5,000 to 20,000.

"Well, gentlemen," remarked the grocer, "you are all wrong. There are approximately 119,000 beans in a bushel."

No one was inclined to believe him until he showed them that it took sixty beans, selected at random, to weigh half an ounce. The rest of the calculation was simple.

"Now, then," said one of the party, "since we are engaged in guessing contests, how many dollar bills would it take to weigh as much as a silver dollar?"

One said 100, another seventy-five, while the grocer, who knew all about beans, put the figure at 300.

"All wrong," remarked the man. "It takes just twenty-two." This was proven to be the case by experiment.

# WITH THE EDITOR.

[GEO. F. HEATH. M. D.]

AN index to Vol. VII will be presented with our January issue.

MANY subscriptions expire with this number. Please make renewal promptly so that no disappointments may follow.

QUARTER eagle pieces ($2.50) of 1845, New Orleans mint, have lately been found, although no coinage that year appears in the Mint Report.

WATCH the 1830 cent. It is much scarcer that the catalogues or the number struck would seem to indicate. In our judgment this date in good condition is the rarest between 1823 and 1857.

MR. HOOPER'S paper on The Coins of the Jews will be begun in our January issue. It will run through four issues and will be illustrated by about forty double cuts. It is a grand paper on a grand subject.

WE are informed by Mr. Proudfoot, of St. Vincent, W. I., that the *genus*, numismatist, is not indigenous to that island. That British coins mainly circulate there, the four pence being peculiar to the West Indies and British Guiana.

EX-SECRETARY TATMAN writes that he will issue in January his No. 3, American Numismatic Series, which will be his Association paper on "The Beginnings of United States Coinage." Mr. Tatman has lately been admitted to the Massachusetts bar, and we are sure that all A. N. A. members will join us in wish him not only much practice but a good deal of business.

IT is reported from Washington that Mr. J. M. Clapp of that city has by purchase from a western collector recently completed his set of three dollar pieces of all mints. And this reminds us of a piteous wail we heard among some Detroit collectors not long since when they learned that a stranger from away east had been among them and purchased from a local collector, many dates of our three dollar gold pieces, a few of them rare. These pieces would have brought higher prices at home had it been known they were for sale. Up to this time Mr. Farrington, of New York State, and Mr. Heaton had the only complete sets known.

A SUPPOSED 1838 O mint half dollar sold in the stock of a deceased French coin dealer of New Orleans, has lately been found to be an altered piece, as were many in that unreliable individual's display. It is now in a saloon keeper's possession there.

THE 1846 dime and half-dime are considered rare pieces: only 31,300 of the former and 27,000 of the latter being struck. In good condition these pieces are sold usually at from $3.50 to $5 respectively. We notice in Frossard's 130th sale over a hundred of these dimes, and eleven half dimes in good to fine condition are offered.

YE Editor at this period has no time or space to indulge in retrospective, flights or future fancies. To all he can say, that THE NUMISMATIST has never stood on firmer ground, or better fitted to battle for our science than it does today. To all who have in any way contributed to this result it is his fondest desire that the benefits he may have been able to obtain for our beloved science may in their merited measure be reflected upon you. A Merry Christmas and Happy New Year, and many of them, to you all.

WHEN we place Lyman H. Low as the best known numismatist in this country, we only utter the consensus of opinion of the guild. By those who personally are acquainted with him he is pronounced genial, cultured and affable. At the head of the numismatic branch of the Scott Stamp and Coin Co., he reigns supreme; as a numismatist in general information regards our science, he is among the leaders; as a specialist in the study of the coinage of the Spanish American peoples, he easily leads. THE NUMISMATIST takes pleasure in presenting his portrait to its enlarged circle of readers, and to those who would desire to know more of him would refer to its issue of January, 1892 for biographical sketch.

PRESIDENT HEATON writes us as follows: "The communication of Mr. Bennett in the October Numismatist (With the Editor) regarding 1880 S. mint dollars shows the opportunities bankers sometimes have for gaining desirable coins,—especially in the dollar series, as such pieces are apt to remain for years in bank or mint vaults until a chance demand brings them into circulation. But large pieces often undergo several transfers without the bags being opened, while collectors are hunting in vain for desirable specimens. Could numismatists delve into treasury and bank reserves there would at times be great discoveries, not only in mint marks but in Philadelphia coinage and prices of some dates would have the bottom knocked out. This has occurred and will again, by the grace of our banker collectors, but the under bags earliest put in vault are seldom reached and export and recoinage add to the doubt that gives coin hunting a fascinating uncertainty."

## A Confederate Dime.

A silver token, probably struck over a U. S. dime, made its appearance at the Massamore sale, New York, Oct. 25th. It was at first thought that this was like the Confederate token sold some years ago in one of Ed Frossard's sales, but investigation developed the fact that material differences exist between the two pieces; besides the latter was of the half dime or perhaps three cent size, while this is exactly of the dime size with the reeded edge. The following is a correct description of this Massamore piece: Maize and Tobacco plants, side by side, between their stems the date 1861 incuse on a small oblong tablet. Rev.—Blooming cotton plant in open wreath. So far as now believed this piece is unique; at least if other specimens exist, they have not yet crept into numismatic circles. It sold for $13.25.

---

Subscriptions for Membership Medal: (See November number.)

Silver:—Joseph Hooper, Dr. Heath, Dr. Fisher, James Kavatagh, James M. Yates.

Bronze:—Jeremiah Zimmerman. Chas. A. Lentz. H. E. Deats, Phil S. Bonney, W. H. Taylor.

Metal not named:—J. E. Morse. W. K. Hall. Geo. W. Rode.

---

Changes in address:

C. W. Stutesman. Peru, Ind.

A. E. Docherty, Box 143, Buffalo, N. Y.

Daniel L. Emery. 33 Warren St., Taunton, Mass.

---

Congressman Johnson, of North Dakota, has just fallen into a bit of good luck through one of his constituents who is a clerk in the treasury department. Some time ago a lot of pennies were presented at the treasury department for redemption. Among them was a new coin which was rejected. The treasury could not give a cent for it. A clerk in the office redeemed it and gave it to Congressman Johnson, who sent it to the Smithsonian to be identified. Today he received word from the Smithsonian that the coin is of the mintage of the year 284 A. D., and circulated in the time of the Emperor Diocletian. It is a very valuable relic, worth many times its weight in gold.—Washington Star.

# QUERIES.

**This Department is open to all the readers of The Numismatist. A *nom de plume* may be used if desired in either the asking or answering queries.**

**A saying we here commend to you**
**Ye learned. ye wise ye great ye small;**
**Far better to have aimed and missed,**
**Than never to have fired at all.**

45—I wish you would some day give us a brief explanation regarding "pattern pieces," and why the Government allows these pieces to pass out of its hands in the various metals. C. I. C.

Ans.—"Pattern pieces", to a large extent, were those for which the dies have been designed and cut by order for "a proposed coinage", as models, afterward submitted to the mint authorities for approval, and for various reasons discarded, (fault in design, etc.,) these dies are not used on coins for general circulation, but a limited number of strikes have been permitted for numismatic purposes only, by special favor, and purchase to collectors, now while this explanation holds good to a large extent. Yet we find pattern pieces which have had no rivals to fill their "wanted position", this occurs in Wm. 4th Crown of England 1831-7. ($100 was offered a friend for his proof piece of this type) in my own effort to fill this gap in my series of Crowns $75 was the best it could be done for, in fair condition only, there are two varieties of these crowns which have not gone into general circulation and are held as "pattern pieces," the Gothics: Queen Vic: smooth and lettered edge were pattern pieces in mint proof condition sold at my private sale $12 smooth edge, $8 lettered. Among the coins of the U. S. there occur a number of patterns in "the Washingtonians," Fugios, Myddleton Kentucky, Continental currency, Nova Constellatios, and others see catalogue reports Scott, Chapman, Frossard, etc., in Canada we have pattern smooth edge 20c, 10c. 5c, of 1858 then there are a variety of other nationalities: Mexico, Haiti, France, Ireland, Belgium, Russia, Siberia, Cambodia, etc., in British Columbia we have two pattern gold pieces. Obv.—Government of British Columbia (with crown in center of field). Rev.—"20" "DOLLARS" "1862" in three straight lines surrounded by wreath of lauel; the $10 gold piece has the same. Obv. and Rev. (but numerals 10) the issue of these pieces were stopped by the authorities but not before a few pieces were struck. the dies are now in the Museum at the New Westminister B. C.

JOSEPH HOOPER.

46—In your valuable paper—the November, issue—you state that coinage ceased at the Carson mint in 1893. In today's Evening Report (S. F.) I note "Bullion shipped to arson mint assay value, $41,087.75. Bullion now on hand about $28,000 sent from Con. Cal., and Va. mines. Is not the same turned afterwards into coinage at same mint? I enclose clipping from Daily Evening Report (San Francisco). E. E. GAMBS.

Bullion may be received and disposed of at any of the U. S. mints. This does not necessarily imply coinage at all. In this case certainly does not. No coins have been struck at the Carson City mint since 1893. When coinage will be resumed there is indefinite. Nevada is one of those states that seems to be "progressing backwards" and the repeal of the Sherman Bill has aided in doing the rest.

## THE WORLD OF FAD.

A collection of Australian stamps has just been bought by a London dealer for $50,000, the largest price ever paid for a stamp collection. The collection was begun in 1892, and includes stamped envelopes, postal cards and wrappers.

Many hundreds of manuscripts have been recovered at Pompeii. They were charred rolls, but by the exercise of patience and ingenuity some have been unrolled and read. Nothing of importance has been discovered in their contents.

Some curious objects have been unearthed from Etruscan tombs, the use of which for a long time was conjectural. It was at length ascertained that they must have been the heads of walking canes, probably belonging to the dudes of 2,500 years ago.

Many razors have been found in the ruins of Pompeii. They are of different shapes, some resembling knives, others being not unlike the razors of the present day. The barber shops of antiquity were also provided with bottles of perfume and boxes of pomatum.

Among the many queer fads of royalty is one possessed by both the late czar and his brother-in-law, the duke of Saxe-Coburg-Gotha—namely, a craze for collecting models of ships, especially cruisers. In the case of Duke Alfred, they are all of silver; there are some sixty or seventy of them, several being from three to four feet in length, and they form an imposing fleet in the long gallery in which they have been placed in his palace at Coburg.

Those of the late emperor of Russia, while merely of wood and brass, make up in perfection of finish and detail what they lacked in intrinsic value, and one of the last addition to the collection was a model over seven feet long of the Cunard steamer Lucania, constructed at a cost of over $8,000.

Dr. F. M. Palmer, of Los Angeles, Cal., has for fifteen years past been collecting relics of the primitive days of the southern section of Alta California, including the counties of Los Angeles, San Luis Obispo, Ventura, Santa Barbara and San Bernardino, and the channel islands of Catalina, San Clemente, San Nicolas, San Miguel, Santa Rosa and Santa Cruz. His collection now numbers several thousand objects, and is of the greatest interest.

An auction sale of Napoleonic relics in New York has developed a remarkable crop of Napoleonic cranks, and the $50,000 realized at the sale does not indicate that there is a scarcity of money in Gotham. A first empire bedstead in mahogany, on the headboard of which were two gilt bronze Egyptian heads, was sold for $480. A Louis XVI drawing-room suit brought $310, and an empire center table $185. An empire pedestal in mahogany $101. The main interest in the sale was, however, in the miniatures, and the price ranged downwards from $115, paid for a portrait of the little king of Rome, to as little as $10 for some truly ugly and inartistic specimens, which here and there mar the otherwise exceptionally fine collection. One man paid $100 for a miniature of Napoleon, signed "J." and dated 1804, and the same price was secured for "Floersea Corsy," by Fabrigni. Other miniatures that sold were: "The Duchesse de Cheremse," $85; a Mme. Recamier, $75; Mme. de Parabere, $70; "Napoleon at St. Cloud," $85; Mme. Turenne, $62.50; Mme. Louise, $60; and Henriette Bourbon-Conty, $ 2.50. The ninety-eight miniatures sold brought $5,423.

The passion of mankind for curios is almost universal and very various, says James Payn, in the Illustrated London News, and what to one man is an object of desire, for others has not the smallest attraction, they even touch their foreheads with significance when they see him poring over his "collection," and wonder that his friends permit him to be at large. It is one of those cases where the proverbial maxim of "put yourself in his place" is impossible to be employed. To one person a copy of the first edition of a book, especially if it has errors in it, is worth all the others put together, including rhe *édition de luxe*. Another gloats over a stamp from the Cannibal Islands, which is all the more valuable if it has been used. These people are not mad on other matters, and may even have great intelligence. Sir Walter Scott laid immense store upon the wine glass out of which George IV drank when he visited Edinburgh, and had it not (one is glad to read) been broken in his pocket, would have added it to his "collection" at Abbotsford. These things are a matter of taste, and can never be argued about: but people may have "a good deal of taste and all bad." This must have been the case, I think, with the purchasers of the late Mr. Deeming's personal property at Melbourne. The axe and knife with which he murdered his victim fetched £4 15s., we are told, and the spade with which he dug her grave a guinea. "His clothing was eagerly bid for, even down to half a dozen pairs of patched socks;" This is strange enough, since while he was awaiting his trial nobody would have stood in his shoes for anything.

## Valuable Bibles.

Daniel K. Cassel, the Mennonite historian, whose home is in Nicetown, is the possessor of a valuable collection of Bibles, some of which are very rare and can scarcely be duplicated. Among them is one that is said to have been printed at Basle, Switzerland, in 1778, and another in 1798, at the same place. A valuable old Bible to be found in the library is one that is known as the Martin Luther Bible. It is a copy of the fourth edition, and was printed at Wittenburg in 1682. It contains marginal explanations on the Biblical books by S. D. Hutterl, and an introduction by the Theological Faculty of Wittenburg. The first edition of this work was printed in 1546. Perhaps the rarest volume in this collection is a copy of the Polyglot Bible. It was printed at Nuremberg, Germany, in 1609, by Elias Hutterl. This Bible is peculiar in that it is printed in twelve languages, namely, Syrian, Italian, Hebrew, Spanish, Greek, French, Latin, English, German, Danish, Bohemian, and Polish. It is said there is not another Bible of this kind known to exist.

---

## Expensive Stamps.

The Philatelic world has been fluttered by a recent important event, for it is announced that the vice-president of the London Philatelic Society has sold all his stamps. The affair certainly becomes interesting when we learn the price commanded by the few thousand little bits of paper.

A firm which deals in these light and airy trifles secured the vice-president's entire collection, and gave no less than $50,000 for it.

This, we understand, is the largest price ever paid for a collection of stamps though it is said that the treasures in this sort recently bequathed by a member of parliament to the British museum would have fetched a higher figure if put up to public auction.

A London establishment is just now advertising a single stamp valued at $22,500, but whether any intending purchaser will be found willing to receive it in exchange for that sum remains to be seen. The duke of York, already known as a keen connoisseur, is said to be anxious to purchase this great stamp.

Experts declare that there is no better investment for money nowadays than stamps. If that be so they will become an object of fascination to many who at present take little delight in them — Black and White.

## Columbian Half Dollars.

Washington, December 11—Secretary Carlisle recently gave notice that the $1,785,880 in Columbian exposition silver half dollars may be had in any quantities in exchange for gold coin. The half dollars are now in the treasury at Washington and in the Chicago and Philadelphia subtreasuries.

# Exchange Department

— FOR THE —

## A. N. A.

For Rules see September or November NUMISMATIST.

ADRAN, MCH. W. J. LUCK, Ex. Supt.

### U. S. DOLLAR.

| No. | Date | Price | Description | Condition |
|---|---|---|---|---|
| 81 | 1796 | $ 3 00 | Small date | fine |
| 82 | 1798 | 2 00 | Without knob to 9. | very good |
| 83 | 1799 | 2 00 | 13 stars—6 facing | fine |
| 84 | 1802 | 5 00 | 2 over 1 | uncirculated |
| 85 | 1803 | 4 00 | Small 3 | " |
| 86 | 1842 | 1 50 | | fine |
| 87 | 1843 | 1 10 | | good |
| 88 | 1845 | 2 00 | | fine |
| 89 | 1847 | 1 75 | | uncirculated |
| 90 | 1849 | 50 | | fine |

### U. S. ½ DOLLARS.

| No. | Date | Price | Description | Condition |
|---|---|---|---|---|
| 91 | 1842 | 1 00 | O mint, drapery to elbo | fine |
| 92 | 1853 | 30 | O " | fair |
| 93 | 1854 | 75 | O " | good |
| 94 | 1857 | 50 | O " | fine |
| 95 | 1857 | 30 | P " | good |
| 96 | 1865 | 25 | S " | fair |
| 97 | 1866 | 30 | P " | good |
| 98 | 1868 | 30 | S " | good |
| 99 | 1873 | 40 | S " S in angle | fine |

## F. E. MERRITT,

61 EAST AVE., ROCHESTER, N. Y.

Dealer in

## U. S. AND COLONIAL COINS, CENTS

and Half Cents a specialty. Correspondence solicited. 9

## HERBERT E MOREY,

Wholesale and retail dealer in

## American Coins, Medals,

And Paper Money. Importer of Ancient and Foreign Coins and Medals.

Send 25c. for 3d annual catalogue of 40 papes, and quarterlies to be issued in 1894.

**HERBERT E. MOREY,**

31 Exchange St., Room 1. BOSTON, MASS.

# Coins and Stamps

## FOR SALE!

Can furnish anything in this line. Send list of wants.
J. B. GOLDSMITH,
53 Hale St., Beverly, Mass.

## A. P. WYLIE,

**PRAIRIE CENTER, ILL.**

*Dealer in*

+ Fractional and Colonial Currency. +
Free Trade rates. Send for lists.

## SCARCE COINS OF THE U. S.

BOUGHT AND SOLD.

Approval Packages sent to responsible Parties. **1799** Fine Cents a Specialty. Good stock on hand.

SEND FOR NEW CATALOG.

## A. E. MARKS, WOODFORDS, ME.

# HAVE YOU ANY

# Desirable Coins

## To Sell at Reasonable Prices?

An "ad" in the Numismatist will do it! There is no other medium to compare with it.

# Wants, to exchange, etc.

This department gratis to all our readers.

Wanted.—Early issues of Rhode Island paper currency. Geo. C. Barton, Box 163, Providence, R. I.

Wanted.—Uncirculated U. S copper cents. Give date and price. Clayton C. Herr, Bloomington, Ill.

To Exchange.—A Hall type writer for 20 dollars, dates prior to 1873. J. A. Heckelman, A. N. A. 6, Columbus, Botetourt Co., Va.

To Exchange.—Foreign coins for numismatic literature or U. S. money (paper or metallic) medals or tokens. W. H. Taylor, North Wales, Pa.

Wanted.—Cheap American sale catalogues, with plates and priced, also plates for Parmelees, and Woodward's 69 sale. R. Archer Jr., 15 Prussia St., Dublin, Ireland.

The signature of Sir James Outram, K. C. B., the Bayard of India, for American coins. Also Asiatic stamps, coins and war medals. Major Adam Smith, Poona, India.

To Exchange.—Columbian stamps 2 to 50c for any of the following dates U. S. cents 1793, 95, 96, 99, 1804, 21, 24, 25, 28, 30, 44, 56. F. R. Ebright, Melrose Highlands, Mass.

To Exchange—Set of English post stamps, ½—£1 unused for U. S. Coins or U. S. and good foreign stamps, (coins preferred.) Scott's Catologues the basis. All letters answered. Also a Hall Type Writer, good as new, cost $40.00, to exchange for $20.00 worth of good U. S. Coins or U. S. and Foreign stamps. E. S. Ward, 306 Superior St., Toledo, Ohio.

To Exchange.—1793 and 1804 cents for 1804 cent. E. B. Root, 20 Munson St., Watertown, N. Y.

To Exchange.—"Hard Times" tokens and half-dollars to exchange for hard times tokens not in my collection. I make them a specialty and will give good exchange part or wholly cash for those I lack. For particulars, address Wm. Ross, A. N. A. 135, Chaplin, Ct.

To Exchange.—U. S. cents 1793 fair; 1799, very good, date weak but visible; 1800, good; 1796, fair; 1808, good; 1810, good; 1812, 1814, both good; 1857, fine. Wanted—½ dimes 1794-97-1800-03-05; dimes, 1796-97-98, 1800-01-02-03-04; 5c. nickle, 1877. J. B. Goldsmith, Beverly, Mass.

To Exchange—Isabella quarter (fine) for U. S. dollar of 1861. Set World's Fair souvenir tickets for U. S. dimes of 1837, 38, 61, or for a quarter of 1815. Columbian half dollar for half dollar of 1806. I also have a fine coin cabinet to exchange for coins not in my collection. C. W. Statesman, A. N. A. 4, Peru, Ind.

To Exchange.—Dickeson's Numismatic Manual, plates complete, Humphrey's Manual, and the Coin Collector's Journal for 1877, 79, 80, 81. Will take in exchange Greek or Roman coins, or American historical medals not in my collection. Also wanted Chinese temple and razor money, and plate XIX to Dickeson's Manual. M. H. Stafford, Marquette, Mich.

To Exchange.—Half dollars, fine, 1823, 31, 32, 33, 59 o, 61 o; uncirculated, 30, 32; proof, 79, 83, 86, 87; for half dollars of any date prior to 1818, 25, 36, milled edge, '37, 39, 41 to 45 inclusive, 48, 50 to 53 inclusive, 56, 57, 60, 62 to 65 inclusive, 67, 68, 72, 73, 74, 76, 78, 80, 81, 82, 84. Dates since '60 must be uncirculated or proof and all others strictly fine. Will pay difference if any, in exchange, or will buy if price is right. Dr. A. L. Fisher, Elkhart, Ind.

www.ingramcontent.com/pod-product-compliance
Lightning Source LLC
Chambersburg PA
CBHW030314270326
41926CB00010B/1364
* 9 7 8 3 7 4 1 1 4 3 3 1 1 *